# Creative Computer Graphics

# Annabel Jankel · Rocky Morton

**Writers**
Robert Leach
Neil Wiseman
Tim Glauert
Tony King
Andrew Pullen
Martin Hayman

**Researchers**
Peter Dean
Jon Tubman

**Designer**
Clive Challis

# Creative Computer Graphics

**Guild Publishing**
*London*

# Acknowledgements

This edition published 1984 by
Book Club Associates
By arrangement with Cambridge University Press

© Cambridge University Press 1984

First published 1984

Printed in Great Britain by W. S. Cowell Ltd, Ipswich
Bound by Hunter and Foulis Ltd, Edinburgh
Text setting by Wyvern Typesetting Ltd, Bristol
Colour origination by East Anglian Engraving, Norwich

The nature of computer graphics has meant that many people have been involved in compiling this book. We are grateful to everyone involved for their enthusiasm and support throughout the project.

First we wish to thank Robert Leach for his work in originating and organising the text. His knowledge of both film animation and computer graphics, and his appreciation of the relationship between artist and computer, have added much to the book.

We thank Neil Wiseman, Tim Glauert, Tony King and Andrew Pullen from the Computer Laboratory, University of Cambridge. Their skill in presenting complex technical ideas in simple language has proved invaluable.

Also many thanks to Martin Hayman, to our researchers Peter Dean and Jon Tubman for their work in the US and UK, and to Clive Challis for designing the book.

To everyone who has contributed pictorial material to *Creative Computer Graphics* we bestow our sincerest thanks. It goes without saying that without these images there would be no book and we hope that these pictures will stimulate an even greater interest in the subject.

Finally, thank you to New York Institute of Technology Computer Graphics Laboratory for 'User Friendly', who appears on the front cover, and to International Information Inc. for the image on the back cover.

*Annabel Jankel*
*Rocky Morton*

**Contributors**

Robert Abel & Associates
645 Madison Avenue
2nd Floor
New York

Acorn Soft
2nd Floor
Betjeman House
104 Hills Road
Cambridge

Activision
184–186 Regent Street
London

Addison Wesley Publishing Co.
Reading, Massachusetts

Alan Kitching & Jim Harper
Antics
Grove Park Animation
Grove Park
Camberwell
London

Atari Inc.
1399 Moffett Park Drive
Sunnyvale
California

Atari Laser
Windsor House
185–195 Ealing Road
Wembley
Middlesex

Rick Balabuck
280 Wychwood Avenue
Toronto
Ontario
Canada

BBC Photo Library
12 Cavendish Place
London

Turner Whitted, Dave Weimer,
Frank Sindon
Bell Laboratories
Holmdel
New Jersey

Barsky De Rose Dippé
University of California, Berkeley
Computer Graphics Laboratory
505 Evans Hall
Berkeley, California

Blavy
Crossway House,
Lutterworth Road
Blaby
Leicestershire

Loren Carpenter
Boeing Aerospace
PO Box 3999
Seattle
Washington

Harry Holland
Carnegie Mellon University
5000 Forbes Avenue
Pittsburgh
Pennsylvania

Commodore
675 Ajax Avenue
Slough

Computer Animation
100 Chalk Farm Road
London

Computer Effects
14–15 D'Arblay Street
London

The Association for Computing
Machinery
11 West 42nd Street
New York

Control Data
27 Cour des Petites
Ecuries Lognas
Marna La Valla
France

Roy Hall, Chas Verbeck
Cornell University
Program of Computer Graphics
120 Rand Hall
Ithica
New York

Malcolm Cox
15 Brookfield Road
Chiswick
London

Cranston–Csuri Productions
Charles Csuri, Don Stredney
The Cranston Centre
1501 Neil Avenue
Columbus
Ohio

Joanne Culver
633 North 13th Street
Dekalb
Illinois

Scott Daly
1200 Bearmore Dr.
Charlotte
North Carolina

Mike Newman
Dicomed Corp
9700 Newton Avenue
South Minneapolis
Minnesota

Joe Pasquale
Digital Effects Inc.
321 West 44th Street
New York

Digital Pictures Ltd
185 Drury Lane
London

Brad de Graf
Digital Productions
3416 South LA Cienega Boulevard
Los Angeles
California

Bob English, Gijis Bannenberg
Electronic Arts
Unit 2, 6
Erskin Road
London

Evans & Sutherland
PO Box 8700
580 Arapeen Drive
Salt Lake City
Utah

Feigenbaum Productions Inc.
25 West 43rd Street
New York

Pergamon Press
Hedding Hill Hall
Oxford

Bob Fisher
228 North Allegheny
Bellefonte
Pennsylvania

Focal Press
31 Fitzroy Square
London

Ford Motor Company
Scientific Research Staff
2000 American Road
Dearborn
Michigan

Darcy Gaberg
PO Box 413
Old Chelsea Station
New York

L. Gartel
152–18 Uman Turntike
Flushing
New York

Graham McCallun
Hairpiece
Logica
64–68 Newman Street
London

C. Cantwell, J. Dunn
Hewlitt Packard & Dunn Instruments
King Street Lane
Winnersh
Wokingham
Berkshire

Hiroshima University
Electronic Machinery Laboratory
Faculty of Engineering
Saijocho
Higashihiroshima
Japan

James Hockenhull
SW 205 Snowdrift Court
Pullman
Washington

Herve Huitric & Monique Nahas
24 Rue Theodore Honoré
Nogent sur Marne
France

Benoit Mandlebrot, Richard Voss,
Alan Norton
Thomas J. Watson Research Centre
PO Box 218
Yorktown Heights
New York

IBM Research
John Whitney, Jr, Gary Demos
Information International Inc.
5933 Slauson Avenue
Culver City
California

S. Cohen
Intelligent Light at Austin Electronics
17–01 Pollit Drive
PO Box 950
Fair Lawn
New Jersey

James F. Blinn
Jet Propulsion Lab
California Institute of Technology
4800 Oak Grove Road
Pasadena
California

Ken Brown Films
Wedgewood Mews
Greek Street
London

Lang Systems Inc.
1010 O'Brien Drive
Menlo Park
California

Laser Vision

Mark Snitily, Nelson Max,
Arthur Olsen
Lawrence Livermore National
Laboratory
University of California
Livermore
California

Legend
PO Box 435
Station Road
London

Litton Educational Publishing Inc.
Van Nostrand Reinhold
450 West 33rd Street
New York

Institut National de L'Audiovisual
4 Avenue de l'Europe
Bry sur Marne
France

Llama Soft
49 Mount Pleasant
Tadley
Hampshire

Lodge Cheeseman
191 Wardour Street
London

Margot Lovejoy
166–04 81st Street Avenue
Queens
New York

Alvy Ray Smith
Lucasfilm
PO Box 2009
San Rafael
California

Magi
3 Westchester Plazza
Elmsford
New York

Magi Sythavision
1560 12th Street
Santa Monica
California

Manchester University
Morphanalysis Unit
Oxford Road
Manchester

Mike Marshall, Fred Polito
3351 Bryant Street
Palo Alto
California

Alyce Kaprow, Gregorio Rivera,
Joel Slayton, Lynn Smith
Massachusetts Institute of
Technology
Visible Language Workshop
Room N51–138
275 Massachusetts Avenue
Cambridge
Massachusetts

Byte Books
McGraw-Hill
Peterborough
New Hampshire

David Fraser
Microsoft Corp.
Piper House Hatch Lane
Windsor
Berkshire

Manfred Mohr
20 North Moore Street
New York

David Morris
156 W. Burton Pl.
Chicago
Illinois

Moving Picture Company
25 Noel Street
London

Nippon Hosai Kyoko

Alvy Ray Smith, Paul Heckbert,
Rebecca Allen, Fredrich Parks,
Ned Greene, Bill Maher,
Dick Lundin, Kenneth Westey,
Ed Emscheller
Computer Graphics Laboratory
New York Institute of Technology
Old Westbury
New York

Yoichiro Kawaguchi, Hitoshi
Nishimura, Yoshi Fuknshima
Osaka University
2–1 Yamada-Oka
Suits
Osaka
Japan

Richard Chaang
Pacific Data Images
550 Weddell Drive
Suite 3
Sunnyvale
California

Paramount Pictures
5555 Melrose Avenue
Los Angeles
California

Parker Bros
Palitoy Company
Owen Street
Coalville
Leicestershire

Phaidon Press
5 Cromwell Place
London

Psyon
22 Dorset Square
London

Quantel Ltd
Kenley House
Kenley Lane
Kenley
Surrey

Ramtek Inc.
2211 Lawson Lane
Santa Clara
California

Al Barr
Raster Technologies Inc.
924 Executive Park Drive
North Billerica
Montana

Real Time Design Inc
Copper Gilloth
531 S. Plymouth Court
Chicago
Illinois

Rediffusion Simulation
Michael Potmesil
Rensselaer Polytechnic Institute
9 Executive Park Drive
N. Billerica
Montana

Robinson Lambie Nairn
41 Great Marlborough Street
London

Brian Reffin Smith
Royal College of Art
Kensington Gore
London

Sandia Labs
Albuquerque
New Mexico

Lillian Schwartz
Murray Hill
New Jersey

Scientific American Inc.
415 Maddison Avenue
New York

Sega Laser

Sinclair Research
25 Willis Road
Cambridge

Sogitec
32 Boulevarde de la Republique
Boulogne
France

South Glamorgan Institute of Higher
Education, University of Wales
Institute of Science
Cyncoed
Cardiff
Wales

Barbara Sykes
3911 N. Greenview
Chicago
Illinois

Synopsis Video
4531 Greengate Ct.
Westlake Village
California

Edward Zajec
Syracuse University
516 Kensington Road
Syracuse
New York

Systems Simulations Ltd
16–50 Russell Square
London

Philippe Bergeron,
Nadia Margaret Thalman,
Daniel Thalman
Universite de Montreal
Ecole des Hautes Etudes
Commerciales
5255 Avenue Decelles
Montreal
Canada

Syd Mead
Walt Disney Inc.
500 So. Buena Street
Burbank
California

Williams
3401 North California Avenue
Chicago
Illinois

Mark Wilson
PO Box 23
West Cornwall
Connecticut

Dean Winkler, Tom de Witt,
Vibeke Sorenson
111 N. Pine Avenue
Albany
New York

Frank Dietrick,
Zsuzsa Molnar
Zsuzsa
4214 East Broadway
Long Beach
California

Joel Slayton
940 Arlington Avenue
Studio 12
Oakland
California

Linda Freeman

Sally Cushing

Parker Bros.

Llama Soft

Dyson

Bell Telephone Laboratories

Kenneth Knowlton

**It has proved particularly difficult at times to establish ownership of copyright and to gain the necessary permissions. The authors have made every effort to follow normal procedures, but would apologise to, and be pleased to hear from, any person or company who may feel that they have not received an appropriate acknowledgement.**

# Contents

## Introduction 8

**About this book · some definitions · tools and techniques · some applications · computer-aided engineering · scientific simulation · fine art · feature films · television · video games**

## 1 History 18

**Beginnings · pioneers · vector displays and wireframe models · raster displays · interactive graphics · scientific filming · cartoon animation · television logos · image processing · games**

## 2 Modelling Techniques 30

**Types of model · curves and surfaces · processing dimensional data · procedural modelling · constructive solid geometry · human figures · natural forms · fractal geometry · growth algorithms**

## 3 Views 42

**Types of display · points, lines and polygons · hidden-line removal · colouring · illumination · texture mapping · transparent objects · aliasing and anti-aliasing**

## 4 Design and Industry 54

**Computer-aided engineering · industrial design · operation · robots and automation · plant control · decision making**

## 5   Science and Simulation 64

Science and computer graphics · visualization and display · languages and mathematics · medical applications · simulation models · shipping and flight simulators

## 6   Art 80

Computer graphics as fine art · creations and productions · image quality · languages · illustrations, art work and experiments · interaction and participation · art and home computers · gallery

## 7 Feature Films 110

Predecessors and pioneers · special effects · technical systems · vehicles · environments · notable sequences · human faces and figures

## 8 Television 122

Production and reception hardware · early approaches and attitudes · wireframes and solid surfaces · notable examples · show reels · music videos

## 9 Video Games and Home Computing 136

Beginnings · arcade games · home computer games · hardware and capability · programming · developments and prospects

# Introduction

An airline pilot under training overshoots the runway while attempting to land and hits a house. All that is damaged, however, is the pilot's self-esteem, since the scene is completely generated by computer. A goal at a football match is celebrated by the score, the scorer's name, a picture of the trophy cup and a flashing football being drawn on a huge array of lights under computer control. The screen of a computer cashpoint invites us to touch that part of it which contains the description of what we actually want to happen to our money.

Images in one way or another generated by computer are being ever more commonly seen, are performing a greater diversity of functions and are starting to change the way we live. Computers are powerful tools. Vision is a powerful medium. The union of the two is a revolutionary means of communication: computer graphics.

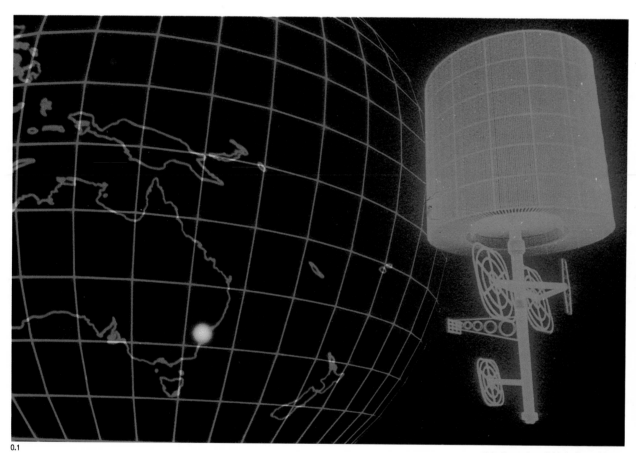

0.1

0.2

**0.1**: A nearly-solid 'wireframe' image of a satellite orbits the Earth. The computer draws only outlines, but when outlines are close the appearance is of a solid surface.
*Computer Effects, London.*

**0.2**: **Times Square, New York**. The dimensions of buildings and streets in photographs taken during the 1930s were entered as data, and the result was a nostalgic journey around Times Square in an entirely computer-generated (and computer-coloured) movie sequence.
*Digital Effects Inc.*

**0.4**: An artificial landscape seen from a flight simulator cabin.
*Computer Graphics by SOGITEC, France.*

The way in which a video game can, by the use of bright primary colours, movement and sound, compel us to play it is just one example of the power of computer-generated graphics. Compelling also are the fantastic images produced for television and motion pictures by some most creative people; combining their unbounded imagination with computer graphics, they enable us to see impossible things.

This book is entitled *Creative Computer Graphics.* It is about the ability of computer graphics to enhance the creativity of people who work in industry, engineering, art and science. It is also about the creations of the people whose work is computer graphics; the machines they have built, the techniques they have developed, and the pictures which they have produced.

The nature and quality of an image is necessarily highly dependent on the machine which generates it. Personal microcomputers costing less than the domestic television set to which they are coupled can assemble pictures from coarse 'lumps' of colour. The graphics associated with the Teletext service and with the early 'space invader' games also exhibit this lumpiness. Slightly more sophisticated machines can display pictures with a finer grain so that figures composed of lines, curves and shaded areas can be rendered. At the other end of the scale are enormously powerful computers costing many millions of pounds, which spend hours calculating the exact intensity and colour of each one of millions of points of light and assembling them to form pictures of stunning detail and realism. And between these extremes there are numerous and diverse machines, techniques and applications.

Although computer graphics is a young

**0.3**: This apparently computer-generated image was in fact hand-coloured from computer-generated outlines. Wire frame outlines are less complicated and less costly than solid surfaces.
*'Outer Spacers'* KP Commercial by Lodge-Cheeseman Ltd

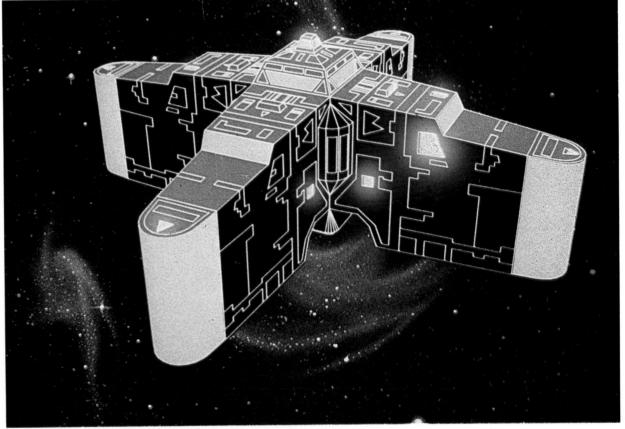

0.3

0.4

0.5

**0.5**: DNA molecules. Complex and convincing creation for the TV series *Cosmos* presented by Carl Sagan. *Dr James F. Blinn & Jet Propulsion Laboratory.*

discipline it is growing so rapidly that it is beyond the scope of this book to explore it in all its aspects. Instead we shall describe the main techniques and applications, and print some beautiful images.

The images in this book have been chosen for their visual appeal, imaginative content and for the way in which they demonstrate different techniques. They are arranged to serve as illustrations for the text. The first chapter, History, traces the progress of electronic and computer technology from the 1950s to the present day and describes how it has driven the development of computer graphics. Modelling Techniques together with views examine the important idea that the description of an object which we give to the computer (the model) is a separate matter from how we instruct the computer to render the object on its screen (the view). The rest of the book is concerned with the principal applications of computer graphics. Industry and Design and Science and Simulation discuss how computer graphics has changed the way people work in these areas. Art, Feature Films, Television, and Video Games and Home Computing describe how computer graphics has emerged from the laboratory and is now making an impact in the wider world of entertainment.

What, then, is computer graphics? Why is it such an important, challenging and exciting subject, whether your standpoint is commercial, scientific or artistic? In the rest of this chapter we shall sketch out, albeit using fairly broad strokes, some answers to these questions.

Computer graphics can be defined as comprising **modelling** (describing an object in terms of coordinates, lines, surfaces or solids), **storage** (of the model in the memory of a computer), **manipulation** (changing the model in some way, for example by altering its shape or merging two models together), and **viewing** (the computer adopting a particular viewpoint, looking at the model from this viewpoint and depicting on its screen what it sees).

This fundamental definition holds true throughout computer graphics, but there are many areas of specialization within the subject. In interactive computer graphics the importance of a fast, effective dialogue between the human user and the computer is stressed (a video game is an example). On the other hand, in the quest for realism, time, trouble and expense are of little importance as long as the final image looks good. Everybody wants to put an image on the screen. But the answers to the questions 'why is the image made?', 'what does the image represent?', and 'how is the image made?' may vary enormously depending on whom you ask.

One way of gaining access to the subject is to look at some of its applications. To do this, it is helpful to draw a line (albeit somewhat arbitrary and unreliable) between those images which may be described as 'functional' and those which are 'representational' in some way. 'Functional' images make no pretence at realism, but instead communicate things about the real world to us through symbols, in much the same way as words do (but often with far greater potency). 'Representational' images, by contrast, communicate to us through their resemblance to the familiar forms and laws of nature. We shall begin our survey of the applications of computer graphics with those which make use of the former type of image and, bearing in mind the unreliability of the line, move on to those which illustrate the latter type.

Computer-aided engineering (CAE) is a term embracing the related areas of Computer-aided design (CAD) and Computer-aided manufacturing (CAM). In CAD the **model** which is stored in the computer memory represents the object the designer is designing. The **view** which he sees on his screen may or may not be a realistic rendering of the object in question; the electronic circuit designer might want to look at the waveforms produced by his circuit, whereas the car body designer would want a realistic three-dimensional image. The designer is provided with various controls which enable him to communicate with the computer in an efficient way and which he uses to **manipulate** the model to his satisfaction. The circuit designer may move a wire; the car body designer may smooth out some contours. These controls, which we term **input tools** and shall describe shortly, are things which can be pushed, pressed, and rolled, and whose movements are readily sensed and interpreted by the computer.

Once the model is finished it can be used as a blueprint for manufacturing. This is the province of CAM. As CAM is not intimately dependent on computer graphics, we shall say no more about it here.

CAE was the first significant application of computer graphics. Nowadays the turnover in CAE in the US alone is more than a billion dollars, in the rest of the world about twice that figure. The enormous economic advantages which accrue from making use of CAE techniques have been a major driving force behind the development of computer graphics. One rapidly developing area is man–machine communication. An important question in industrial design is how the highly-skilled and highly-paid designer can make best use of his time, so that the company can get the most for their money, and design changes can be

**0.6**: Dr James F. Blinn of the Jet Propulsion Laboratory, Pasadena. Jim Blinn is undoubtedly one of the leading creative forces in computer graphics today.

0.6

most quickly and easily effected. The answer to the question involves not just the use of computers but more particularly how well a human being can communicate his ideas to them. This is the realm of interactive graphics, which we shall briefly look at now.

Every use of a computer involves, to a greater or lesser extent, engaging in a dialogue with it. The dialogue may consist of submitting cards to a card reader on Tuesday and collecting the results on Thursday, or typing something at a keyboard and having the computer immediately print the response on a screen. There can be no doubt that the second example is preferable from the human user's point of view, and the keyboard is accordingly a familiar example of an **input tool**.

However, if there is an image on a computer screen which we want to alter in some way, is a keyboard the best way of communicating to the computer what we want done? Certainly we could give the feature in question a name and then type something like 'move square 5 right' – but this is cumbersome. It would be nice to be able to do it simply by pointing at the screen. The **light pen** enables us to do just that. The first input tool to be designed for interactive graphics use, it consists of a light-sensitive component which generates an electrical pulse when the spot of light tracing out the picture on the screen passes directly beneath it. The electronics controlling the display sort out where the spot of light was when the pulse occurred and pass this information to the computer, which can thus tell at which part of the screen you are pointing and take the appropriate action.

Continually holding a pen up to the screen was found to be tiring, however, and light pens could not be used to trace around drawings to

**0.8**: **Pirelli Tyres**. The tyre was entirely computer-generated by Digital Effects Inc. New York. (See chapter 8 for a full sequence from this TV commercial).
*Directed by Jankel and Morton for Cucumber Studios.*

0.8

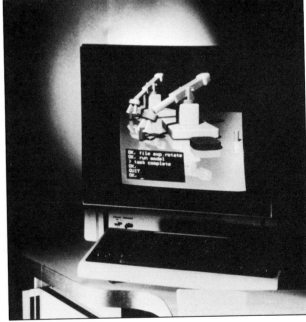
0.9

**0.9**: A computer graphics workstation with VDU and keyboard.
*Raster Technologies Inc.*

**0.7**: Wheel hub. An example of computer-aided industrial design.
*Control Data, France.*

0.7

0.10

0.11

0.13

0.14.1

0.14.5

0.12

**0.10**: Today Nadia Magnenat-Thalmann and Daniel Thalmann are generating walking, talking robots on the screen with their MIRA system at the University of Montreal. In the future much more human mannequins will be accepted as a matter of course.

**0.13**: A demonstration of simulated exterior daylight at an airport. Note the tone gradation in the sky and the shadows and highlights on the two aircraft, a Boeing 707 and a Concorde.
*S. Cohen, © Intelligent Light 1984.*

**0.11**:**Still Life** by Turner Whitted and Dave Weimer, showing a successful depiction of complex curves and reflections.
*Bell Laboratories, New Jersey.*

**0.12**:**Bottle in window**. The window and the bottle were generated independently. A line showing one edge of the bottle in silhouette was revolved to create the shape of the whole bottle which was then coloured. The window was calculated piece by piece. The two elements were brought together by a bit of inspired guesswork which is completely convincing.
*Designed by Turner Whitted at Bell Telephone Laboratories, New Jersey.*

**0.14.1–8**: An analog computer, the Quantel Mirage, distorts the original manually-generated images for a television commercial.
*Coca-Cola Corporation.*

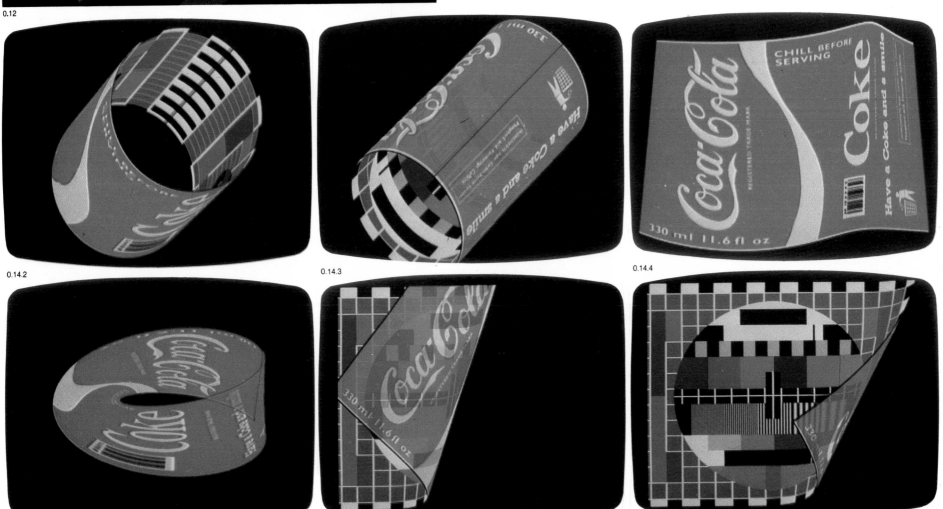

0.14.2

0.14.3

0.14.4

0.14.6

0.14.7

0.14.8

enter them as models into the computer. Thus the **digitizing tablet** is now finding favour as an alternative to the light pen. The digitizing tablet usually comprises a shallow box of sensing electronics with a smooth top surface, and a stylus. As the stylus is moved over the surface of the tablet, which is usually placed in front of the screen, the electronics pick up and inform the computer of its movement. The tablet may vary in dimension from notepad size up to the scale of an engineer or architect's drafting table.

The **joystick** and the **tracker ball** are two further examples of input tools. The tracker ball consists of a hard plastic sphere about the same size as a tennis ball which is set into a console and mounted on rollers to allow it to rotate about any axis. The rollers can sense the direction in which the ball is rotating, and this information can be made available to the computer which typically uses it to move a marker around the screen. A joystick is a lever which can be pushed in any direction and is made use of in much the same way as a tracker ball. Both have been fitted to amusement arcade video games.

The final input tool we shall look at, and the one which is currently the most fashionable, is the **mouse**. This small beast essentially consists of a tiny tracker ball, like a ball-bearing, set in the bottom of a plastic housing containing some electronics. The housing is conveniently shaped for the hand to rest on and has one to three buttons on its top surface. As the mouse is pushed around on a flat surface the ball-bearing spins and the electronics relay the direction of travel to the computer. Again it is primarily used to control the position of a marker on the computer's screen.

Although we have talked about interactive tools in the context of industrial design the same techniques are of course used in other applications. The digitizing tablet is now a familiar tool for the computer artist, the mouse is now being used for document preparation in the 'electronic office' and the tracker ball has for a long time been seen in front of the radar screens of the air traffic control.

Science too has found computer graphics a useful tool. First made use of in astronomy and mathematics, it is now an accepted means of presenting scientific data. *Disc of Stars* was an early film about astronomy produced at the Atlas Computer Laboratories in England, and demonstrated theories of galactic growth and decay. A model of a galaxy was created, consisting of half a million pieces of matter, each with its own mass and momentum, and viewed as half a million white dots on a black background. The computer manipulated the model in accord with the physical laws described by the theory, and at each step a frame of the film was exposed. The result was a film of just over one minute's duration showing the birth, life and death of a galaxy: a solid white globe flattens out into a disk and fragments into a whirling spiral pattern, which then grows out across space and finally collapses in upon itself under the pull of gravity.

This technique of using a computer to predict how a model of a physical system will behave is called **simulation**. In computer graphics it has found its ideal partner to show us the results. Simulation is used in CAE to predict, for example, the behaviour of a nuclear reactor or of an electronic circuit. In science it can show the way a complex molecule will vibrate, or predict the effect on a forest of over-population of deer. Simulation is a very powerful tool, but without computer graphics we would always be faced with the dreadful prospect of examining thousands of numbers on line-printer paper in order to make proper use of it.

One physical system which has been extensively modelled and simulated is an aircraft and the space through which it may fly. Flight simulation combines the techniques of interaction with those of simulation. The trainee pilot is confronted by a large number of what are effectively input tools but look like the controls of an aircraft. He uses these to manipulate the computer model of the system, to control the values of speed, altitude and direction fed into the model. An instructor is also able to manipulate the model – to make an engine fail or a tyre burst – if he feels suitably malicious. The computer causes the simulation to proceed and displays a view of the scene for the pilot as it develops. The image displayed is usually quite realistic and so enables the pilot to gain experience of flying in various light and weather conditions.

There is an application of computer graphics now familiar to us all – video games. The fascination they hold for millions of players and spectators all over the world is undeniable. From unpromising black and white tennis games they have evolved with startling speed to the imaginative colourful and dynamic games we see today.

Games are an example of the way computer graphics has progressed from being a tool for doing something else to being an end in its own right. We are starting to appreciate that the images which come out of computers can be enjoyed. It is now time to cross the line we drew earlier, from 'functional' images over into 'representational' ones, and look at art and realism.

The work of Dr James F. Blinn can serve as our starting point. Trained as an artist, he is now one of the foremost research workers in the field of computer graphics. Blinn has developed brilliant techniques for rendering surfaces, textures and reflections, and has demonstrated the effectiveness of his techniques by producing some superb images. When NASA wanted a favourable public response to their launch of the Voyager deep space probe, Blinn's imaginative sequence of images simulating a journey past Saturn caught the public's imagination even more strongly than Voyager's subsequent authentic transmissions from space. Blinn also created a sequence for Carl Sagan's television series *Cosmos* which showed how the two helices of the DNA molecule interlock, and won for him an 'Emmy' award – television's equivalent of a film 'Oscar'.

We have indeed come a long way since IBM and Honeywell sponsored the first highly-privileged artists to make computer art films and still pictures almost two decades ago. At enormous expense in machine time, they demonstrated the human face of computing to a doubting public. The pictures produced these days are accepted as examples of a serious art form – as evidenced by the establishment of a computer art gallery in New York.

All the styles used by artists working with traditional media have been eagerly embraced by the computer artist: portraiture, landscape, still life, as well as psychedelic, abstract expressionism and op art. A pointillist view of Brooklyn Bridge, after Seurat, was created by Digital Effects Inc. for Harris computers. Lillian Schwartz's *Pictures from a Gallery* and other examples of her work give a prismatic, cubist view of her subjects. The abstract work of Hans Richter and Oskar Fischinger probably inspired Stan Van Der Beek's linear scratches. Eastern art is another source of inspiration. John Whitney Sr, perhaps the first artist to make significant use of computer graphics, often turns to the mandala, a focus for Hindu and Buddhist meditation. The ability of computers to produce pictures which are lifelike but which nevertheless seem to defy gravity and other natural laws has inspired many surrealistic images. It seems to be Rene Magritte's pipe which Turner Whitted generates in his still life (chapter 0). The landscape with sphere, cone and cube from Information International Inc. (also chapter 0) pays homage to Dali, De Chirico and Ernst.

Another notable consumer of computer images is the motion picture industry. Hollywood's welcome to computer graphics was at first hesitant. George Lucas rejected computer-generated images of the X-wing fighter for his first *Star Wars* film, preferring instead to use models, although he now funds one of the leading computer graphics research centres. Walt Disney Inc. were not prepared to back Steven Lisberger's idea for the film *TRON* until $300 000 had already been spent on it. *TRON* went on to become the first ever feature film to incorporate a large proportion of computer-generated images and was critically and financially successful. It will certainly not be the last of its kind. Other films which make use of computer-generated sequences are *Star Trek II – The Wrath of Khan* and *Star Wars VI: Return of the Jedi.*

It may be thought that television, and in particular television advertising, with its incessant demand for novel and striking images, would be an enthusiastic user of computer-generated graphics, but this has not always happened. The cold and sinister connotations which computers have in some advertiser's minds are still to be overcome. There are some worthy pioneers –

Britain's Channel 4 identification sequence is one – but the medium is waiting for many more.

We have now looked, if briefly, at some of the areas in which computer graphics plays a role. We shall look at them again in more detail in the following chapters. All that remains to be done here is to stress once more that the essence of creative computer graphics is **communication**. We live in a world where the amount and complexity of information which is available to us, and which it is necessary for us to comprehend, is growing daily. Computer graphics can hardly fail to have immediate and growing relevance to our lives.

To convey a proper sense of the progress of computer graphics, the ingenuity of its practitioners and the possibilities it opens up for the future would be a dificult task indeed if we had to rely on words alone. Fortunately we do not have to: we have the pictures as well.

0.15: An engineer using a digitising tablet and stylus to input graphics for display on the VDU. Other commands can be entered with the keyboard. *Courtesy Evans & Sutherland Computer Corporation.*

0.16: **Mountain**, Benoit Mandelbrot and Richard Voss. The realism of the mountainside and its infinite detail give an indication of future scope for in computer graphics. *IBM Research, New York.*

0.15

0.16

0.17

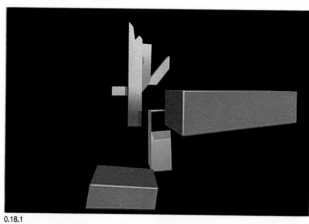

0.18.1

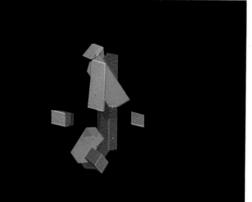

0.18.5

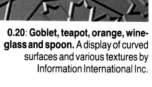

0.18.6

**0.17**: Simulation of Saturn and Voyager probe created before the probe was launched. The extraordinary realism is typical of Blinn's brilliant computer graphics.
*Dr James F. Blinn & Jet Propulsion Laboratory.*

**0.18.1–9**: The first television station identification for Channel 4 (UK). Designed by Robinson Lambie-Nairn and executed by Systems Simulation Ltd in the UK and Information International Inc. in the USA.

0.19

0.20

**0.19**: **Sphere, cone and cube on a textured floor.** An influential image from Information International Inc. The sphere, cone and cube appealed to ancient Greek geometers for their mathematical properties, to Cezanne for their artistic potential and to computer graphics people for both.

**0.20**: **Goblet, teapot, orange, wineglass and spoon.** A display of curved surfaces and various textures by Information International Inc.

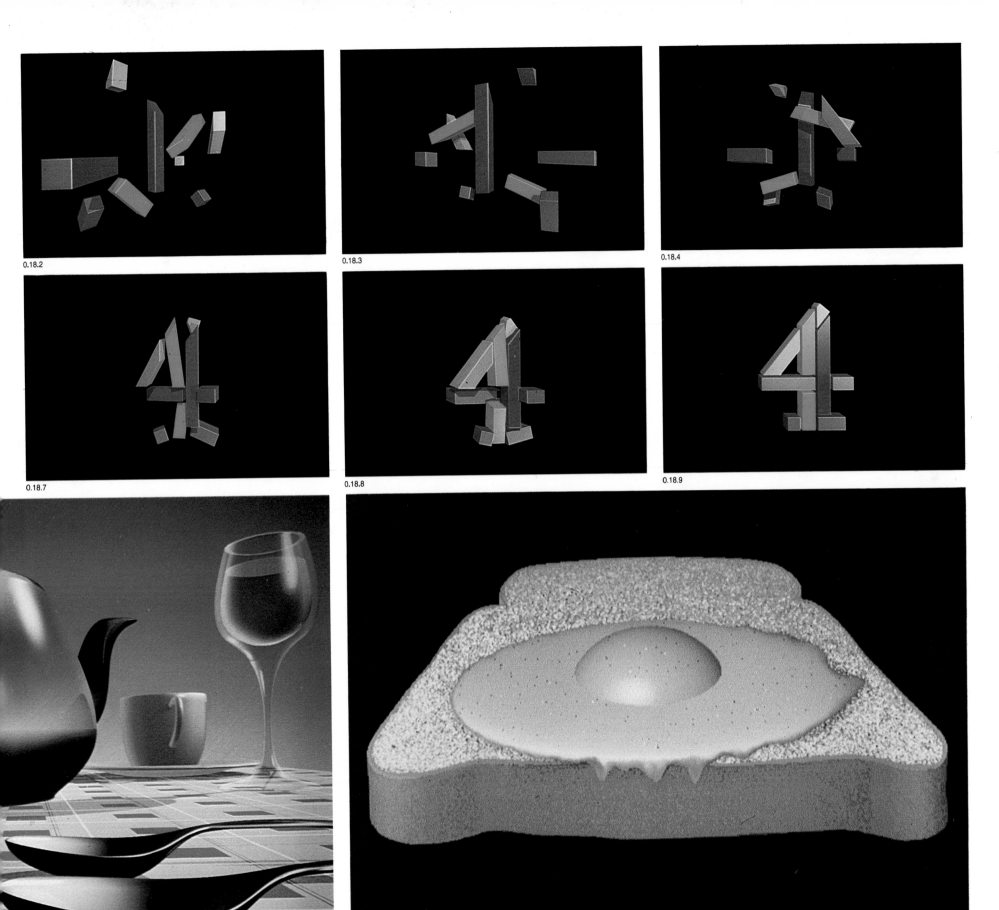

0.18.2

0.18.3

0.18.4

0.18.7

0.18.8

0.18.9

0.21

**0.21: Fried egg on toast.**
*Alvy Ray Smith, Computer Graphics
Laboratory NYIT*

# 1 History

As with any new technology, it is difficult to pinpoint dates for the various stages in the progress of computer graphics. The walls of many computer rooms in the 1960s were decorated with images of nudes, faces or patterns printed out in quiet moments. Though of little aesthetic or practical value, these did lead some programmers to keep a look out for relevant graphics technology and applications. The first use of computer graphics though was probably much earlier than this. The EDSAC computer at the University of Cambridge, which was probably the world's first electronic stored program machine (1949), carried on its front panel several cathode ray tube displays, intended to reveal the electronic operations of the hardware for diagnostic purposes. Programmers naturally used them to display simple graphics (David Wheeler recalls a highland dancer animation made around 1950). In the early 1950s the Whirlwind computer at Massachusetts Institute of Technology (MIT) was fitted with a cathode ray tube display specifically for plotting pictures, which could then be photographed to produce images on paper. It also carried a light pen which allowed a degree of interaction with the displayed picture, an idea developed further in the SAGE air defence system. The computers of the 1950s were expensive, slow and unreliable and the pictures they were called upon to make were mainly simply point plots of numerical data. In those days no one foresaw the use of computers in art or the entertainment industry as anything more than a joke, given the high cost of machine time, the programming effort involved and the poor quality of the results.

The SAGE air defence system, introduced

1.1

1.1: **Mural**. This nude was photo-scanned and the tones are made up of micro-patterns consisting of communication symbols. *Kenneth Knowlton and Leon D. Harmon, 1966.*

1.2.1: These vector lines all have the same brightness value. The illusion of depth is given entirely by the perspective convergence of the lines.

1.2.2: The brightness of the lines is reduced as the line apparently recedes, giving an illusion of greater depth. This 'depth cueing' makes vector displays slightly more demanding on computing power.

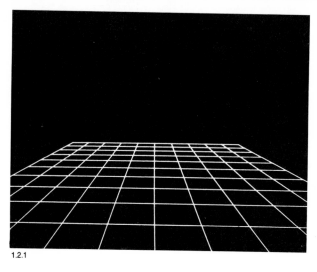

1.2.1

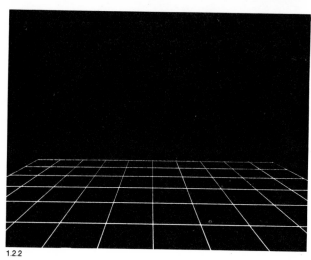

1.2.2

by the US government in the mid 1950s, provides the first example of a production system that relied on the use of interactive computer graphics. Missiles and aircraft were detected by radar and their positions displayed on screens. Operators at these screens examined the images and decided which targets were interesting; these were indicated to the computer by pointing at them with a light pen. The computer then performed tracking and interception calculations, and relayed the results to command stations elsewhere. The SAGE system was interactive in the sense that the computer acted on instructions received from the operator, who worked at the screen, but of course the operator could not actually direct the movements of the targets. It was some time before computers could process information quickly enough to change the image on the screen as fast as the operator's hand could move – that is, in 'real time.'

The father of real time interactive computer graphics is Ivan Sutherland, whose doctoral dissertation 'Sketchpad: a man–machine graphical communication system' (MIT Lincoln Laboratory, 1962) was most influential on early work in computer graphics. It presented in embryonic form a methodology for computer graphics which gave the subject its name and began its evolutionary development.

A Sketchpad drawing was based on lines, arcs and points. The operator held a light pen in one hand and specified the relationships of graphic elements (e.g. angles, sizes) using a keyboard with the other hand. If the light pen drew a line that was not quite straight, the computer could straighten it. Rough circles could be improved to perfect roundness, and a vague squiggle could become a neatly drafted electronic symbol. For the first time operators could use the light pen as a drawing instrument and draw freely on the screen as if it were magic paper. Even better, a number of geometric figures (circles, ellipses, squares) and symbols (arrows, crosses), were held in a 'library' and could be made to appear on the screen at the touch of a button on the keyboard.

An important contribution of Sketchpad to the development of software techniques for graphics was that the view displayed on the screen was derived from an internally stored model of the thing represented. Interactions were between user and model and the use of the display was to close the feedback loop, not simply to reveal the answer. This separation of the model of an artefact from its picture is of fundamental significance, as is explained in more detail in chapters 2 and 3.

'Sketchpad III', a development of Sutherland's ideas by Timothy Johnson (also from MIT Lincoln Laboratory) allowed the operator to draw and visualize objects in three dimensions.

The impact of Sketchpad was most immediate in the fields of computer-aided engineering, although most workers seriously underestimated the amount of innovation, development and sheer programming effort that would be needed to build anything really effective. Many vehicle and aeroplane manufacturers made use of, and indeed contributed to the development of, experimental design systems that taught important lessons but solved few problems. A notable design system known as Digigraphics was supplied by CDC to General Motors in the mid 1960s for car body design. Amongst the many fruits of that system came the first ideas about 'user friendliness'. It was found that interactive graphics systems provide a truly enormous challenge to the systems programmers in achieving ease of use and rapidity of action. It was not (and is not) easy in a complex screen display to help the operator keep his attention focussed, to recognise the implications of a changed image, and to know what to do next.

Research in computer graphics around 1970 proceeded in an atmosphere of expectation and excitement not seen in the subject before – nor likely to be seen again! Several years elapsed before much was achieved which might be said to be of real practical value, but the methodology advanced in a spectacular manner.

The first displays plotted points on a CRT primarily in order to be seen by an attached camera. For each point the phosphor was stimulated once and the flash of light decayed away while the next point was being prepared. Using the persistence of vision and a bit of imagination, simple pictures could be viewed (briefly) with the naked eye. When, later, displays were intended to be viewed by eye for any length of time, it became necessary to draw the points over and over for as long as the image was wanted. This process is called 'refresh' and it made rather heavy demands on the computers of those days just to send all the data to the display some 50 times per second so as to produce the appearance of a steadily lit image. It soon occurred to somebody that the amount of data to be sent could be dramatically reduced if lines instead of points were used. Each picture was then generated through a sequence of movements and drawn lines; the resulting display was called a 'vector' display because all the visible effects were composed from lit vectors (line segments) displayed in turn. The pictures most suitable for such vector displays were clearly

1.3

**1.3**: John Whitney Sr, an early user of computer graphics, with his analogue M-5 gunsight computer which he adapted for experimental computer animation (see chapter 7).

those that easily decompose into line segments. Much engineering drawing is of this kind, stemming as it does from the draftsman's equivalent of the vector display, the pencil and the drafting machine. As the detail in the picture generated by a vector display increases, the time to draw it also increases; at some degree of picture complexity, the screen will flicker in an objectionable manner (for most displays this is when the refresh is less than about 20 times per second). This severe restriction on the amount of detail which can usefully be shown was the driving force behind many ingenious, and expensive, displays made during the 1970s, with the common objective of drawing as quickly as possible.

Until the mid 1970s the great majority of graphics systems were based on the use of vector displays, and the pictures which typify the era are 'wireframe' models of buildings, airframes and car bodies. The representation of three-dimensional objects through such vector displays utilized any of three methods. First, the object (or the viewing position) could be progressively rotated so that the projection on the screen revealed some depth information from the relative movements of the parts. Although ambiguous, this often provided a powerful and sufficient impression of the shape of the object. Second, the more distant parts could be drawn with less brightness than the nearer parts. Third, if the object was a solid, the view could be processed to remove the edges in its wireframe image which were obscured by nearer parts. This provided a more realistic view, but at the expense of much computation. As better methods and faster computers were put to the task, so the expectations of picture complexity increased and faster displays were developed to serve increasingly sophisticated applications.

**1.4**: A wireframe image on the left, a solid model on the right, this space shuttle is colour-coded to accentuate the component parts.
*Created by C. Cantwell (Hewlett Packard) and J. Dunn (Dunn Instruments) on a Hewlett Packard HP 9874 Digitiser and HP 9845C Desk Top Computer, recorded on a Dunn Instruments Camera.*

1.4

Just as acceptably high speeds seemed to be in sight, the whole situation was overturned by the arrival of framestore driven raster displays.

The first raster displays were introduced to the computing scene in the late 1960s as replacements for character printing teleprinter terminals. They were called 'visual display units' (VDUs) and could do little more than show ugly characters in 80 columns and 24 lines, with the same sort of serial function as a teleprinter – that is, the keyboard behaved as if driving the mechanical carriage of a teleprinter and the screen worked like the paper roll.

The word 'raster' refers to the manner of drawing the picture on the screen. The beam visits in turn every possible position on the screen, scanning row by row from top to bottom, as in a domestic television receiver, and varies the spot brightness as it goes to create the desired image. The whole screen can be envisaged as composed of an array of small squares or 'pixels' (from 'picture elements'), each of which can be shown at a separately specified brightness. With a colour display each pixel can be shown at a separately specified colour. For a VDU every character has an associated rectangle of pixels which, when lit in the specified manner, produces a picture of that character. Fairly reasonable characters can be shown with a $7 \times 9$ rectangle of pixels for each one and the VDU electronics contains the definition of a whole alphabet of say 96 characters as a set of these rectangles of pixel patterns. Besides knowing the alphabet definition, the VDU also has to store the characters being shown on the screen at any one time. For 80 columns $\times$ 24 lines this requires storage for 1 920 characters, a modest number which, though memory was then expensive, accounted for only a small proportion of the VDU electronics cost.

Owing to dramatically falling costs of electronic components, it soon became possible to increase the memory in a VDU by several factors and to envisage storing separately each pixel value on the screen. The resulting store is called a 'framestore' and allows the display to show arbitrary pictures (within the limits of the pixel resolution, of course), not just characters. This opened new horizons; the picture could now include coloured or shaded areas as well as line segments. In such a display, the screen is refreshed continuously from the framestore and there are no flicker problems related to the complexity of the picture.

Recent developments in computer graphics are mostly based on raster displays; many are concerned with achieving more realism in images, manipulating pictures faster and reducing the cost in hardware or computer time to obtain given effects. At the present time, pixel resolutions of $1024 \times 1024$ are common, with each pixel able to take on any of a few hundred to a few million different colours. However, it may take a few seconds to transfer a picture to the screen but a few hours to compute it in the first place. There is plenty of room for development!

Behind those developments, the available technology has been the important enabling factor. For example, users of framestore driven raster displays had to wait for the cost of memory to fall to reasonable levels because there is such a lot of memory needed to build one (a million bytes or more). The computer power needed to show real time animation of complex subjects is still nowhere in sight, but will be snapped up when it emerges.

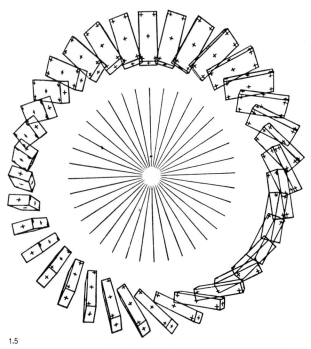

1.5

1.6.1

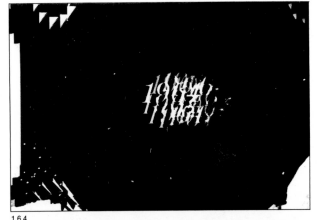

1.6.4

1.6.2

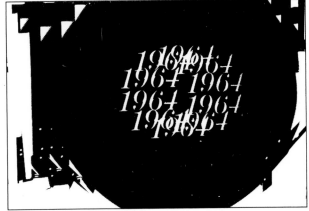

1.6.5

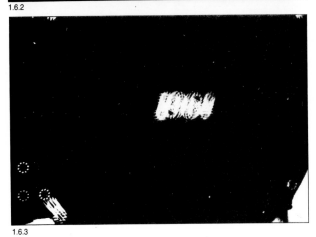

1.6.3

**1.5: Simulation of a two-giro gravity-gradient attitude control-system** by E. E. Zajac, 1963. The first film to popularise scientific uses of animated computer graphics. It shows how the attitude of a satellite can be altered as it orbits. This picture shows every fifth frame of one section of the film, made on an IBM 7090 computer.

**1.6.1–5**: The date '1964' is graphically manipulated by Whitney's analogue computer to create a graduated series of forms.

While the technical basis for the subject was being hatched, John Whitney Sr was interesting himself in the aesthetic possibilities of using a computer to create pictures. Whitney was first an experimental film maker, then a director of engineering films for guided missile projects. He also directed films for UPA (United Productions of America, a group of independent film animators who broke away from Walt Disney) and worked on the title sequences for Alfred Hitchcock's *Vertigo*. In the 1950s he bought an M-5 anti-aircraft gun

director, which served as the basis for a mechanical analogue computer. This he used to control many different movements of camera and artwork after the manner of a modern rostrum camera. The result was a film entitled *Catalog* (1961), a display of abstract but apparently organic patterns that grow, decay and revive in an ever-changing cycle. Although the artwork was all created by hand, the distinctive quality of computer processing meant that *Catalog* had more in common with modern computer animation techniques than with any hand-produced effects.

The finest developments of Whitney's analogue computer was achieved by his brother James with *Lapis* (1963–6). Glass plates were painted with fields of dots and mounted on tables. These rotated both on their own axes and round one another, while the camera also moved. The result is an extraordinary abstract

1.7.1

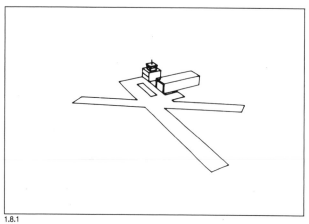

1.8.1

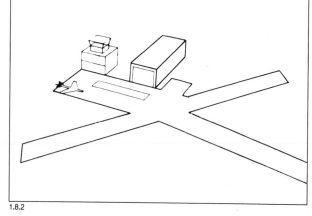

1.8.2

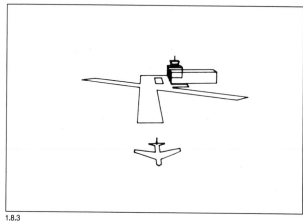

1.8.3

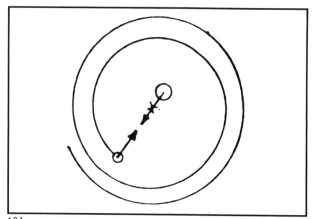

1.9.1

1.9.2

**1.9.1–2: Force, mass and motion**, by Frank Sindon at Bell Laboratories. The first specifically educational computer-generated film. In the first image, two bodies orbit each other as seen from the centre of mass. In the second is a visualisation of a cubic force law of interaction.

**1.10.1–4: Hummingbird** by Charles Csuri, Ohio State University, 1967. A line drawing of a hummingbird breaks up into small pieces and re-assembles. This simple but magical film was widely seen and led on to the current leading position of Csuri's firm, Cranston–Csuri.

1.10.1

**1.7.1–4**: **Lapis**, by James Whitney. This six-minute film was probably the best work achieved on his brother John's original analogue computer as adapted by the artist. It took three year's work from 1963 to 1966 and has a unique atmosphere which reflects the combination of analog. computer technology with meticulous craftsmanship.

**1.8.1–6**: Approach to airport and rotation. HICAMPER language devised by Sherwood Anderson in 1968 at Syracuse University. Operated on an IBM 1130/2250 stand-alone system.

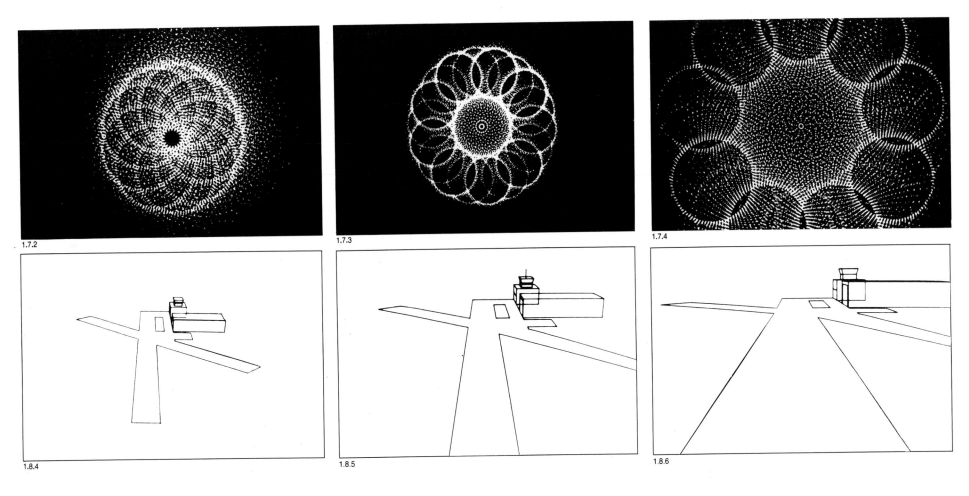

1.7.2

1.7.3

1.7.4

1.8.4

1.8.5

1.8.6

1.10.2

1.10.3

1.10.4

**1.11.1–5**: Frames from a film by Kenneth Knowlton, showing the initials BTL (Bell Telephone Laboratories) proliferating on the screen with his 1972 computer-movie language, EXPLOR (for Explicit Patterns and Randomness), a development of the earlier BEFLIX.

1.11.1

1.11.2

1.11.5

**1.12.1–6**: Titles and rotating satellite by HICAMPER, language devised by Sherwood Anderson in 1968 at Syracuse University, operated on an IBM 1130/2250 stand-alone system.

film of great complexity, and a great artistic achievement.

The use of vector displays for scientific film making was popularized among scientists by E. Zajac, whose computer graphics film *Simulation of a two-giro Gravity-Gradient Attitude Control System* (1963) was widely seen by scientists, at least in the form of still pictures published in the journal *New Scientist* (10 February 1966). The film showed a box, representing a satellite, orbiting the Earth at various angles according to a mathematical model of the Earth's gravity. The *New Scientist* article demonstrated the technique and its effectiveness, and gave examples of similar work using computer graphics for applications in research, such as *Flow of a Viscous Fluid* and *Propagation of Shock Waves in a Solid* from the Lawrence Radiation Laboratory and *Vibration of an Aircraft* from Boeing. Bell Laboratories became a major centre for this sort of work with Zajac, Frank Sindon, Michael Noll, Kenneth Knowlton and others working in the field. The scientific community must have been much encouraged by Zajac's claim that the cost of filming 42 seconds of his film was a mere $30! An interesting educational application of this kind of computer graphics was seen in Sindon's film *Force, Mass and Motion*, which showed Newton's laws of motion in operation and demonstrated the inverse square law.

Programming the computer to produce an animated film sequence was a pretty tortuous job

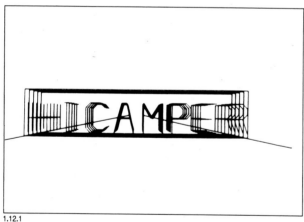

1.12.1

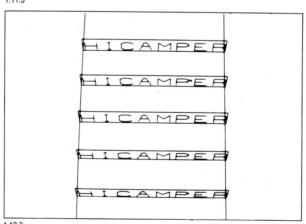

1.12.2

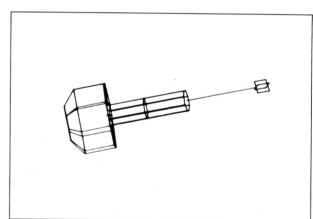

1.12.3

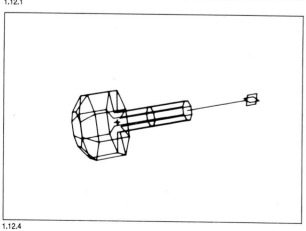

1.12.4

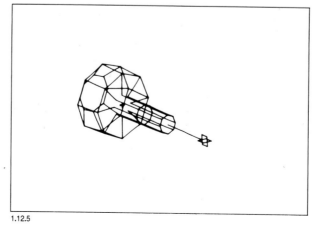

1.12.5

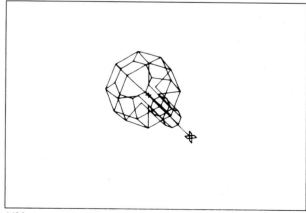

1.12.6

in the early days and only enthusiastic computer users would do it. Help was at hand. First, special languages could be developed allowing situations and actions to be described to the computer which would then compute and send the picture sequences to be filmed. Second, interactive graphics could be used to enable the artist to construct and animate his work directly on the screen, rehearsing the action until it was ready to be filmed. There are many examples of each approach dating from the 1960s and 1970s which helped the methodology along but are all now superseded: CAMP (computer-aided motion pictures) and CAMPER, BEFLIX and EXPLOR, GENESYS and GENESYS II, CAFE, ANTICS, SHAZAM . . . it is a long list. Some, but not all, failed to anticipate the arrival of raster technology and thus faded from the scene along with the vector devices they supported. Others were experiments in the manage-

**1.13**: Car wheel and suspension system using 'close vectors' and colour coding.
*Courtesy Evans & Sutherland Computer Corporation.*

1.11.3

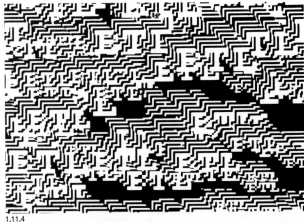

1.11.4

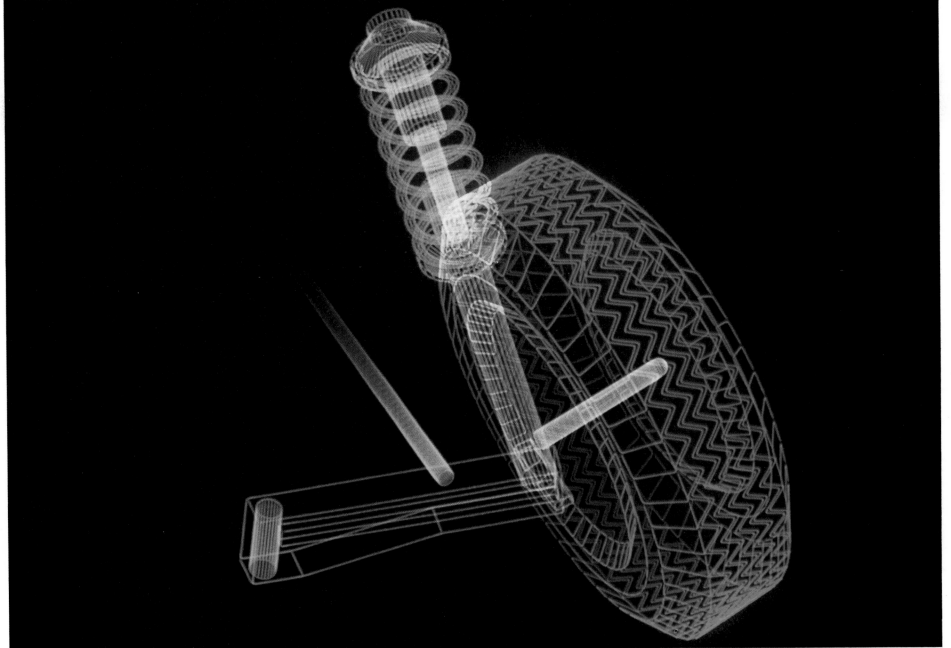

1.13

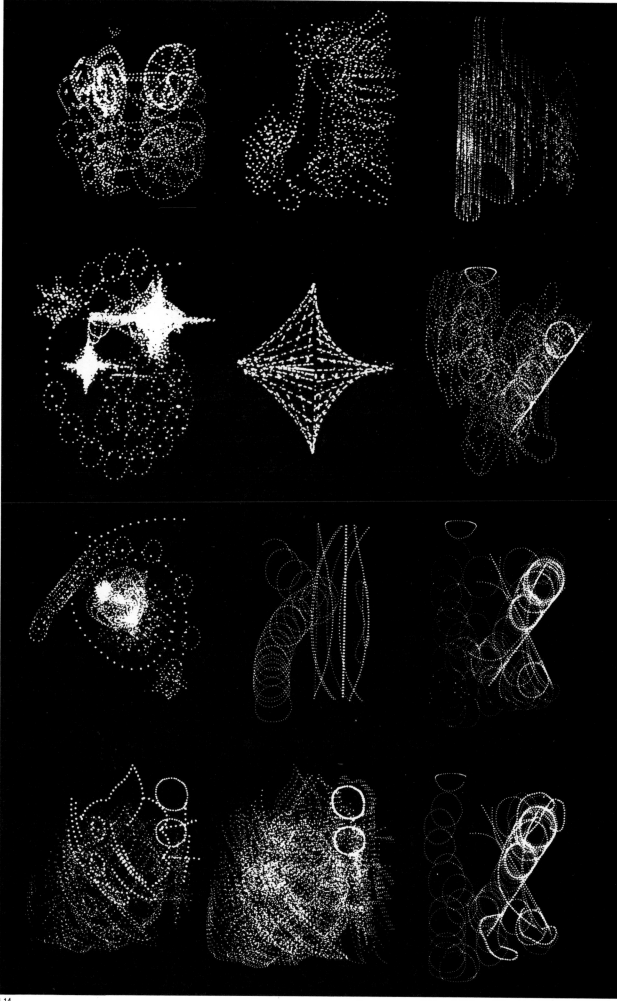

1.14

ment of interactive computing and were devised just to try out an idea.

The real problem however was that the marriage of art and science is not easy: neither side fully understood what the other was saying and in consequence there were many false starts. It would take a brave reporter indeed to claim that the situation is satisfactory even now, though for some this is a source of comfort, ensuring that there are still important subjects left for research. As an amusing aside, it is worth noting that misunderstandings between the two sides can lead to original discoveries. Lynn Smith had been trying to use the GENESYS system (built by Ronald Baecker at MIT in 1969) to draw cartoon characters, when she noticed that the afterglow of the dots of light forming her figures were more appealing than the figures themselves. By a sort of misuse of GENESYS she was able to explore this idea and develop a new style: a computer scientist would normally think of afterglow as an undesirable aspect of the presentation which should be removed as soon as technology permits!

By the end of the 1960s computer graphics had influenced some large and diverse areas and its methodology was pulling together nicely. But it had not reached the general public. There were no commercially available video games, practically no computer graphics on television and no awareness of what computer animation could do. For the scientists who developed wireframe animation though, it was natural to imagine that computer graphics would soon eradicate the repetitive manual work of cartoon animation, so that computer animation could take over a large part of the motion picture industry.

The quest for computer-originated cartoon movies dominated some aspects of computer graphics research, possibly with too much emphasis on imitating hand-drawn cartoons rather than seeking new directions. It is still not really cost-effective to use computers for cartoon animation, despite many attempts, and as yet aesthetically pleasing computer-drawn cartoon characters are few. User Friendly, on the front cover of this book, is one, however, and others may well come from the New York Institute of Technology (NYIT), whose Computer Graphics Laboratory is conducting a well funded campaign to develop the tools and techniques alongside real users and artists in film making. NYIT have an important research programme for two-dimensional cartooning, as well as some exciting and innovative work in three-dimensional modelling.

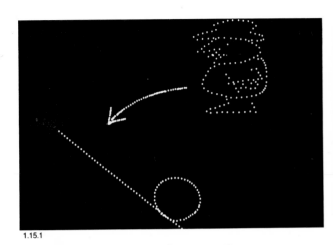

1.15.1

1.15.2

1.15.3

1.15.4

1.15.5

Their *tour de force* is a film entitled *The Works* with an electronic cast of very convincing three-dimensional robots, the result of close cooperation between artist, scientist and computer. Other sections of this book report on such achievements, which point to a rosy future in this area (see Feature Films).

The Computer Image Corporation was largely responsible for introducing computer graphics to television. The first generation of commercials for television using the techniques of computer graphics were made with their three successively more sophisticated systems – ANIMAC, SCANIMATE and CAESAR. SCANIMATE was sold to Madison Avenue by Dolphin Productions in New York, and to London by Scanimation Ltd. These systems were based on processing of hand-made artwork and offered a novel visual fillip to company logos and brand names. Words and symbols could be made to rotate on any axis, zoom into the distance or overhead, stretch or squash – in fact, do many of the things now thought of as video graphics and seen in mainstream television. In 1970 however, these kinds of images were the only computer graphics widely seen. CBS ran sports promotions with them and Bell Telephones made commercials with a rotating Bell logo. For a time it seemed that computer graphics had really arrived in the world of film and television, but the expectation was premature. The high cost and lack of variety in these systems meant that their popularity with producers was transient. Scanimation ceased trading, but the seeds of its successors had been sown. Cooperation between media people and university scientists, artists and hardware designers, system builders and users had begun.

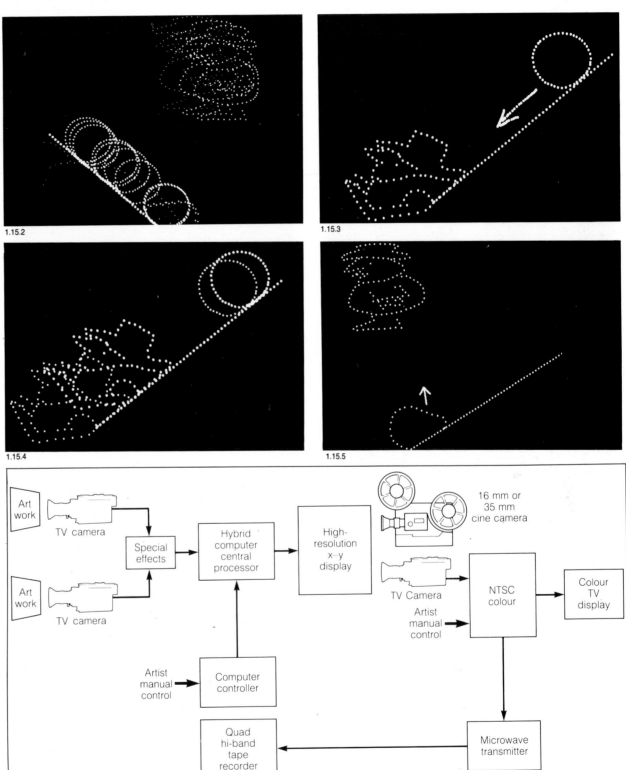

1.16

**1.16**: An analog computer modulates original artwork; a digital computer constructs a model in its memory. The diagram shows an early SCANIMATE analog computer system 1970. The Scanimate computer distorts, rotates and flips over original photographic or hand-made artwork. This was the only high-profile computer graphics method of the 1970s, and it brought computer graphics to the attention of television producers and advertisers.

1.17

Stan Hayward, one of the few people in the world to make a living from writing cartoon films, and Tony Besant, Tom Jebb, Peter Chandler and Tony Diment, whose backgrounds were in computer-aided design, started working together at Imperial College, London. The ideas they developed there were later exploited commercially through Electronic Arts Ltd (formerly called Video Animation) and EMI to make profitable computer-animated films. Their first successful television commercial was for electricity, appropriately entitled *Think Electric*. It was designed by Ken Brown in 1976 on a DEC PDP11/40 computer with a Tektronix storage tube display and a D-MAC digitiser/plotter for input and output on paper. This system also made the titles for the *New Avengers* television series and the 1980 World Cup football matches. Like Zajac's film, it was based on wireframe graphics, with the out-

**1.17**: **Think Electric** a 1976 television commercial designed by Ken Brown. Computer animation by Electronic Arts Ltd in London.

**1.18**: Meteosat image of the Earth from space. The satellite scans three images every thirty seconds.

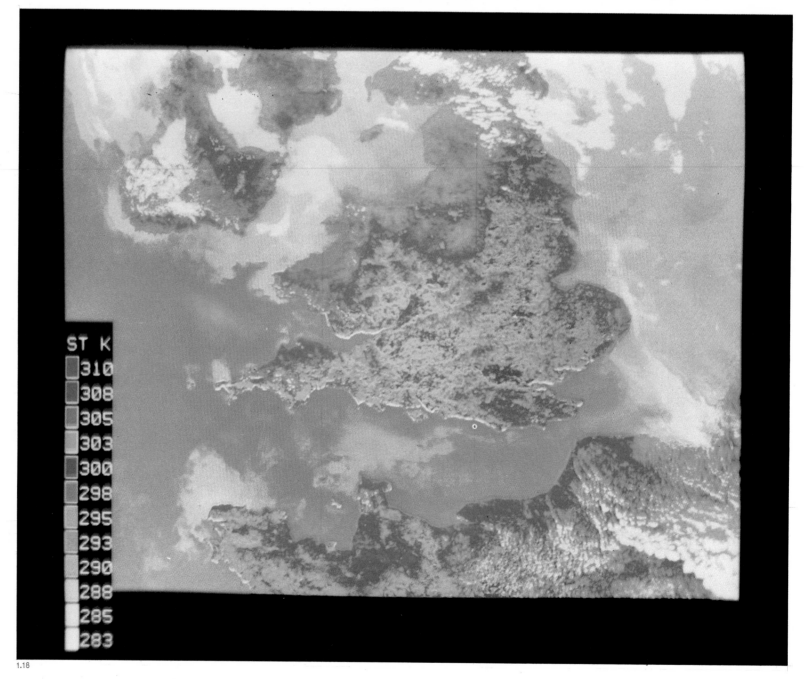

1.18

lines subsequently coloured by hand or treated by photographic means. Costs now favour raster methods of course, and there are several commercially available systems well suited to this sort of work.

Another field of computer graphics is sometimes known as computer imaging or image processing, more easily identified by the acronym PRIP (pattern recognition and image processing), which refers to the processing of an input picture to meet some specified requirement. An example might be to build up a panorama from unmatched single frames of a landscape, or to recolour an image (old black and white movies are being reprocessed to colour in this way). Weather satellites have provided the best known PRIP images since Meteosat was launched in 1978 to monitor the Earth's weather. Signals from the satellite are received in Germany and processed to remove distortions; colour is then added to make clouds white, sea blue and land green. Television weathermen use these images daily.

Finally, the most pervasive computer graphics of all – video games. The video game explosion started with *Pong*, a black and white simulation of table tennis. Programmed and marketed by Atari in 1972, *Pong* had immediate success in bars and amusement arcades. By 1978 home video games were well established and over two million *Pong*-type games were sold in the US in that year. The graphic components of *Pong* were very simple: white rectangular paddles on each side of the screen that could be moved up and down, coupled with a white square that could bounce around the playing area to serve as the ball. The simplicity stemmed from the limitations of cheap electronics of that time, and the public was soon to tire of the game and the spectacle as better things became possible.

*Space Invaders*, a game developed in Japan and sold worldwide by Atari, became so popular that the word for a video game machine in Japan and France was a 'space invader'. Early versions were still in black and white, but the complexity of shapes and movements were far superior to *Pong. Space Invaders* and its variants were the leading video games until Namco in Japan produced a game with a more homely flavour, *Pacman*, in 1980. *Pacman* became the most popular children's character in the US in 1981 and 1982. There have been 100 000 *Pacman* games in American amusement arcades alone and over 30 companies have had franchises for associated goods. Popularity apart, *Pacman* did not represent any step forward for the technical aspect of video games – it made use of existing technology and the visual design was simple.

A different game, *Zaxxon*, which came from Gremlin Industries of San Diego in 1982, gives an appearance of a three-dimensional landscape, over which the operator flies a plane and bombs enemy targets. The image resolution is not high, owing to the problems in performing the game calculations with so little computing power, but it is a significant advance.

Almost every day now sees the release of a new processor, a new game, a new home graphics kit, a new book explaining how to make it all work. The 'hobby' computers are improving such that in the world of home computer graphics there will soon be pictures made which rival the best in this book, many of which took millions of pounds worth of equipment to make. Where will it all end?

**1.19.1–3**: Pistol shot animated on the giant scoreboard at Oakland stadium. The image had a resolution of 80 × 130, and was plotted on the ACIANS (Artist-Computer-Interactive) system by Oscar Vigano.

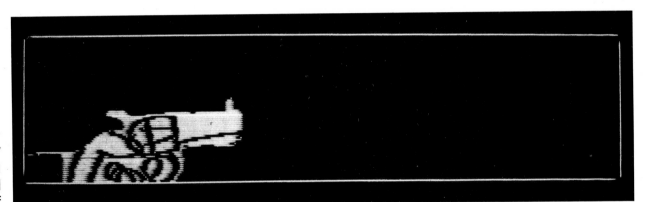

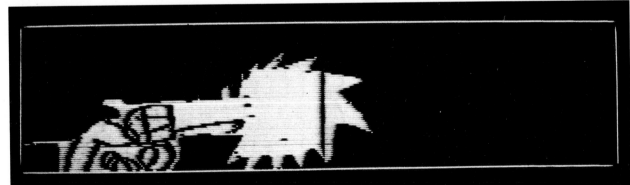

1.19.1–3

# 2 Modelling Techniques

When people see a computer-generated picture very few of them consider how the picture was produced. How was the computer told what to draw? It seems somehow natural to most people that computers should be able to produce pictures. It is therefore easy to underestimate the sweat, tears and computer time which may have been necessary to produce the image they see before them. Producing a picture is basically a two-stage process: first the computer must be told what to draw, secondly it must draw it. The first process normally involves setting up some sort of model in the computer's memory which, to the computer at least, represents the world to be viewed. At a later stage, any desired views of this artificial world may be displayed. The viewing process is described in detail in the next chapter and so will not be dealt with here. Rather, this chapter will describe techniques used to produce the initial, abstract model in the computer's memory.

The final image produced on a graphics screen is always two-dimensional; when we talk of three-dimensional graphics, we are referring to the underlying model used to generate a picture, not the picture itself. It is possible to generate a picture without a model at all, but it would then be very difficult to alter the picture in any way if it is not quite what is desired. The computer must always hold some representation of the picture, even if there is no actual model. At the most fundamental level a vector display must have a list of vectors (straight lines) to be drawn; a raster display needs a bitmap, or quadtree perhaps. It may be possible to perform some operations on these directly but most operations will not be possible. It is the ability to alter a model after it has been created, together with the possibility of generating many different views from a single model which account for the importance attached to modelling techniques.

Models may be divided into two basic types – two-dimensional models and three-dimensional models. It is also possible to have models with dimension greater than three, though the final image will always be a projection of the model onto a two-dimensional viewing screen.

Two-dimensional models are normally used for objects which are essentially flat (two-dimensional). For example, consider an artist drawing on a digitizing tablet using an electronic stylus. The computer model of this picture would probably consist of a list of points (vertices) and a list of which points should be joined to form line-chains. A curve would be approximated by a series of short straight lines. Thus for each line-chain, all that need be stored in the com-puter's memory (or on disk or magnetic tape) would be a list of the coordinates of the points along the line-chain. If the picture is to be shaded it may be necessary to define polygons to be filled in a certain colour. This could take the form of a list of vertices or line-chains to be joined, thus defining the perimeter of the polygon, together with a colour value.

Computer models may also have some hierarchy involved in order to save space or facilitate manipulation of the picture. To create a model to be used in a game of *Space Invaders*, for example, the model would perhaps be on two levels. At the top level the computer would store the positions of the 'invaders' on screen, together with the position of the 'tanks' and 'shelters'. In this way, as an invader moved across the screen it would not be necessary to update all of the coordinates of its outline; all that is needed is to move some point which represented it, say its centre. Only when the image is actually being drawn do we need to know the shape of the invader.

It was stated earlier that a curve could be approximated by a series of short straight lines. If the curve is to appear smooth, the number of line segments required would be very great, which would use a large amount of computer memory. The degree of detail required would depend on the maximum resolution at which the image was to be displayed. For example, consider the outline of a letter S to be drawn on a vector graphics display with a physical height of 10 cm. It may be necessary to specify 100 line segments around the outline of the S for it to appear acceptably smooth. If it is later required to display the S at a height of 3 cm, perhaps 30 points would have been sufficient. The extra 70 points are still taking up memory space, however. This may not matter if spare space is available, but is wasteful none the less. The problem is worse if after specifying the model, expecting it to be displayed at a height of 10 cm it is then decided to display it at a height of 25 cm. The 100 line segments may not be sufficient to give the illusion of a smooth curve; at this resolution the individual straight lines may be visible, and it may well be too late to change the model. This leads to the idea that it would be desirable to have a model which could produce a smooth curve at any resolution, but without the necessity of very large numbers of data points being stored.

Various methods exist for specifying a curve (in two or three dimensions) whose shape is determined by a small number of data points. These have names such as Overhauser curves, Bezier curves, Hermite curves and B-splines. The last three of these are examples of parametric cubic curves. They differ in the details of how the curves are specified, but all allow extra points to be generated along the curve if the resolution of the final picture demands it. The decision as to how many line segments should be used need not be made until the picture is finally displayed on some output device. Instead of joining the points in the model using straight lines, the coordinates of the points may be used in a formula to generate extra points on the curve. This saves computer memory since unnecessary coordinates need not be stored. The shape of the curve is specified exactly by the control points used in the model. In three dimensions, these ideas generalize to bicubic patches.

Another way of displaying detail greater than that stored in the model is what Loren Carpenter calls *stochastic interpolation*. This is a method whereby a complex object, such as the coastline of Britain, is approximated by a crude polygon. Possibly 20 or 30 line segments would be specified in the model. When the map is to be displayed on a graphics terminal, extra line segments are generated in a pseudo-random manner to produce the effects of inlets etc. The way this would be achieved is as follows. Each line chain in the original model is divided in half by the addition of an extra point at its centre. This point is then displaced by a randomly determined distance. Thus, the original straight line will form a shallow V-shape. These new line segments are repeatedly subdivided in a similar manner until the maximum line length is less than some predetermined value, at which point the process is halted. In this way a suitably lumpy coastline may be generated from a few input data points. It obviously will not be an accurate map of the coastline of Britain, but will be much more

recognisable than a picture formed by joining the original points by straight lines. This process is based on what Benoit Mandelbrot calls 'fractional Brownian motion.' Mandelbrot calls curves of this type 'fractal curves'. They are 'self-similar', that is, they are equally jagged at any resolution, and hence have 'fractional' dimension (we shall say more about such curves later in this chapter).

We now turn to the subject of three-dimensional computer graphics. As has been stated before, all computer images are essentially two-dimensional; the difference is in the underlying model. In two dimensions, a model could consist of points and lines. This is also true in three dimensions. However, when a picture modelled in this way is drawn there can be no indication of solidity – what will be produced is a wireframe figure. Since lines have negligible thickness no other lines will be obscured, so the effect will always be of X-ray vision. To avoid this problem a shape's surface must also be modelled. Surfaces obscure anything behind them. This suggests the idea of adding facet (polygon) information to the point and line model. Models defined in this way are called 'polygon meshes'.

When the time comes to display the picture algorithms exist which avoid displaying surfaces and lines that are hidden from the viewer. This gives the impression of a solid three-dimensional object (more on this follows in the next chapter).

This method is very useful for describing such things as the exterior of buildings or, in fact, any object with flat surfaces. A problem arises when the object to be modelled contains curved surfaces. In much the same way that, in two dimensions, curves may be approximated by a series of short straight lines, three-dimensional curved surfaces may be approximated by a large number of flat polygons. The disadvantage of this technique is that the representation is only approximate. The error can be made arbitrarily small by using more and more polygons, but this uses up computer memory and also increases the computer time necessary to manipulate or display the model.

Methods have been developed which define curved surfaces in a way analogous to the parametric cubic curves described earlier. Parametric bicubic patches define the coordinates of points on a curved surface by using three equations, one for each $x$, $y$, and $z$. Each equation has two variables (parameters) and terms for all powers of the parameters up to the cube are used (hence 'bi' and 'cubic'). The boundaries of the patch are parametric cubic curves as mentioned above. These patches can, in general, be larger than the polygons which would be required to define a similar curved surface.

A few control points can be stored in the model (in a similar way to cubic curves) in order to define the shape of the patch exactly. When the picture is being drawn, extra points may be generated on the surface and used in equations to determine shading etc. Thus any level of detail can be generated at display time, although only the coordinates of a limited number of points are stored explicitly in the model.

Thirty six beta-spline patches were used in the model of *Array of bottles* by Barksy, De Rose and Dippé from Berkeley. Beta-splines are a special form of the B-spline that have the ability to vary the tension of the curve but still be described by the same control points. In the bottle example, as the tension increases from left to right and top to bottom the underlying control points of the curve make themselves more and more obvious.

The above methods are very useful in computer modelling; but how are polygons or patches input to the computer? Three-dimensional input is a problem since most input devices, such as digitizing tablets or light pens, are inherently two-dimensional. This makes it very difficult to specify three-dimensional objects by direct methods. It is possible to input three-dimensional information by carefully digitizing several (perhaps three) meticulously drafted engineering-type drawings by tracing them on a tablet, leaving the computer to decide which points in the various views represent the same three-dimensional position. By comparing the position of corresponding points in different views, a three-dimensional 'fix' can be obtained on the point's coordinates for entry into the three-dimensional data base (model). This is obviously a tedious process and can be quite error-prone, especially for complex objects, requiring extra time to be spent editing the model. An even more time-consuming and error-prone method is merely to enter coordinates of vertices, together with line and facet information, via the keyboard. To give some idea of how time consuming these processes can be, in the model of Red Square used for the *Weekend World* title

sequence (see chapter 8), days were spent generating a very accurate model of the Kremlin clock, which, as things transpired, never appeared in the final sequence.

Various methods have been developed to speed up the input of three-dimensional information into the model. To produce a complex symmetrical shape it may be possible to draw an outline in two dimensions, on a tablet for example, then rotate this curve in three-dimensional space to produce points on a surface. These points may then be used to define polygons or patches as desired. This can involve considerable saving for shapes such as bottles, since it is easy to draw the outline of a bottle but not so easy to specify points on its surface in three-dimensional space. Shapes produced in this way may be called 'surfaces of revolution'. The ashtray and the wooden trim of the clock, in the image *Cat Clock* by Glen Entis,

were modelled in this way. 'Swept surfaces' may be created by taking a two-dimensional shape and extending it in a certain direction, effectively 'dragging it out of the page'. For example a cube may be formed by 'sweeping' a square in a vertical direction. In *Cat Clock* the cat's tail is initially modelled as a single curved line; a cross-section is then specified at one point and 'swept' along the curved path.

Another way that a three-dimensional model may be built is by use of specific program procedures, the so-called **procedural modelling** technique. Here a computer program is written which defines in general terms how a certain object should be drawn. Certain key values (parameters) are left to be specified at a later stage to produce a particular version of the object. For example, a procedure may be written to produce a model of a staircase; parameters to be specified

**2.1**: **Cat Clock**. Glen Entis, Pacific Data Image, 1983 Three-dimensional scene rendered on VAX II/750 at 512 × 486 pixels and matted in frame buffer over a sunrise sky and graded tones of the wall. The Pacific Data Images script system models objects with primitives, B-spline bases spheres and anti-aliasing for polygons.

2.1

later may include, where the staircase should be placed, how many steps it should have and the size. A procedure to produce windows may need the position and size to be specified. Large numbers of windows could be produced for a model of an office block, by repeated calls to this procedure. If at a later stage we want to change the style of the windows on the office block, it would not be necessary to alter all of the window coordinates in the model by hand; a simple change in the procedure as to how windows should be drawn is all that would be required. Procedural modelling can be a very powerful tool if a feature is to be modified often.

A slightly different approach to three-dimensional modelling is to work directly with solid shapes. This is called 'solid modelling'. In the techniques described so far in this chapter, only the surfaces of three-dimensional objects have

2.2

**2.2: User Friendly**. The first computer-generated TV presenter. Part of a moving sequence created at New York Institute of Technology Computer Graphics Laboratory. *Computer Scientist: Carter Burwell. Designer: Bill Maher.*

**2.3: Beta-spline bottles with increasing tension values and different textures**. The title refers to the mathematical expressions used to make the curve sharper or smoother while going through the same reference points (e.g. the shoulder and top of the bottle). As tension increases the bottle becomes thinner, as tension decreases, it becomes stubbier. The textures demonstrate a range of texture-mapped effects. Produced by Barsky, De Rose and Dippé, University of California at Berkeley, 1983.

2.3

**2.4**: A Koch curve – four stages in making a snowflake, one of nature's simpler 'fractal' shapes. The snowflake is constructed by mounting an equilateral triangle on each side of an original triangle, and adding more triangles *ad infinitum*. The mathematical paradox is that the length of the sides approaches infinity, but the area remains roughtly constant. This leads to the notion of a 'fractal dimension' – not a one-dimensional line, nor a two-dimensional plane, but somewhere in between. A Koch snowflake has a dimension of 1.26181.

**2.5**: **White Sands**, Alvy Ray Smith, Lucasfilm Ltd. Particle systems, as used for the wall of fire for *Star Trek II*, can also create quite different effects. In this image they provide the grass. The impression of grass is caused by showing the entire parabola of a particle's lifetime as a streak or blade of grass. The lettering in the top left-hand corner is the artist's name in Chinese characters. The flowering plants are grown in three dimensions from a single cell, using an alogrithmic computer model written by the artist and based on mathematics by Paulene Hogeweg. The compositing was accomplished using software by Tom Porter.

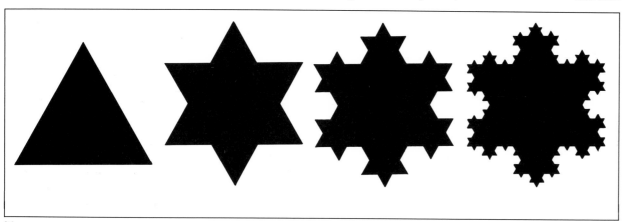

2.4

been modelled; a solid object would in fact be modelled as a closed hollow shape. Solid modelling techniques, by contrast, may be used to represent the object as an actual solid. Objects may be built using solid primitives such as cubes, spheres, cones and cylinders, which are combined using operators such as 'move', 'union', 'difference', 'intersect', 'rotate', 'assemble'. This technique is called constructive solid geometry (CSG). Solids of revolution or swept solids, as described earlier, may also be used in some

Using CSG a ball-bearing with a hole through it could be modelled as a sphere with a cylinder subtracted from it. More complicated objects may be modelled in similar ways. This technique is not easily used when free form curves are required; a teapot, for example, cannot easily be modelled using such primitives. Solid modelling is very popular in computer-aided

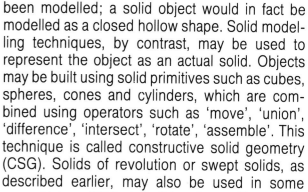

2.5

engineering, not least because many of the operations it employs are readily translated into machine tool actions. For example, subtracting a cylinder from a sphere is equivalent to drilling a hole through it. Again, a model may be generated for the mould necessary to make the object, by subtracting the model of the object from a cube. The robot arm by Al Barr (chapter 4) was modelled using solid modelling techniques based on CSG.

Similar methods have been used to create crude models of human figures using ellipsoids – small ellipsoids being used for the various finger sections, larger ones for forearms, thighs or heads. The figure can then be articulated by allowing suitable rotation about the joints such as elbows, knees or ankles.

The modelling of human beings has long held a special fascination for computer modellers everywhere – ever since it was originally thought that computers may be able to take over the task of character animation (which as noted above has since turned to be much more difficult than anyone imagined). Work is going on at the Computer Graphics Laboratory at NYIT to digitize accurately a sample pair of human figures, one male and one female. A realistic model is being developed of how human joints behave, including such details as the individual vertebrae of the spine. This is a very time-consuming process. An earlier version of the female model was used in making Rebecca Allen's *The Catherine wheel* (see chapter 6). In this piece a computer-generated figure dances alongside a human dancer. The movements of the computer model were determined by studying human dancers. Although this model did not allow for curvature of the spine, the movements of the computer-generated figure are most realistic – a great tribute to the intricacy of the model. The final picture produced was of a wireframe figure with some of the lines removed, very much as though a real dancer had been filmed wearing a black body stocking and hood with green lines painted on it. In fact, so accurate were the movements that it would have been easy to assume this was the case had it not been possible to see through the figure. When a complete model is available, this may be used to define movements for human figures, perhaps by interacting with a 'stick man' image on the screen, to decide on the poses required before the model is 'fleshed out' with clothing and facial features. The modelling of expressions on a human face is a major project in its own right (see chapter 7).

The modelling of human figures may be considered as an attempt to model natural forms. Computer artists are by no means limited to reality in everything they produce; computer models may include impossible objects in unknown environments, without consideration of gravity or other physical laws which must be taken into account when building physical models. Nevertheless, a great deal of energy is being directed into the quest for realism.

Unfortunately, nature exhibits very complex forms which would take an eternity to model by conventional means such as those outlined above. This led several people to the idea of trying to 'grow' models in a naturalistic way but controlled by a limited amount of data specified by the modeller. An example is the modelling of a range of mountains. Mountains are extremely craggy objects and would require a vast number of polygons to be specified to model the surface in sufficient detail. This is obviously impractical. However, it is not normally necessary to model an existing mountain range exactly. Any shape will be sufficient as long as it may be recognized by its overall features; the positions of individual outcrops of rock is immaterial. This being so, if an overall shape can be specified using a few data points and polygons, more data may be generated using some random method which can represent data from the physical world reasonably accurately. Such a technique has been developed by Mandelbrot and described in his book *The Fractal Geometry of Nature* (Mandelbrot calls objects created in this way 'fractals'). Other algorithms which may be used to 'grow'

**2.6**: A mandrill's face wrapped around a ball was a familiar sight to participants at SIGGRAPH 83, the annual meeting of the Special Interest Group on Computer Graphics of the American Association for Computing Machinery. These colourful apes have now been wrapped around glass balls and golf balls, boxes and bottles. This one is by Michael Potmesil, Rensselaer Polytechnic Institute.

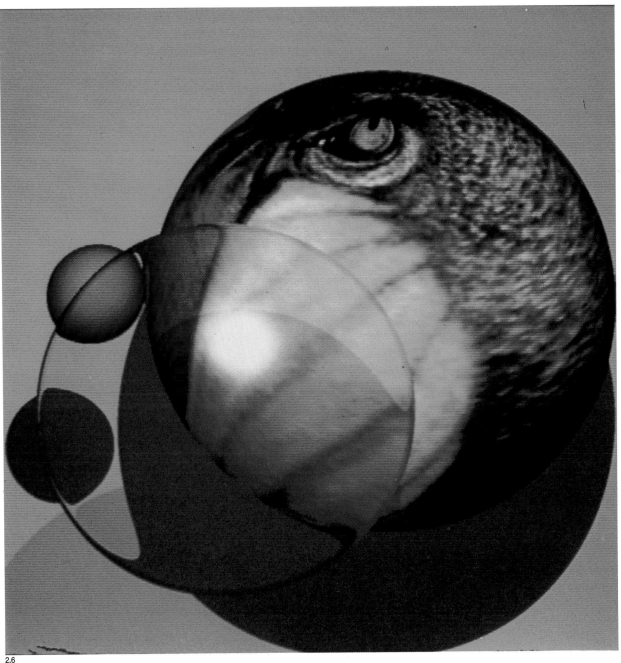

2.6

objects starting from a few data points include 'particle' systems developed by Bill Reeves, and Yoichiro Kawaguchi's 'growth' algorithm. Particle systems are capable of modelling such complex objects as smoke, fire or grass, whereas Kawaguchi's growth algorithm is often used to create models of objects such as flowers or spiral shells. These are all complex objects which may loosely be described as 'natural forms'.

Fractal geometry is perhaps the most exciting theoretical starting point for exploring natural forms. It is based on the concept that dimensions need not always be considered in whole numbers, (one, two, or three dimensions), but can be broken into fractions as a means of obtaining functions much truer to the natural world than the Euclidean geometry of point, line and surface.

A striking illustration of Mandelbrot's ideas is provided by a snowflake. The snowflake in question was discovered by Helge von Koch in 1904. Von Koch took an equilateral triangle, mounted a smaller equilateral triangle on each side, and repeated the process until he could go no further – though in theory the number of triangles is infinite. Mathematicians of Koch's time were disturbed by this curve (in mathematics, bent lines are called curves) which they called 'pathological' or 'monstrous' because it offended against orthodox mathematical theory. The line of the curve becomes longer and longer as more and more triangles are built on, but the area it encloses tends to a limit. At infinity, there would seem to be an infinite length of line enclosing a small, finite area of snowflake; the snowflake's perimeter does not adequately describe its shape, nor does its area. What is needed to provide an adequate description is a number which can be used in a formula to generate a snowflake-like curve. Such a number is what Mandelbrot calls the fractional or fractal dimension of the object – this particular snowflake has dimension 1.26181 . . .

Mandelbrot believes that statistically self-similar curves provide basic tools for analysing and representing (by computer graphics) an enormous variety of physical phenomena. A coastline is wiggly on a map, and wiggly on the ground, down to the smallest pebble of the beach. A mountain is rugged in its silhouette and rugged in each individual crag. A cloud is globular in its general looks, and globular in its smallest puffs. Throughout nature, Mandelbrot has identified a range of phenomena and natural forms which exhibit self-similarity, and therefore fractal dimension. Even price changes in economics and changes in the weather can be shown to follow a fractal pattern.

According to fractal geometry, there are infinite numbers of curves whose dimensions are between one and two. One of these, which Mandelbrot calls his 'snowflake sweep', both fills Koch's snowflake with a space-filling curve and demonstrates the natural forms of the leaves on a tree and the blood vessels in a lung.

As fractal curves between one and two dimensions show remarkable resemblances to natural forms, so fractal surfaces display many more such resemblances. A fractal surface has dimension between two and three. It can look like a mountainside, a cloud or foliage, depending on the dimension. Roughly speaking, the more convoluted the elements in a curve, the higher the fractal dimension. Mandelbrot is sufficiently experienced with fractals to be able to guess with a high degree of accuracy the fractal dimension of any fractal shape he comes across. For those with less experience, he has produced the 'Mandelbrot set', a combination of all the formulae necessary to produce a range of fractal surfaces.

The most commonly seen fractal surfaces are ones used to represent hills and valleys. Hills are easier than valleys since valleys are always smoother and smoothness is not a quality associated with fractals. A contouring algorithm may be applied to make valley floors decently smooth, instead of a mass of ravines, or alternatively a 'truncated fractal' may be specified, in which an arbitrary zero is set at some 'water level'

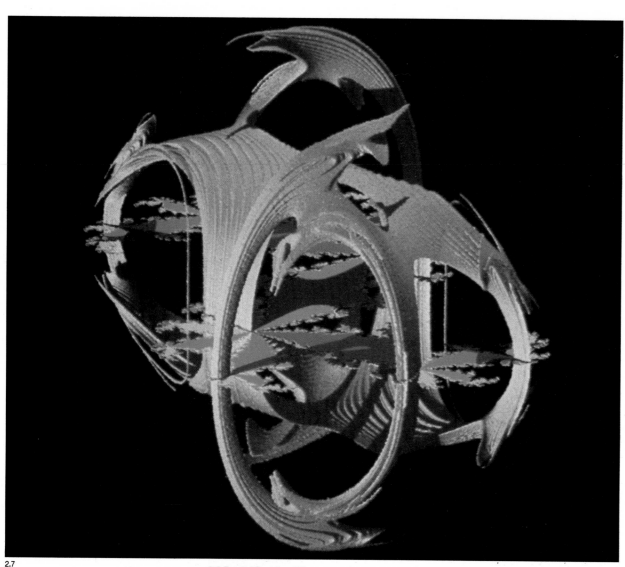

2.7

**2.7: Fractal Construct V,**
Alan Norton, IBM Research.

and no growth occurs below it. The water itself is then produced by other means.

The simplest way to represent a hill by fractals is to specify three parameters (not including those for illumination and the viewer's position). One parameter is length. If you double this parameter, the altitude of the hills will double. The second parameter is a kind of randomness, or rather a choice among a finite number of fractal growth patterns; this parameter is called a 'seed'. The third parameter is dimension. The dimension for a surface will fall between two and three: a dimension nearer two produces smooth hills with pimples growing on them, a dimension nearer three produces a range of jagged hills of the same height. For a relatively realistic mountainside (provided that it is slightly smoothed), dimensions of about 2.3 are useful.

One method in which these parameters may be used is 'polygon subdivision'. Consider a scene in which all surfaces consist of triangles. This type of model is often used to represent real-world data which has been acquired automatically. Each triangle can be subdivided into four smaller triangles by connecting the midpoint of its sides. These midpoints can then be displaced by a randomly determined distance to form a bumpy surface. Such subdivisions can be continued until a scale is reached in which no triangle has a side exceeding a specified length. The original triangle is now a fractal triangle whose irregular surface consists of many small triangular facets. A quadrilateral can be subdivided in a slightly more complex way by generating the midpoint of each of the four sides, together with a central point, and displacing these points as before. In this way, a fractal quadrilateral whose

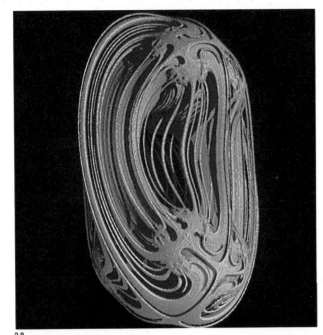

2.8

surface is composed of many quadrilateral facets is produced.

With the extraordinarily small amount of input described above, any number of realistic fractal landscapes can be created. Only colour and shading (illumination) need be added. These landscapes are, of course, more or less random in appearance. The designer cannot accurately predict which crag will come where. However it is possible to set positions for mountain peaks by suitable choice of the initial triangles or quadrilaterals.

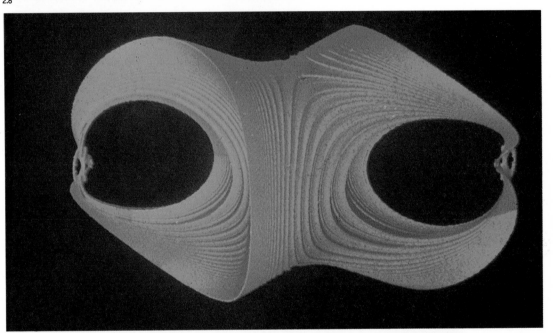

2.9

2.10

**2.8/9/10: Fractal Domains of Attraction**, Alan Norton, IBM Research. Alan Norton writes:
*These mathematical shapes result from the dynamics of simple formulae in three-dimensional space. Repeatedly applying such a formula is like a process of erosion: We see here what remains after the process is repeated many times. The resulting object is a fractal, possessing roughness and fragmentation at all scales of magnification. The generation technique effectively simulates the erosion process inside the memory of a computer, then displays the resulting shape by simulating the reflections of light from such a surface. Calculations were performed on an IBM 3033 computer using an FPS 190L array processor. Pictures were displayed at resolution 1024 × 1280 on a RAMTEK 9400 system.*

has been crossed the pixels are coloured until a second boundary is crossed. This process continues until the rightmost pixel is reached, at which point the process starts again on the next line down. If a count is kept of the number of times the boundary has been crossed we can see that the pixels are coloured if the count is odd and they are ignored if the count is even.

Obviously there are problems with polygons which have horizontal edges and at the points where the boundary crosses itself, but these are fairly easily overcome. This method takes advantage of the 'coherence' of a raster picture by assuming that the colour for one pixel on a scanline is probably similar to the colour for the next pixel on the scanline. The assumption is wrong when the scanline crosses a polygon boundary, but this happens only a few times on each scanline, even for fairly complicated polygons.

Using these drawing primitives we can take a simple model and produce a picture by drawing raster lines for points which are joined in the model to form a 'wireframe' picture, and filling raster areas where there are polygons defined in the model to produce a 'solid' picture. This will produce reasonable pictures for two-dimensional models such as maps and graphs but will be unacceptable for three-dimensional models where a vaguely realistic image is required. The problem lies in the fact that the whole model has been displayed to give an X-ray view of the object. We have all seen a wireframe drawing of a cube, in which it is impossible to tell which corner of the cube comes out of the page, and where the cube seems to twist and tumble in front of our eyes. In real life some parts of the model would be hidden by other parts; we must draw only the visible parts of the model, a process called 'hidden-line' or 'hidden-surface' removal.

There are two distinct forms of hidden-line removal, depending on the way the model is drawn. The first method is used for wireframe drawings and involves removing lines or sections of lines which lie behind visible surfaces (see *Evolution of a Goblet*). The second method is used where the model is defined as a number of planar surfaces, or facets, defined by polygons, and starts by rejecting all polygons which face away from the viewpoint and are therefore not visible. The remaining polygons are painted onto the display starting at the back of the model, the point furthest from the viewpoint, and working forwards. The result is that distant polygons appear only if they are not over-painted by nearer obscuring polygons and a full three-dimensional effect is produced. There are problems with this method when polygons overlap in awkward ways

**3.1.2**: Island and waves in moonlight.

**3.2.1**: Applying flat shading to a raster display, the scan lines intersect the outlines of the house, shading will be added. At the apex of the roof, the scan line intersects only once and no shading is called for.

**3.2.2**: When the scan line intersects twice, it begins to shade in the wall of the house. At the level of the window, it intersects four times and in this case only shades in between the first and second and the third and fourth.

**3.2.3**: When the scan is complete the whole wall is successfully shaded.

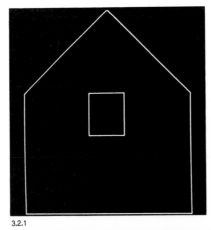

3.2.1

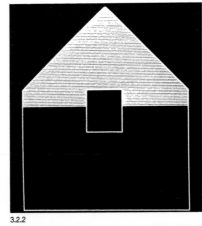

3.2.2

3.2.3

3.1.2

**3.3**: Lighting simulation for interior design.

**3.5**: Lighting simulation for a building. Nakamae, Nishita and Ohbayashi, Hiroshima University. These two companion pieces demonstrate pools of light around the lamp post in the exterior scene and from the wall lights in the interior. There is also apparently natural light and other light sources. The combination of different light sources in one image is a new and complex achievement. 1983.

3.3

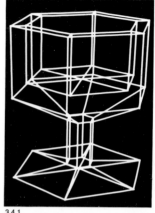

3.4.1

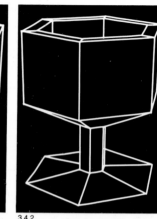

3.4.2

3.5

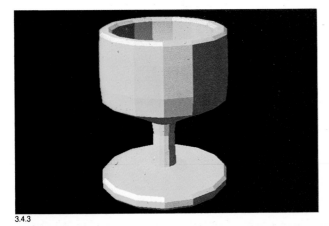

3.4.3

3.4.4

3.4.5

**3.4.1–5: Evolution of a goblet.** Five images to demonstrate basic computer graphics techniques. Dr James F. Blinn and Jet Propulsion Laboratory.
1. The wireframe skeleton.
2. Hidden lines are removed.
3. Solid surfaces and illumination are included.
4. Smooth shading 'sandpapers' the edges.
5. Texture is added.

**3.6: Stools on a floor.** Al Barr, Raster Technologies Inc. The stools are made by Constructive Solid Geometry, and the grooves in the floor are there to show that the shadows are genuine projections onto a non-planar suface (real shadows).

**3.7/8:** Two seascapes with clouds generated by Nelson Max at Lawrence Livermore National Laboratory.

3.6

3.7

3.8

**3.9/10: Sunstone**, Ed Emschwiller
with Alvy Ray Smith (NYIT).

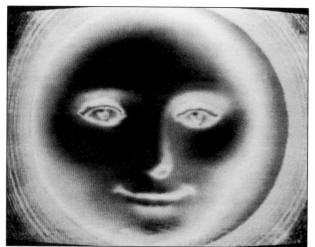

3.9

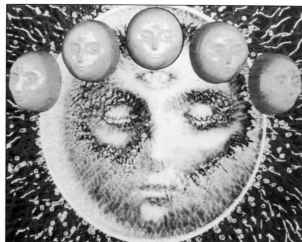

3.10

3.11

**3.11: Foggy Chessmen.** Turner Whitted and Dave Weimer. As an alternative to ray tracing, scan-line algorithms provide a cheaper method of lighting computer models. The imaginary light source's position decides if any pixel is in shadow and the illumination is built up line by line down the screen. Scan-line algorithms cannot handle reflections, however: the mirror chessmen are in fact the original ones turned upside down and toned down to give the effect of reflection in a marble chessboard. The chessmen were designed interactively by David Weimer, Bell Telephone Laboratories, New Jersey.

and the process also involves drawing a large number of extra polygons which are destined to be overwritten by nearer ones. But it does have the advantage of relative simplicity.

The next stage in producing a realistic image is to decide the colour to be used for each of the different facets of the model. The simplest technique is to colour them all the same shade, but this leads to a very plain image in which it is very difficult to tell the direction a facet is facing or how it lies relative to nearby facets. In the real world this information is gained from the exact shade of the different facets, because facets reflect different amounts of light at different angles. So an attempt must be made to relate the shade of the facets to their position relative to the imaginary light source. When drawing a curved object, such as a wine bottle, this gives rise to highlights or 'specular' reflections on the surface where the light source is strongly reflected. Having only one point light source would give a very sharp high-contrast image, so another factor in shading a facet is the ambient lighting, which gives rise to 'diffuse' reflections. Early researchers such as Bui-Tuoung Phong, and more recently others such as Jim Blinn, have produced complex models describing the reflection of light from surfaces such as different types of metal and plastic.

The illumination of the model, which is separate from the model itself and is only decided when the picture is drawn, also gives rise to the problem of shadows that would appear in the real world. In fact the problem of shadow is relatively simple because it can be calculated in exactly the same way as hidden lines. If a point can be seen from the light source it should be well lit, with specular reflections; if it is hidden from the light source and so lies in shadow, it will show only dimly and will have only diffuse reflections. It is necessary to calculate shadows early in the drawing process, before highlights are added; otherwise the effect is as in badly shot 'day for night' scenes in films where the actors fumble along dark streets but every reflecting surface betrays the sun and the lighting.

More advanced forms of lighting are beginning to be developed for specific applications where the restriction to a single point light source is unacceptable. Dino Schweitzer of the University of Utah has produced images of cars with the lighting distributed as carefully as by any advertising photographer. His system controls the light directions, specifies the concentration of light from spotlights to floodlights and masks off unwanted spillage from all these sources. Hiroshima University is a major computer graphics centre and Nakamae, Nishita and Ohbayashi have shown dramatic progress in multiple light sources

46 ■ Views

with their *Lighting Simulation of a Building* and *Lighting Simulation for Interior Design*. These pictures come close to the actual inclusion of a strong direct light source in the image, which has not yet been attempted in computer graphics.

Nelson Max has produced very effective images of *Puffy Clouds*, which are modelled using mathematical equations rather than the more complicated fractals. He has produced algorithms which calculate only the light which reaches the viewer's eye and take into account the sunlight at the top of the cloud, its path through the cloud and the way that the light is scattered and absorbed by the cloud.

So far we have been able to take a model containing many polygonal surfaces and produce an image which shows evidence of lighting in the form of shadows and highlights. This can produce reasonably convincing images, for example Al Barr's stools on an indented floor. However, the appearance of the surfaces is too perfect; they show no texture or irregularity and so appear artificial. The most obvious solution to this problem would be to create a very complicated model containing every little surface detail of the object, but this is clearly impractical because of the inordinate amount of computing power which would be required to generate even the simplest picture. Jim Blinn has produced a very workable solution for simulating rough textures. Rather than stippling the actual surface of, say, a doughnut he uniformly varies the illumination of the surface, which produces a similar effect. The silhouette of the doughnut is not stippled but this is hardly noticeable and would not worry most people.

The *pièce de résistance* of surface detail is the process of 'texture mapping', in which an arbitrary picture can be mapped on the surface of any object. Two stunning examples of this process are given by Ed Emschwiller's film *Sunstone* and Michael Potmesil's mappings of the face of a mandrill on to the surface of a cube, a sphere, the inside of a box and around a flask. The former case actually involves mapping previously computer-generated images on to a surface to create a new image.

The texture mapping process can be used to create all kinds of surfaces from brick walls to patterned bottles, and can also be used with a fine pattern to lend a little realism to an otherwise totally flat surface. Texture mapping also improves the quality of an image by giving perspective clues, since the texture detail is enlarged for objects near the camera but reduced for objects further away.

One difficult area in drawing pictures not yet considered is the representation of transparent objects. This requires the handling of refraction of light passing through the transparent object, like a lens, and the attenuation of light from objects behind the transparent object caused by any translucency in the object. The most successful approach has been devised by Turner Whitted and the classic example of his methods is his picture of a checker board with glass spheres. His approach is called 'ray tracing' and solves most of the problems of hidden lines, shadows etc. at the price of considerable computation cost. The computer follows imaginary rays starting at the viewpoint and heading towards the model passing through one of the pixels on the way, and the passage this ray takes through the model will determine the colour of that pixel. If the ray hits a solid surface then a fraction of the ray, derived from the properties of the particular material in question, is reflected off and the rest is absorbed by the material. If this reflected ray heads towards a light source the effect will be to generate a highlight; otherwise, a normal diffuse colour will appear – unless the ray strikes another object, in which case the whole process is repeated. The most interesting case occurs when the ray passes through some transparent material. Some of the ray will be reflected, some of it will pass through refracted and the rest will be absorbed. The path of the two new rays is followed as before and the pixel colour is derived from a mix of the two rays. The rays may collide with other transparent surfaces and be split again, so the value for one pixel could be the combination of a number of separate rays.

Ray tracing is time-consuming; there are faster methods for producing shaded objects without transparency or reflections using scanline algorithms. A good example of the sophisticated effects which can be obtained by such methods is Turner Whitted and David Weimer's *Foggy Chessmen*.

One problem which has been glossed over so far stems from the fact that the display is limited to a finite array of pixels and the final picture is just a mosaic of small coloured squares. During the calculation of the picture the model has been sampled only at points which correspond to the centre of one of these pixels, so the detail lying between the points is lost. This gives rise to the problem of 'aliasing'. One obvious effect of this sampling is the 'staircase effect', obtained when trying to draw straight lines or edges. Aliasing also causes other problems, such as interference effects when thin lines are drawn close together; these effects are similar to the swirling pattern seen on television programmes when a presenter wears a herringbone jacket or closely striped shirt.

The solution to the problem is called 'anti-aliasing'. Essentially, this tries to take into

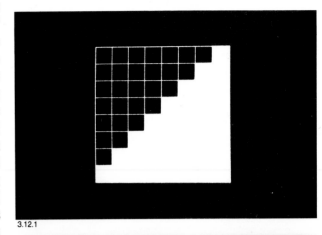

3.12.1

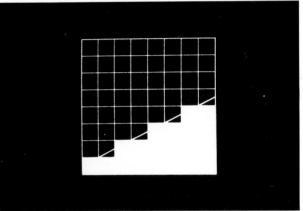

3.12.2

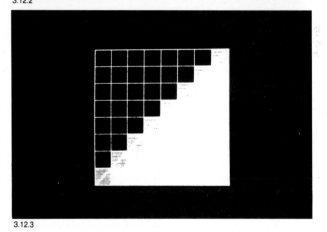

3.12.3

**3.12.2:** If each line of pixels is not aligned exactly with the scan lines, some pixels are lost and the aliasing effect is worse. Pixels are also lost during sampling for hidden-line removal and illumination.

**3.12.3:** At the edge of the slope pixels are given a shade that is an average of two adjacent ones. This 'anti-aliasing' technique makes the slope look smooth. The diagram should be viewed with half-closed eyes for the effect to be noticeable.

**3.13**: **Theme image for SIGGRAPH 1981.** Turner Whitted. The reason this image was chosen for SIGGRAPH 81, the computer graphics convention, was that it is visually appealing and also demonstrates the most elegant method of lighting curved and reflected objects – ray tracing. In ray tracing, the computer calculates the path of rays as if from the viewer's eye, bouncing off surfaces and bending through glass to the imaginary light source. Thus the light from the red and yellow squares is reflected and refracted through the glass ball, and the properties of glass are convincingly simulated. Any material whose transparency and reflectance can be calculated can be created in the same way, but it is expensive in machine time. Bell Telephone Laboratories, New Jersey.

**3.14**: **Sunstone,** by Ed Emschwiller with Alvy Ray Smith's computer graphics. This film is a *tour-de-force* combining vivid hand-painted images with computer graphics 'wrapping' techniques. Computer graphics executed at NYIT Computer Graphics Laboratory.

**3.15**: **Martini glass with dice**, Gray Lorig, Rensselaer Polytechnic Institute.

account all of the model lying within the area covered by one pixel. With anti-aliasing, the colour for the pixel becomes the average colour of a small area of the whole model rather than the colour at one particular sampling point. In practice this often means sampling a number of points within each pixel and taking the average of these values. For example, with the ray tracing method of picture construction the rays are actually sent from each corner of a pixel; the final colour of the pixel is the average of these four corner values. The sampling which is the cause of the aliasing still remains but the effects are reduced to such an extent that the eye can no longer detect them. The same effect could also be obtained by using smaller pixels in the display, but this is not physically possible with current displays except when recording directly to film.

The aliasing problem occurs again when

3.13

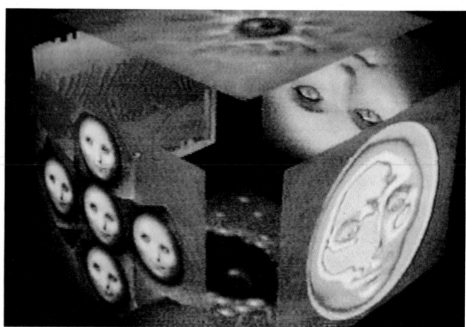

3.14

3.15

individual computer-generated frames are combined to form an animated film sequence. The model is sampled at discrete moments in time, leading to 'temporal aliasing', or aliasing in time, rather than the previous problem, which is known as 'spatial aliasing', or aliasing in space. The solution to temporal aliasing is to make each computer frame show the average picture over a short period of time, in the same way that a film camera shutter is open for a short period of time and captures an average photograph. The camera shutter is open for half the time during camera filming and so the temporal anti-aliasing, or 'motion blurring', should average the picture over a similar proportion of the total time between frames. Thus in Bill Reeves's particle systems sequences, such as the 'genesis bomb' sequence from *Star Trek II: The Wrath of Khan*, the particles are drawn not as points but as lines

**3.16**: **Growth: Mysterious Galaxy**, a short film by Yoichiro Kawaguchi, Osaka University, exhibits a science-fiction landscape or seabed in close up with mysterious organisms constantly growing and interacting with one another. Kawaguchi's growth algorithm, which can produce such shapes as spiral seashells, is similar to fractal techniques in its ability to continue *ad infinitum*. Jim Blinn is also credited for his surface algorithm, with added transparency effects by Kawaguchi: Produced on a Links-64 multi-micro system.

**3.17**: **Teapot**. Rob Cook, Lucasfilm. Teapots are popular modelling examples as they display complex curves.

**3.18**: **Dice and sphere**, Raster Technologies Inc. Dice, like mandrills, are popular images because they demonstrate mastery of difficult techniques. The rounded corners and the hollows for the numerals, each side different, require sophisticated computation. When these are combined with transparent and reflecting surfaces, it is really something to shout about.

3.16

3.17

3.18

**3.19**: Rylos base hangar, from *The Last Starfighter*. Shots of the vast mountainside hangar are intercut with sets detailing activities of the characters. It is not easy to tell what was generated by computer and what was physically built. The spacecraft are 'made' of a metallic alloy – they shine, reflect, register shadows and have the sheen of 'real' spacecraft.
*Digital Scene Simulation by Digital Productions, Los Angeles, California.*

**3.20**: Gunstar with green moon of Rylos, *The Last Starfighter*. Gunstar, the film's mothership, comprises almost 400 000 polygons, four times that of any object previously produced by computer graphics imagery. Each frame takes five minutes, or more to compute on the most powerful computer in the world today, the Cray X-MP.
*Digital Scene Simulation by Digital Productions, Los Angeles, California.*

**3.21**: **Puffy clouds**, Nelson Max, Lawrence Livermore National Laboratory.
Mathematical equations (involving trigonometric series and polynomials) defined the shapes of the clouds. Clouds reflect and emit light and are also partially transparent, so illuminating them is complex. However, Max has written an algorithm for light diffusion, calculating only the light that reaches the viewer's eye, but taking account of the sunlight at the top of the cloud, its path through the cloud and the way that some sunlight is absorbed inside the cloud while some is scattered as it goes through the cloud. Only a proportion of this sunlight eventually reaches the eye and needs calculation by Max's algorithm.

joining the position of the particle at the start of the frame to the position of the particle at the end of the frame. Of course, all such frames must also be spatially anti-aliased, so computer generation of animated sequences is a slow and complicated process.

Co-operation and competition are both intense in the development of computer graphics. A particular technique may be welcomed gladly by some practitioners but reviled as an inadequate substitute by others who think they invented the definitive version. As some techniques gain prominence and others are neglected, it is tempting to see a linear progression from, say, old-fashioned vector displays to modern raster displays but in a complex field like computer graphics this view of developments is dangerous. Benoit Mandelbrot, a mathematician before he began his major contribution to computer

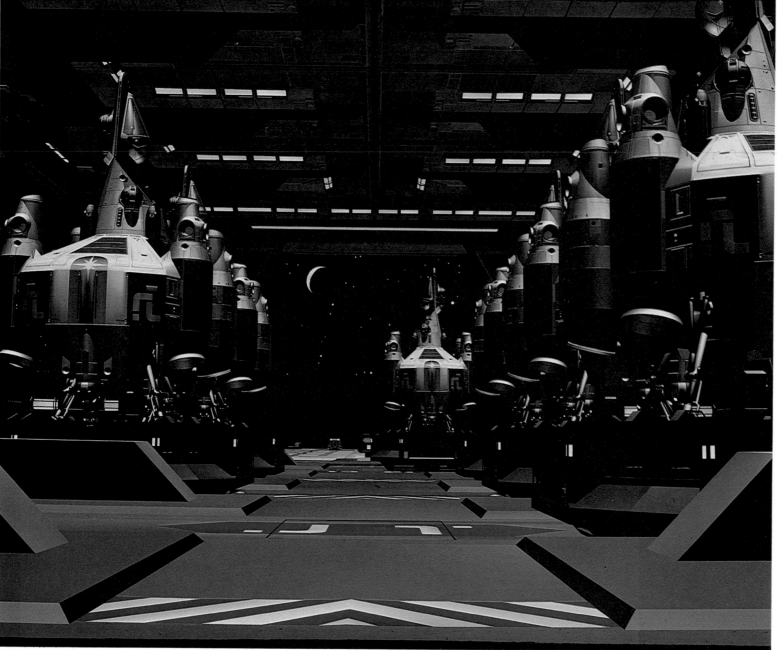

3.19

3.20

graphics, takes great delight in pointing out that the fundamental theories on which he bases his work were complete in 1925 and were ignored as useless until his computer graphics demonstrated their significance. It may be that there are other techniques which, although currently considered to have had their day, will be rediscovered or find some new application no one could have expected.

Digital Scene Simulation is the trade name of a technique which produces very effective computer-generated film, having come to prominence with a short sequence containing the antics of a computer-generated juggler named Adam Powers. The character is modelled using 25–30 000 polygons and impressively animated without the use of any photography or hand drawing. The face of Adam Powers is also used in the feature film *TRON*, where it is texture-mapped

3.21

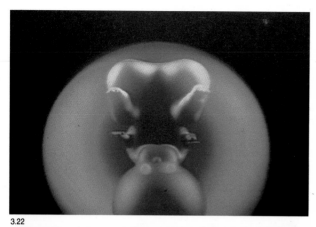

3.22

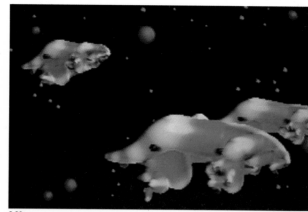

3.23

3.24

**3.22/25**: Further sequences from *Growth: Mysterious Galaxy* by Yoichiro Kawaguchi, Osaka University.

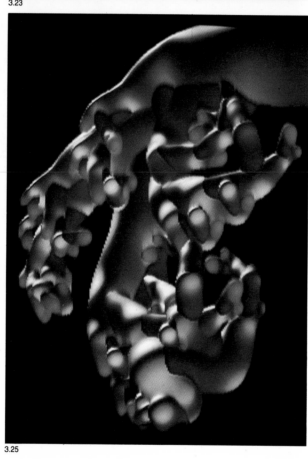

3.25

around a pillar to produce MCP, the imposing evil genius of the computer.

The Digital Scene Simulation technique can now be used with pictures as complex as 1 000 000 polygons, although the computing power required for such images is tremendous. The images are created in six minutes by a Cray X-MP/22, a $12.5 million supercomputer whose main technical superiority lies in a freon gas cooling system to remove the heat generated by the very fast computing circuits contained within this 5.5 ton machine. Such a general purpose computer is used to calculate the camera movement and object animation as well as the actual picture generation. Other centres such as the Computer Graphics Laboratory at NYIT and Lucasfilm use specialized graphics-display computer systems and can use smaller, cheaper machines for the general computing.

Current advances in technology will increase the complexity of computer-generated images through devices such as networks of 32-bit microprocessors and high speed transputers which can be used to spread out the computation among a number of small but very fast processors. The fifth generation 'artificial intelligence' computers will also be useful for the initial model creation and for effective animation of complex scenes where the computer must understand the physical properties of the objects being drawn.

A picture which draws together many of the strands of current research in computer graphics is Lucasfilm's image entitled *The Road to Point Reyes*. Like everything in this picture the word 'Reyes' is artificial, being an acronym for 'renders everything you ever saw'. The road, the sea, the promontories, the fence, the rock face, the flowers and the grass, the puddles, the white lines on the road, the double rainbow and the misty distance are each separate achievements of a wide range of computer graphics techniques.

The picture is credited to Rob Cook, who is given the title of director. The title is well earned, despite the fact that the image is a still photograph rather than a film, because a large team of specialists were involved in creating the separate parts of Point Reyes. The parts have been composited to form an image as close to a natural photograph as has yet been achieved. The solids in the picture are modelled using polygons and patches; the sea, promontories and rock face were produced using fractals; the forsythia bushes and the fence were drawn using procedural models. The ripples in the puddles were produced separately by David Salesin; the grass by Bill Reeves, using his particle systems. Rob Cook wrote the lighting model for the rainbows and produced the texturing and shading for the road, hills and fence as well as the shadows of the fence and the reflections in the puddles; Loren Carpenter dealt with the fractals and also wrote the atmosphere program for the sky and mistiness in the distance. Visible surfaces were dealt with by Carpenter, anti-aliasing by Cook and compositing by Tom Porter. The whole picture was produced using a 4000 × 4000 pixel display.

The large amount of computing power required to create detailed images such as *Point Reyes* is not available to most researchers and so much of the work being done in computer graphics is concerned with the use of new and existing technology to create graphics-oriented machines and new types of display. For example, Tektronix Corporation is studying the use of plasma displays, electro-luminescence and a range of flat panel displays as well as high speed refresh displays. Considerable research is also being carried out on ways of consolidating the current ideas to generate faster methods of producing the same results.

We must bear in mind that the complex realistic images seen in the pages of this book represent the result of a vast amount of computing time. Even short sequences of film can take years to complete. The actual use of graphics is thus limited by the speed with which images can be generated. This poses as many interesting problems as the realistic drawing of natural objects, as we shall see when we turn to the practical uses of computer graphics.

**3.26**: **The Road to Point Reyes**, Lucasfilm Ltd, 1983. This landscape was defined using patches, polygons, fractals, particle systems, and a variety of procedural models. The various elements were rendered separately and later composited. The piece is very much a team effort, a one-frame movie. Loren Carpenter used fractals for the mountains, rock, and lake and a special atmosphere program for the sky and haze; he also wrote the hidden-surface program. Rob Cook directed the picture, designed the road, hills, fence, and rainbow, and wrote the texture-mapping and appearance factors software. Tom porter provided the procedurally drawn texture for the hills and wrote the compositing software. Bill Reeves used his particle systems for the grass and wrote the modelling software. David Salesin put the ripples in the puddles. Alvy Ray Smith designed and rendered the flowering plants using his procedural software. The picture was rendered using an Ikonas graphics processor and framebuffers, and was scanned onto film with a COLOR FIRE 240, courtesy of Mac-Donald Dettwiler and Associates, Ltd. The resolution is 4K × 4K, 24 bits per pixel.

3.26

# 4 Design and Industry

4.1: A CAE system can conjure up realistic neckties and the pattern can be altered without any physical drawing. All the manufacturing implications, from the tessellations giving maximum amount of usable fabric to the cost implications of short and long production runs, can be tested on the screen before any commitment is made.

*Mike Newman, Dicomed Corporation*

Early computer graphics systems were expensive and relatively feeble. The only cost effective applications for them were those that promised, and delivered, a dramatic improvement over manual methods. Engineering design was one of the first contenders for the sensible application of computer graphics and the 'Sketchpad' experiment seemed to point the way forward. However, it was much harder than expected to get useful results. The technology itself was not ready to support wideband or high rate devices, and interactive computing was in its infancy. Nobody knew how to construct a database able to hold the details of a complex design (such as a ship hull) while several designers continued to work on it. Computer-aided design was the catch phrase but what exactly is it that designers do? And what is the computer supposed to contribute? After a long and quite painful gestation period computer-aided engineering (CAE) became a reality and now touches very wide-ranging activities in many different industries.

Computer graphics forms a prominent and essential component of many CAE installations.

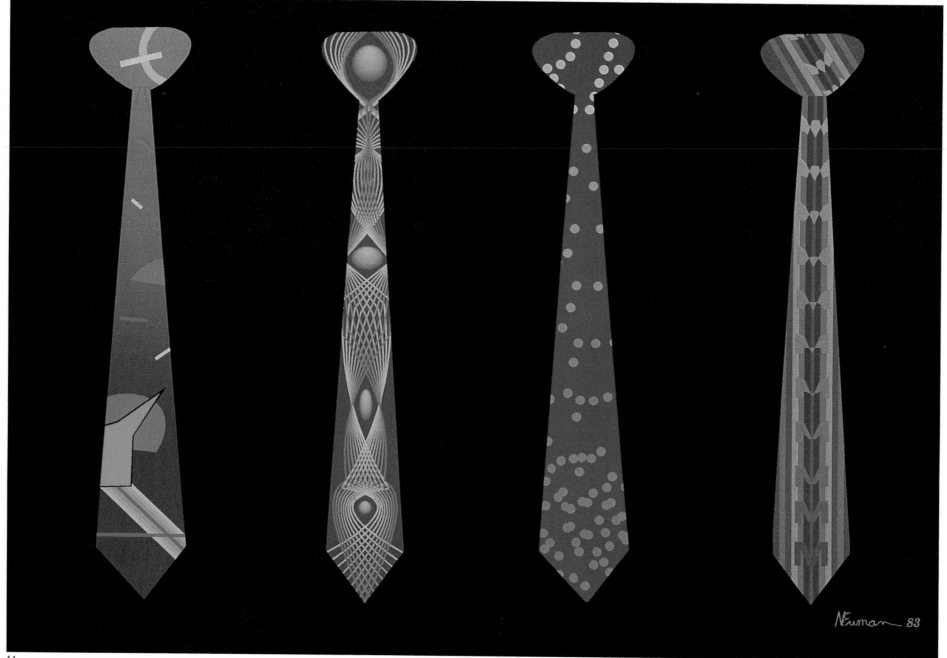

4.1

There is some common ground in the software for interactions management, database manipulation and picture generation. Often, however, the common areas are not clearly visible and different systems (even those serving similar purposes) frequently behave in quite different ways. Researchers do not yet understand the human factors of the man–machine interface well enough to establish effective guidelines for the system builders. Neither have they fully grasped the mechanical, intellectual or artistic aspects of the design activity itself. Nevertheless much useful work is being done: advances nowadays stem more from improvements in understanding than reductions in hardware costs. The past 20 years may be thought of as the period from birth, through infancy (first steps, much falling over), to childhood (lightweight, self-centred but learning fast). Present systems are adolescent (narrow, temperamental and impatient) but maturity will come and with it dominance of the industries that use it – in a few cases one can argue that it has already arrived. When the steam engine was introduced in 1810 it also took 20 years for it to dominate industry, but by then its potential for development was practically exhausted. By contrast the potential for the development of CAE is still enormous and it is hard to see when it will reach exhaustion.

Computer-aided engineering refers to the design (CAD), manufacture (CAM), testing and repair of the products of the engineering industry. There are in addition the many supporting activities, such as progressing, reporting, documenting, and there are also connections to other more traditional computing functions, stock control, management information and forecasting. Of course, the sort of thing being manufactured influences everything, but there are several different reasons why CAE methods are being adopted.

The first is to help cope with complexity. An aircraft, a computer, an integrated circuit have in common a bewildering amount of important detail which designers must create and control, and manufacturers must reproduce and test, and for which a slight mistake could spell disaster. The computer can keep track of such detail and verify that no mistakes have been made.

Another reason is to speed up and simplify experiments. Much design involves some variant of the cut-and-try method, in which the designer changes something and then assesses the change – is it better or worse? Finding an agreeable shape for a telephone handset by carving a model is an example: the computer can simulate the model making, obviating the need for an actual physical model.

**4.2**: Wireframe skeleton for an aircraft on Evans & Sutherland's original Picture System.
*Courtesy Evans & Sutherland Computer Corporation.*

**4.3**: Piston and connecting rod for Ford 1.6 litre Escort engine, as used on SIGGRAPH 83 poster. Produced using Ford enhanced version of the PADL solid modelling system from the University of Rochester.
*Ford Motor Company, Scientific Research Staff.*

4.2

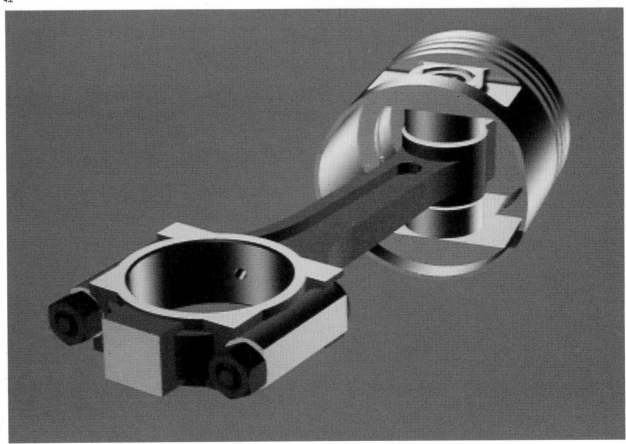

4.3

To coordinate the efforts of many people is a third reason for using CAE methods. When working with paper drawings there is the constant danger that incompatible changes will be made by different designers on their separate drawings. With shared access to a single version of the prime data held in the computer, this danger is greatly diminished – though a fully satisfactory solution remains elusive.

CAE methods offer advantages in mass production and quality control. People are easily bored, and so become inefficient, by dull repetitive work. It is a serious limitation on manufacturing technique if it has to provide an interesting role for each person engaged in it. Robots do not get bored.

Similarly, robots are well suited to dangerous or manually non-feasible job steps. When fitted with small claws with nine fingers, strong arms that lift ton weights, tongs for moving red-hot metal, robots can go places and do things that are impossible for human beings.

Finally, CAE provides methods of analysis and synthesis. Many manufactured objects have an associated mathematical explication which can be used in CAE to allow the computer to discover what would happen (or is happening) to the object under stated (or applied) conditions. Some design can even be done by rule – a specification is automatically turned by the computer into a product design. When applicable such use of the computer is invaluable – indeed, sometimes there is no other way to proceed. A modern integrated circuit could not be made *at all* without computer assistance for design and verification.

Whatever the particular reason may be (and there are others besides those we have mentioned), computer graphics can furnish the means for man and machine to cooperate.

The detail in the picture display is limited to what is necessary for the operation being carried out. There is less emphasis on realism for its own sake and more on the efficient use of symbolism, so as to speed the interactions, to simplify the situation being shown to the operator or to concentrate on some particular feature. Even when generating hard copy for study away from the computer, these considerations still apply – the images are for the engineers to use in advancing their design, not for the board room. Of course it is often the case that the images have a certain aesthetic appeal, and those shown in this book are chosen because they delight the eye, as well as inform the brain. However, it is useful to keep in mind that whereas for some images we can say 'this picture is the answer', for others it is better to say 'this abstraction helps us understand what is going on'.

We might have expected that one effect of the widespread adoption of CAE methods would be the elimination of paper drawings and printed documents. This has not happened, and is unlikely to do so, at least in the near future, although there are important changes in the 'status' of paper materials. What used to be the master drawings, needing manual authority for change, copy and issue, are now entries in the computer database. In some cases they may not even be represented as drawings at all; instead, specific drawings will be derived as needed from the model of the thing being processed held in the computer. This however is a fairly modern idea. In the more common use of computer-aided draughting, each drawing has the same individual existence inside the computer as the paper sheet master once had in the drawing office. What each drawing represents may or may not be 'known' to the computer.

Useful work can be done simply by helping the designers make drawings more quickly. Indeed, this was the main objective of several commercially successful systems, although a comprehensive approach to CAE must aim at much more than that. Modelling the object, instead of just holding drawings of it, makes possible the derivation of all kinds of useful information – how the object is to be built, how well it will fit its intended purpose, what it will weigh and what it will cost. Analysis by the computer can proceed only if it is given a deeper representation than a set of drawings, for their interpretation requires expert knowledge and the background of an engineer. (It is possible that, using the techniques of artificial intelligence, a computer could extract the necessary information from the drawings but it would be an extremely odd way to proceed when the information could all have been made available to the machine at the stage of generation – hardly an efficient use of resources!) The form taken by the model stored in the computer varies enormously with the tasks it is supposed to support. In all cases, however, the facility for computing a property of an artefact being designed within the computer depends on having the requisite data available in its stored model.

The Frenchman Jean-Marc Brun, who designed the Euclid solids modelling project for Matra-Datavision, has remarked that engineering design and the graphic arts were so closely associated with one another during the Renaissance in Italy that Leonardo da Vinci was able to 'create a design technique where graphics, painting and sculpture formed a masterly blend'. Perspective drawings, Brun argues, were descriptions of three-dimensional objects perfectly

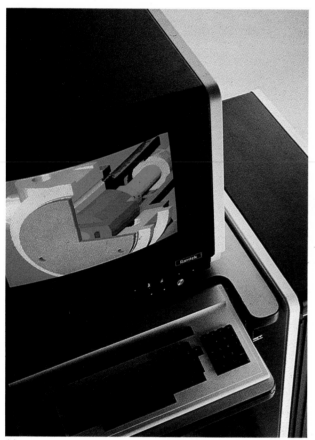

4.4: A CAE graphics work station marketed by Ramtek Inc.

4.4

adequate to guide the minds of designers until the age of mass production inaugurated the blueprint and the table of standard specifications. These two-dimensional representations of objects were better suited to serial production steps and to teams of de-skilled draughtsmen working remotely both from the original designer and the production process itself. Only lately, Brun says, has the sophistication of computer methods enabled the designer to create a model with the three-dimensional solidity of Leonardo's perspective drawings.

Amongst the frontrunners of CAE users, Ford Motors have gone a long way towards integrating design and manufacture and now have 360 workstations based on Prime minicomputers and a further 60 specialized workstations supplied by Computervision. Ford is striving to achieve maximum interchangeability of machine readable data between itself and its suppliers and is urging its component suppliers to adopt compatible systems. Preferably, this compatibility is achieved through the use of standards rather than just working with similar equipment, and although there do exist such standards (for example the Intermediate Geometric Exchange Standard, IGES, for geometrical data) they have not yet been widely adopted. A large corporation can readily face the costs of re-equipping its CAE systems but smaller firms may not find it so easy; standards will be effective only when some degree of acceptance has been established throughout the industry. When it happens the long term effects will be twofold. First, the industry will find it much easier to function, with work flowing from supplier to consumer with less manual red tape and fuss. Secondly, the standards themselves will stifle a certain facility for innovation that might otherwise improve the same work flow. Seeking to standardize too early causes this problem and there has been much argument about when it should be, or should have been, done for the CAE fraternity. When the Pentagon recently proposed replacing its computers the absence of standards for the existing data caused

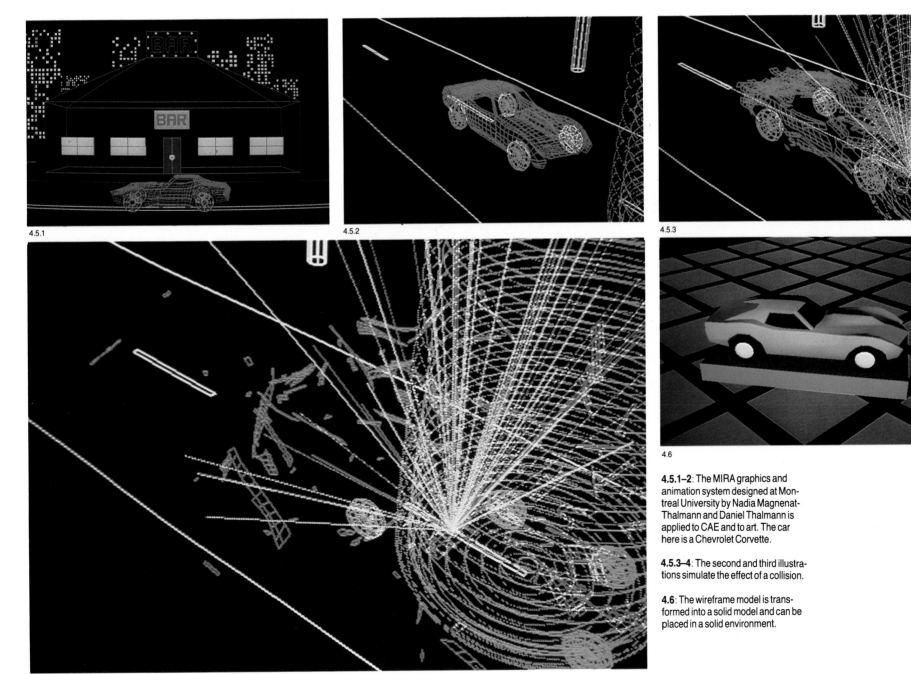

4.5.1

4.5.2

4.5.3

4.6

4.5.4

**4.5.1–2**: The MIRA graphics and animation system designed at Montreal University by Nadia Magnenat-Thalmann and Daniel Thalmann is applied to CAE and to art. The car here is a Chevrolet Corvette.

**4.5.3–4**: The second and third illustrations simulate the effect of a collision.

**4.6**: The wireframe model is transformed into a solid model and can be placed in a solid environment.

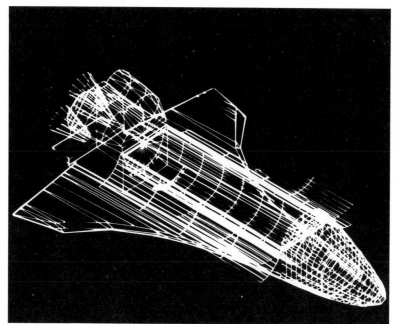

**4.7**: The NASA space shuttle, as represented in a finite element model using PATRAN-G software on an Evans & Sutherland PS 300.
*Courtesy Aerospace Corporation and Evans & Sutherland Computer Corporation.*

4.7

the converse problem – the new computer systems had to be reprogrammed to accept the old data. This was probably a worse situation than using a real, if poor, standard data definition and the old ideas have now been perpetuated until the next time a replacement comes due. What will they do then?

Building a workstation environment suitable for people to work at for many hours each day, week in week out, is a real challenge. Nowhere is it felt more strongly than in CAE applications where managers, engineers and technical workers are all under pressure to act fast and properly. A system which responds slowly will soon seem irritating, an irritated operator will make some mistakes, being told one has made a mistake is itself irritating. Slowness is a highly subjective matter however and it is not necessary for every machine action to be very fast. Indeed, if

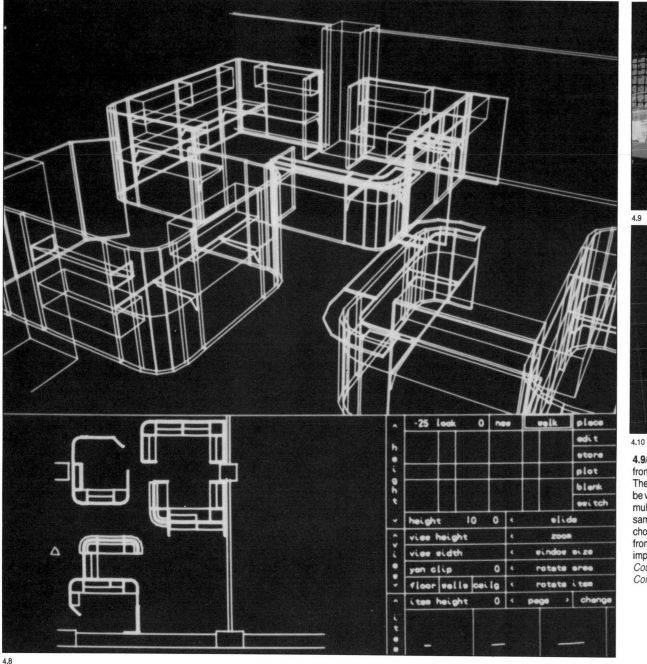

4.8

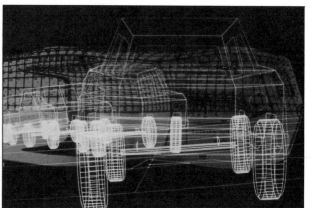

4.9

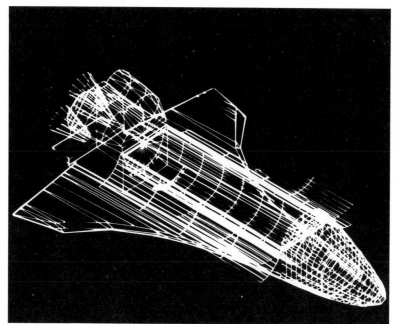

4.10

**4.9/10**: A package of dynamic images from Evans & Sutherland's PS 300. The approach of the automobile may be viewed as a motion picture, or multiple images may be viewed at the same time. The designer may also choose the angle of view. A long view from above gives a more global impression of the car's performance.
*Courtesy Evans & Sutherland Computer Corporation.*

the system is always so fast that the operator never has to wait, he then feels goaded into action which he may not be fully ready to take, and again mistakes occur. The system has somehow to 'feel' right, so that operators are working comfortably and at their own speed. Humans have two modes of behaviour, corresponding with the left and right hemispheres of their brains, which are very different. One hemisphere, the left, processes symbolic information sequentially and is believed to be the area where conscious thought goes on. The right hemisphere controls intuitive behaviour and works in a more 'holistic' fashion. Pattern recognition and subjective matters are dealt with there. The US computer equipment manufacturer Hewlett Packard has conducted experiments on people working at screens and found that their right hemispheres are generally dominant when active pictures are being

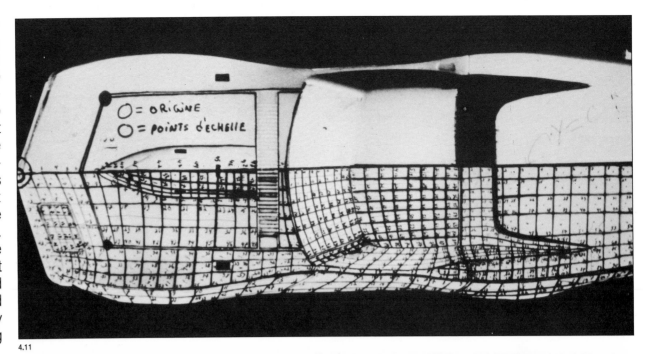

4.11

4.12

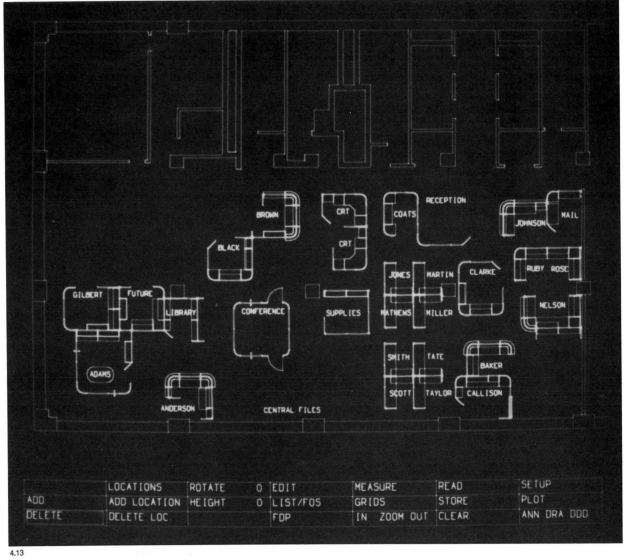

4.13

**4.8/4.13**: Three-dimensional and plan views of layouts for office interiors, on the Evans & Sutherland Multipicture System (MPS). A designer may create the models, alter them and dynamically walk through them. These layouts are from the CORE Division of Herman Miller Inc.
*Courtesy Evans & Sutherland Computer Corporation*

**4.11**: A hand drawing of a Corvette, seen from above, contains notes of all the grid reference points for the computer model.

**4.12**: The back view is similarly treated, here with a solid version juxtaposed. Because the car is symmetrical, only half the reference points are needed.
*Nadia Magnenat-Thalmann and Daniel Thalmann/Montreal University*

observed, but that the left hemisphere takes over when the screen is static or blank. In this mode the brain keeps track of time so the operator is very aware of delays. By contrast, the brain suspends its sense of time when the right hemisphere has control and the operator thus thinks an active screen is working fast. An astonishing fact is that, in right hemisphere mode, a person can discern minute image features that ought to be beyond the physical capability of the human vision system. To demonstrate this, look at a distant line of telegraph wires hanging across the sky. Even at ridiculous distances, you can actually see the wire! The resolution of the eye simply indicates that such a feat is impossible, so there is something quite potent in the facility which our right hemispheres have, to process the image data so well. It will, of course, work on the workstation screen too — people are extraordinarily good at finding tiny faults in the object on display. If pressed to find a long term reason for using computer graphics methods in CAE, when all design will have been turned into the cranking of formulae (it could happen!), then use for this hyperacuity of human vision could be it. To do it justice, really good displays are wanted — very much better than can presently be built.

The observation just made raises another question – why can't computers help assess the object being designed? When 'assessment' is properly quantified then indeed they can, but often assessment is based on issues too subjective to describe properly. The qualitative appearance of an object is not a straightforward computation on the model of that object. We can generate a geometrical projection easily enough by computer, and can shade, colour and shadow the view to reveal it in photographical detail, but the computer cannot mark it out of ten for being fashionable, marketable or pretty. It cannot even

**4.15**: Robot arm, Al Barr, Raster Technologies Inc. The arm was designed by a solid modelling system based on the use of CSG, and again demonstrates the ability of a CAE system to design and manufacture robots. These can then assemble products from any basic components, here symbolized by the pegs and the socket.

**4.16**: (Inset): A robot arm visualized by Lang Systems Inc. When the arm has been designed, it can be engineered and used to manufacture other products which have been designed in the same way. It is almost a self-replicating machine.

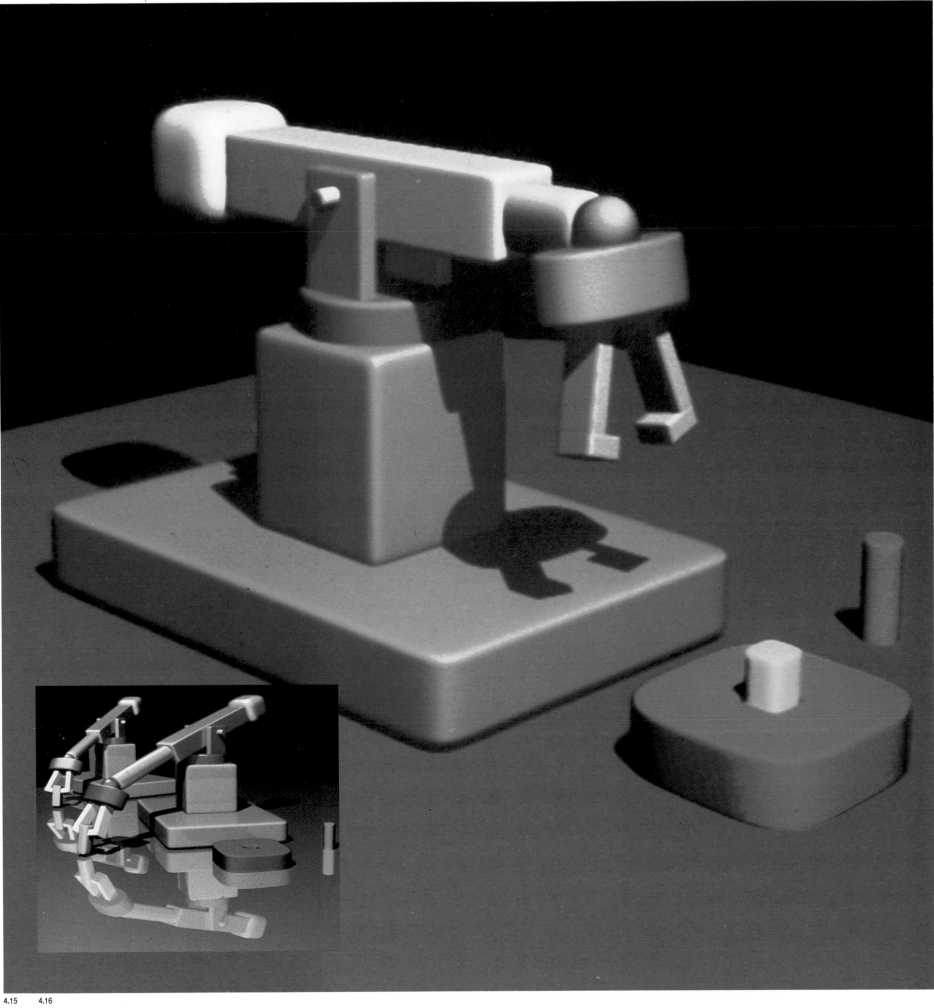

4.15    4.16

■ Design and Industry

: The earliest substitute for time-consuming keyboard input of graphic information was the light pen. Unlike the digitizing stylus it is positioned directly on the VDU screen. *Lundy.*

4.17

4.18

**4.18**: Work station with puck. The cross-hairs on the puck's lens specify the elements of an existing drawing to be input to the data store and displayed on screen. *Envision.*

decide at all easily whether a surface looks smoothly sculpted, though a human operator at the display screen will say it is obvious. The weak links are not only such matters of artistic appeal, but also recognition of the important cues in the image. Pattern recognition and image processing (PRIP) techniques are not as well developed as other aspects of the subject. For the job described this may not be too serious, for people are perfectly well able to do the work instead, but there are other situations where dependence on PRIP is rather more profound. Take for example the robots that participate in the production process.

In electronics assembly robots do the module preparation, component insertion, soldering, inspection and test. In the motor industry, they do assembly work, panel welding and paint spraying. Robots need to sense and understand their environment in order to act properly. By specializing their function the necessary degree of understanding can be made quite modest, but the principle remains that they are often working 'in place of' a human operator and cannot therefore depend too much on manual guidance. The move towards the use of more general purpose robots with more adaptability and sensitivity is being facilitated by advances in artificial intelligence, which allows the computer to understand more about its environment through information received through vision systems, position transducers and tactile sensors. A television camera can deliver to a vision program an overall view of the surroundings for strategic planning of the robot actions, sensors in the robot claw can respond to pressure and orientation for tactical control of the robot actuators. Analyzing the scene picked up by the vision system and finding how the claw has grasped some object (from the pressure image on its fingers) are difficult computations that are the subject of much current research. The wider use of robots and the increasing generality of their function depends on advances in this particular area. There are many hard problems which seem at first sight to be easily solved. An example is a view of something simple, such as a cube, from an arbitrary viewpoint. Without some additional knowledge, no computer can discover that it is a cube at all! It could be a drawing of a cube on a flat sheet of paper. It could also be any of a number of slightly strange three-dimensional objects, for the perspective distortion could be reproduced by differently shaped objects placed at different distances from the viewpoint. Many similar opportunities for visual ambiguity arise in any typical scene and the vision system must be clever enough either to resolve them by calling on additional facts at its disposal, or set some alarm to indicate that it has been confused by the situation. Robots that are too easily confused by poor vision will not find wide acceptance.

The automatic factory has been a dream since the 1930s, but the reality is rather different in its technical characteristics and public appeal from the sort of thing Charlie Chaplin showed us in *Modern Times*. The tightly coupled production line running in lock step, with every station synchronized with the conveyor belt, is the way mass production began. The human operatives were not expected to take decisions but rather to repeat their assigned tasks mechanically. It would be natural to suppose that full automation would go the same way and that the humans would simply be replaced by robots. Not so. The dangers in letting human operatives take decisions is that the whole process will then be dependent on everyone working in harmony with shifting objectives – the variety of products passing along the same line would need to stimulate each operator to alter his job steps to match, and with too much of this 'semi-thinking' activity the operatives would make errors and work disjointedly. Using computer-controlled robots the situation is transformed (strictly one should say 'will be transformed', because these are early days yet). The line needs much less uniformity in its cargo of products because the semi-thinking needed to specialize each job step to the needs of the thing just arriving on the belt is well suited to computer control. The use of robots thus raises the capacity for customising the product and introducing variety.

Our last illustration comes from plant control. A large continuous-flow process, such as an electricity generating station or an oil refinery, will require a mixture of automatic control, electronic monitoring and manual adjustment to function efficiently and safely. The computer control may be through some form of program that models the plant behaviour and knows from accumulated experience and given knowledge how to set the controls to good effect. Such a thing is called an 'expert system'. The use of computer graphics to reveal data and negotiate between the humans and the computers about actions to take is essential. The sort of displays involved are those which show symbolically what is happening in the different items of plant (using mimic diagrams) and which allow alarm conditions to be shown and correction policies to be tried out (both by simulation and 'for real'). Donald Michie, formerly of the Department of Machine Intelligence at Edinburgh University, poses the problem of an expert system which is used to monitor safety on an offshore drilling rig. There is a safety

alert. The official in charge of the rig checks the displays and printouts that tell him what the rig is doing. His intuition says that to avert a disastrous build-up of pressure, a certain relief valve should be opened. However, the computer system, which has been monitoring the events that led up to the crisis, recommends an entirely different course of action. Who knows better? Ultimately the man has to make the decision, although the computer has access to more data (and has more

power to calculate things!). It is important that the computer is able to demonstrate why it recommends its course of action, and allows the operator to experiment with alternatives by simulation before committing him to any action at all. Modern industry is beginning to restore, to most of the people working in it, a role for creative and analytical thinking which has been absent for many years. We can thank the computer, computer graphics in particular, for bringing this about.

**4.19**: Digital restoration of a number plate by PRIP. The number plate is unreadable on the original image, but when it is processed the California registration mark can be distinguished.
*Computation on a CDC 7600, recorded on a Matrix camera. T. M. Cannon and H. J. Trussell.*

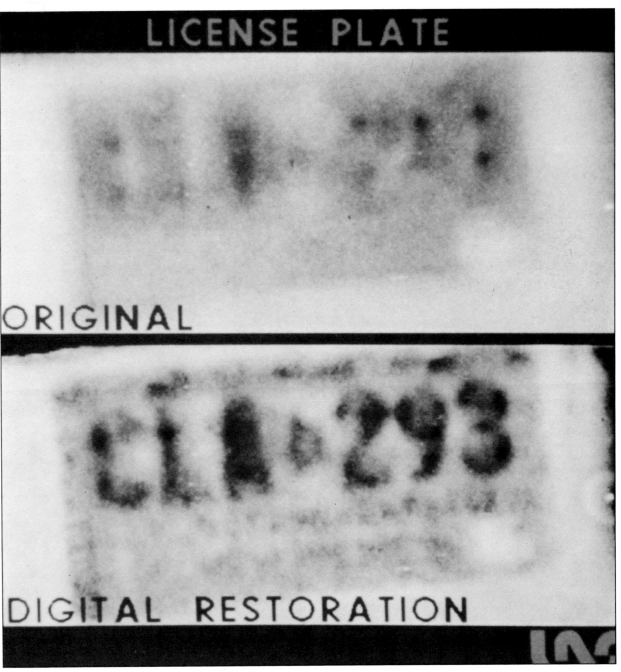

4.19

We have seen how industrial design has found in computer graphics an extremely powerful tool. It could be argued that it is a tool in the sense that the steam engine was a tool in the industrial revolution and that it may have similar implications. But can the same be said about the relationship between science and computer graphics? The answer almost certainly is that it cannot, but that there are, nevertheless, important roles for it to play. In the course of this chapter we shall look at some of them and as we do so we shall come across more extraordinary computer-generated images. We shall also look at simulation and its interrelationship with science and computer graphics and see how flight simulators can produce the illusion of reality that is necessary if they are to be effective as training aids.

What use, then, can science have for computer graphics? The greatest discoveries in theoretical science have been made using pen, notebook and brain – and it seems likely they will continue to be. Experimental scientists have used telescopes to explore our galaxy and streams of particles to investigate the structure of matter. They had produced a good description of the Universe long before the first electronic computer was a gleam in the eye of its designer (in fact they had to, in order to make computers possible at all). So what hope can this upstart have of making an impression on the stately and traditional disciplines of science? Before we can appreciate how computer graphics provides a useful tool for the scientist, it is necessary to understand what he does and how he does it.

Scientists seek to increase the body of knowledge about a particular subject by formulating hypotheses about the nature of that subject and then trying to test the soundness of those hypotheses by collecting experimental evidence. The approach must be highly systematic, and the steps taken and the results obtained must be carefully recorded. It is vital that everything that is done should be presented in a form which fellow scientists can verify and desirable that it is also disseminated in a clear and easily understood manner to the wider public so that any interesting and useful, or alarming and dangerous, developments can more readily be appreciated. And here, in this latter aspect of the work of the scientist, is an obvious role for computer graphics. For, as we shall now show, computer graphics is a powerful means of communication.

The most basic personal computer can be used to display data in the form of bar or pie-charts. Given slightly more sophisticated graphics more imaginative presentations can be made, for example, a map of the world with countries shaded in different colours to represent their mean rainfall. The topology of a three-dimensional object can readily be appreciated if it is plotted as a polar coordinate graph as with Rob Fisher's sculpture (chapter 6). Another imaginative and original presentation is Martin Marietta's

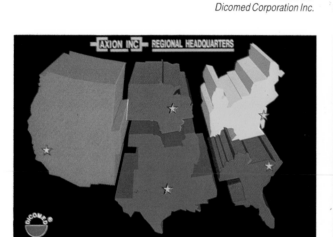

**5.1**: Regions and regional headquarters of the Axion organisation. The three-dimensional view of each region makes their boundaries more memorable than any flat map could do.
*Dicomed Corporation Inc.*

5.1

**5.2**: **Splash**, Yoichiro Kawaguchi, Osaka University. An example of both science and simulation, the image demonstrates the accuracy of the relevant formulae and faithfully reproduces the appearance of a liquid surface after a drop has fallen on it.

**5.3**: Veronese surface sliced by hyperplane and projected from 4-space.
*Branchoff-Strauss Productions, Providence, Rhode Island.*

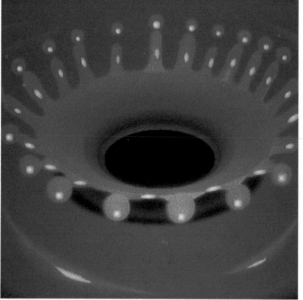

5.2

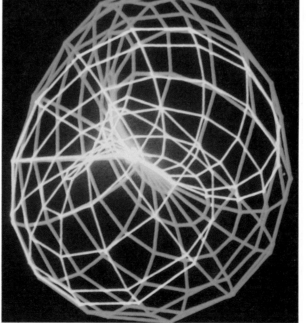

5.3

plot of the positions of satellites relative to each other, to the Earth and to the regions of the Earth for which transmission and reception of their radio signals is possible. The Earth is represented as a flat disk, while each satellite has its own distinguishing colour and is plotted as the apex of a cone reaching down to the Earth, representing its region of transmission or reception.

Computer graphics techniques can help to make sense of an otherwise bewildering amount of complexity of information. But can they help if it is not the meaning of a quantity of data that is wanted, but the meaning of an idea?

Mathematical concepts are often most difficult things to comprehend; it is here that the ability of computer graphics to visualize the abstract can be invaluable. Peano's space-filling curve, Poincare's hyperbolic plane, B-splines and beta-splines are things with odd names and (to the non-mathematician) frightening mathematical descriptions but which seem less intimidating once they are presented in a graphical way. It is not necessary for a layman to understand what the Veronese surface sliced by a hyperplane and projected from 4-space actually is – as long as he is able to appreciate that there can be beauty and symmetry concealed within a mathematical equation. For a mathematician however, an image such as this might clarify his conception of a problem and provide new insight into its solution.

But perhaps an accomplished mathematician has less need of an aid to comprehension than a child who is meeting mathematical concepts for the first time. Children are inveterate explorers: they will learn about a new thing by playing with it, if at all possible. But mathematics is abstract and forbidding and is not easy to play with – which is why 'Turtles' are now part of the curriculum for some schoolchildren. A Turtle is a triangular symbol drawn on a computer screen which, as it moves around the screen, can mark a line so that it is apparent what the Turtle's

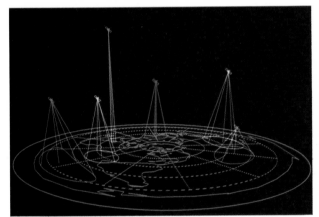

5.4.1

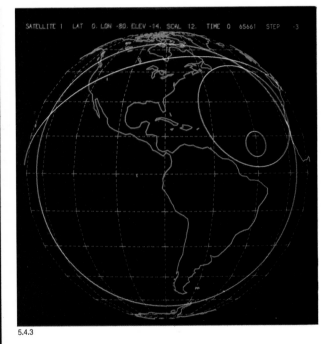

5.4.3

5.4.2

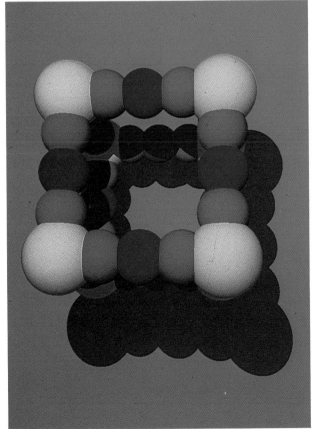

5.5

**5.5**: Molecular model using shadows to give depth in the third dimension. *Intelligent Light*.

**5.4.1–3**: Computer-assisted graphic ingenuity was responsible for this representation of satellite locations and the areas they serve. The Earth is (5.4.1) mapped onto a flat platter, and the satellites are tracked as they move relative to the Earth's surface. Thousands of satellites are included in the model, though it would be confusing to display them all at one time. The display system is a CSM Colour Display linked to an Evans & Sutherland Multi Picture System. Martin Marietta Aerospace, Denver. *Courtesy Evans & Sutherland Computer Corporation*.

**5.4.2**: A real time interactive dynamic simulation of satellites and orbits with an orthographic view of the Earth. Evans & Sutherland MPS & Boeing Aerospace Company. *Courtesy Evans & Sutherland Computer Corporation*.

**5.4.3**: This simulation from the same source shows a satellite in orbit around the Earth from another satellite's viewpoint. Its local horizon is related to those of other satellites. *Courtesy Evans & Sutherland Computer Corporation*.

**5.6** The mathematical expression which forms this particular graph is a simple instruction to the computer. Several hours of calculations and draftsmanship would be necessary for a hand-drawn version.
*Dicomed Corporation Inc.*

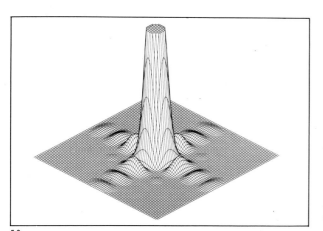

5.6

movements have been. A special computer language called LOGO, which allows the Turtle's movements to be controlled, has been developed by a team at MIT under the direction of Seymour Papert. Using LOGO to control the Turtle is simplicity itself. To move the Turtle forward 20 units you type 'FORWARD 20', to turn right through 90 degrees you type 'RIGHT 90', to raise and lower the pen you type 'PENUP' and 'PENDOWN'. Typing 'HIDETURTLE' will make the Turtle symbol disappear. These, together with any of the other instructions defined in the language, can be combined into a sequence of instructions which will, for example, draw a triangle. The language allows this sequence of instructions, or *procedure*, to be given a name and remembered, then be invoked any number of times and perhaps be combined into a larger procedure which can draw a star using many such triangles.

We have, then, an easily-learnt programming language in which geometrical ideas can be expressed and through which the meanings of those ideas are revealed via the travels of a Turtle. What can this do for us? A very great deal indeed.

Skilful use of a well-chosen procedure as a building block in the construction of a program is the very essence of good computer programming. Similarly, the careful design and repeated use in various ways of one geometrical figure is a way to produce a visually pleasing pattern. LOGO allows the one activity to depend on the other and rewards the author of a well-structured program with a beautiful picture, and, conversely, requires that those who wish to produce beautiful pictures should write beautiful programs. In an age where programs and the people who produce them are becoming ever more in demand, it is important that the embryonic programmer should learn

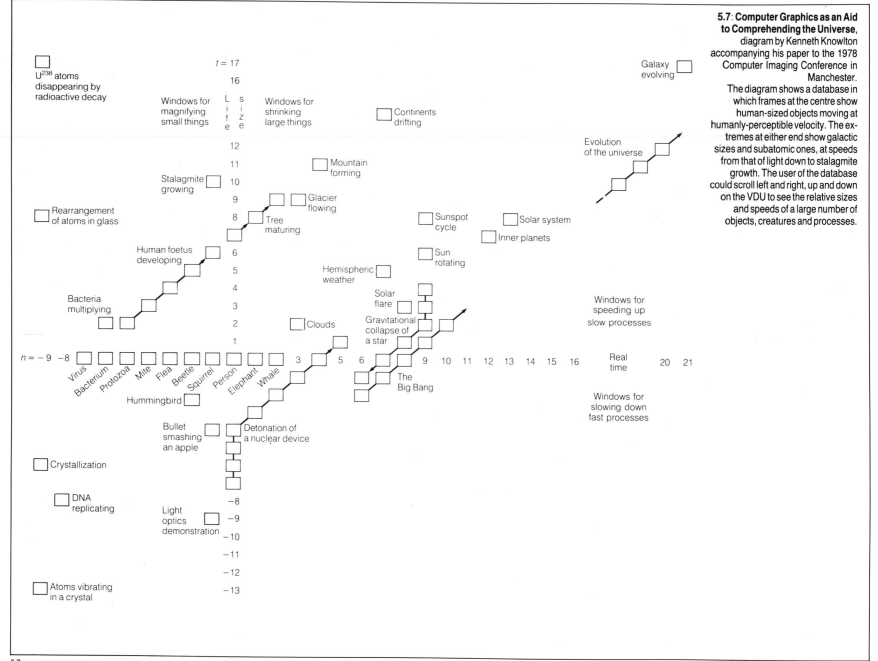

**5.7**: **Computer Graphics as an Aid to Comprehending the Universe**, diagram by Kenneth Knowlton accompanying his paper to the 1978 Computer Imaging Conference in Manchester.
The diagram shows a database in which frames at the centre show human-sized objects moving at humanly-perceptible velocity. The extremes at either end show galactic sizes and subatomic ones, at speeds from that of light down to stalagmite growth. The user of the database could scroll left and right, up and down on the VDU to see the relative sizes and speeds of a large number of objects, creatures and processes.

5.7

good practice from the start, rather than possibly be crippled through the use of the older BASIC or FORTRAN languages. LOGO is by no means a toy language; in fact it is derived from the language LISP, which is important in artificial intelligence applications and can be used, if desired, for serious programming. LOGO and Turtle graphics can, then, be used for programming and for teaching people to program, but there is much more to it than that.

Because typing a command has an immediate visual effect, LOGO and Turtle graphics can act as a medium for exploration, through which ideas can be tried out, modified and tried again. As this is being done a 'mental model' of the world is built up and the problem-solving skills of the explorer are developed. Learning is made active rather than passive. Handicapped children and those with learning difficulties can be especially helped through having an environment which is highly stimulating, which is in no way threatening and which is completely under their control. Geometric concepts are the obvious but by no means the only candidates for Turtle graphics. 'DynaTurtle' is a collection of LOGO procedures which model Newton's laws of motion allowing the Turtle to be pushed from various directions with various amounts of force and the resulting motion of the Turtle observed. Physics undergraduates at the MIT have been taught the general theory of relativity using Turtle graphics.

Another branch of science in which computer graphics is making its presence felt is medicine. In this field, as in the others which we have discussed, it serves as an aid to the interpretation of data or the comprehension of ideas. Cranston–Csuri Inc. are among leading practitioners in producing realistic computer images. In addition to their rendering of a rather morbid skull with a single eyeball smoking a cigarette (see chapter 8) they have produced images of the human torso, eyeball, heart, colon and male sexual organs for use in a television series called *The Body Machine*.

In 1978 the medical students at the University of California at San Diego were treated to an extraordinary journey through the human brain courtesy of computer graphics. A recently dead brain was sliced into sections less than a millimetre thick, the outlines of the various parts traced out and these were entered into a computer model. When this was done the entire brain could be viewed as a three-dimensional structure with each part shown in a different colour. Using images made in this way, an 18-minute film was produced of an impossible journey around, under, and then through the brain.

At the Mallinekrodt Institute at Washington University two doctors have successfully used advanced techniques, originally developed by the McDonnell Douglas Aircraft Company for the design of military aircraft, to investigate cases of severe skull deformation prior to surgery, to help plan surgical operations and to assess the results of those procedures. Previously, these procedures were performed manually by making tracings of X-ray pictures taken from the side of the skull. Making these pictures was a time-consuming process and they lacked detail unless large numbers of scans were taken. Because they were necessarily two-dimensional, the pictures were of limited use to the surgeons who needed a three-dimensional view of the skull beneath the skin.

The technique developed works like this. Between 30 and 64 high-resolution X-ray photographs of sections of the patient's head are taken, each of two-millimetre width and at two-millimetre intervals. These images are fed into a computer and processed so that the boundaries between flesh and bone in each slice are made more apparent. These improved images are then handed to a CAD system, which extracts from them a mathematical description of the way the skull curves and generates a three-dimensional model of the patient's skull. The view of this model on the computer screen can be rotated, compared with normal skulls and the degree of deformation evaluated so that the surgeon may have an

5.8.1

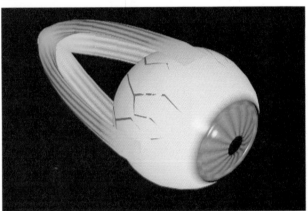

5.8.2

**5.8.1**: Penis with testes, vas deferens and seminal vesicles. Cranston–Csuri for *The Body Machine*.

**5.8.2**: Eyeball and eye muscles. The six eye muscles which control eye movements are shown, together with the optic nerve. An extremely realistic depiction for a general audience, created by Cranston–Csuri for a television series *The Body Machine*, produced by Goldcrest Films. *Images designed by Don Stredney, Animator/Medical Instructor, Cranston–Csuri Productions Inc, Columbus, Ohio.*

**5.9: Mirror Morphine**, Paul Heckbert.
This image depicts a morphine molecule in front of two mirrors, casting soft-edged shadows on a yellow floor. It was computed at a resolution of 2048 × 2048 using the 'ray tracing' technique, requiring the eight days on a AX 11/780 computer. *NYIT Computer Graphics Laboratory, 1983.*

5.9

accurate idea of what sort of reconstruction is necessary.

Another medical application is morphanalysis. This is a way of recasting the facial structure of a patient with such conditions as a cleft palate, severe burns or a broken nose. The technique is similar to the previous example: a computer model of the damaged face is compared to a normal one, the differences quantified and this information used as a guide during subsequent plastic surgery.

We have seen how computer graphics can display scientific data in an easily comprehensible manner and also how it can do more – how it can take a collaborative role and actively help us to understand abstract concepts. Can it participate in science in an even more profound way? We said that doing science involves formulating hypotheses about the nature of a subject. In order to

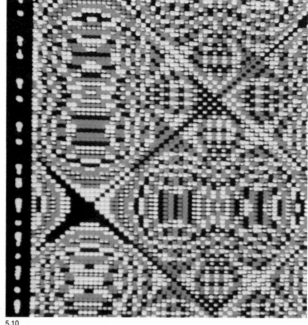

**5.10**: Graph of $\dfrac{(ax^2 + bxy + cy^2)\bmod K}{d}$ with different tones for different values of $K$, by Charles M. Strauss, from an idea by Kenneth Knowlton.

**5.11/12**: Two views of the human brain (front and side), showing cerebellum, brain stem, cerebral cortex, ventricles and basal ganglia. Colour filters and multiple exposures were used to create the film of which they are part, because only a monochromatic display was available. The Evans & Sutherland PS 2 generated the images, digitized from slices of actual brain tissue. University of California at San Diego. *Courtesy Evans & Sutherland Computer Corporation.*

5.10

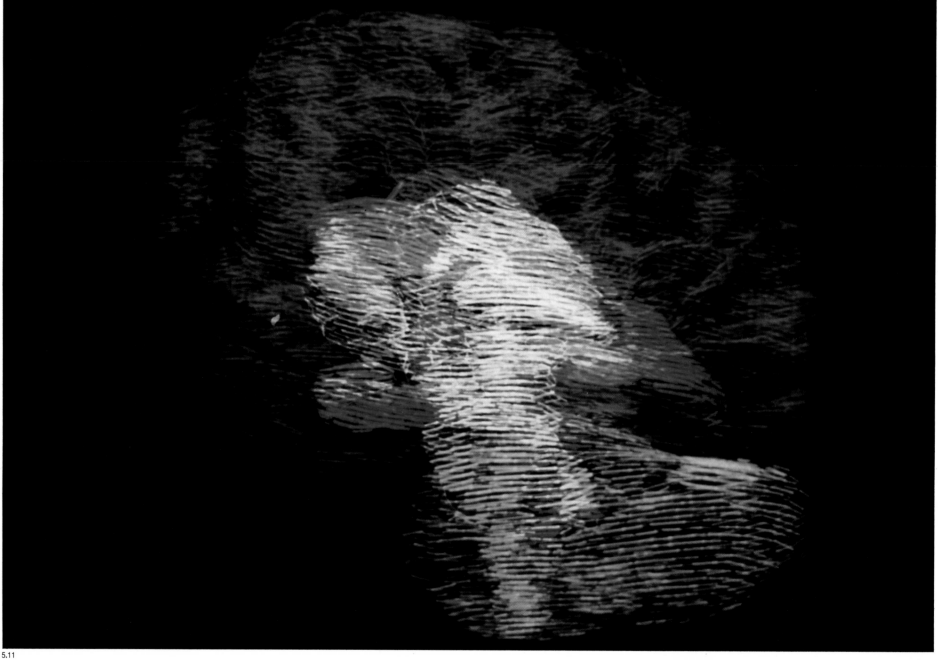

5.11

formulate these hypotheses the scientist must investigate his subject matter thoroughly – by looking through telescopes or down microscopes, by weighing, by measuring, by recording. The scientist is concerned with the real world – how can a computer help? The answer lies in the use of models. Is it possible to conduct a scientific investigation using a computer model of something rather than the thing itself? It is, and the campaign against the tomato bushy stunt virus provides us with an example.

The tomato bushy stunt virus is an organism that attacks tomato plants. It consists of 180 amino acid chains which are connected and coiled around to form a spherical structure. It propagates by attaching a specific site on its surface to a specific area (the receptor) on the surface of a tomato plant's cell. It then uses material from its victim to make copies of itself, which in turn infect neighbouring cells and so destroy the plant.

The first step in combating the virus was to determine where the active sites lay and what they looked like. The structure of the virus was investigated by X-ray crystallography and a data library built up of the information obtained. At the Lawrence Livermore National laboratories in America Nelson Max used this to model the virus on a computer and view it as a realistic assembly of spheres complete with hidden surfaces removed, shading and highlights. The results were displayed using raster techniques and a film made which demonstrated the structure of the virus. This helped the scientists both to get to know their enemy and to advance to the next stage of the research, which was to design a vaccine which would resemble a small part of the virus' surface and would prompt the host to generate antibodies (the natural self-defence mechanism) to kill the invading virus.

Another computer model was created and the virus viewed in a more diagrammatic way using a vector display. This time each group of three amino acid chains was represented as a triangle and the entire organism displayed as 60 such triangles. The objective was to identify those parts of the virus which would be vulnerable to a water-soluble vaccine. To this end, a computer model of a water molecule was created which consisted of a sphere defining the extent of the zone of influence of the water molecule. This was 'rolled' (in the sense that the computer manipulated the two models) around the surface of the virus and the points where the two could touch were marked by dots. The pattern of dots on the surface of the virus clearly showed the areas vulnerable to a water-soluble vaccine and so helped scientists to design a vaccine that would

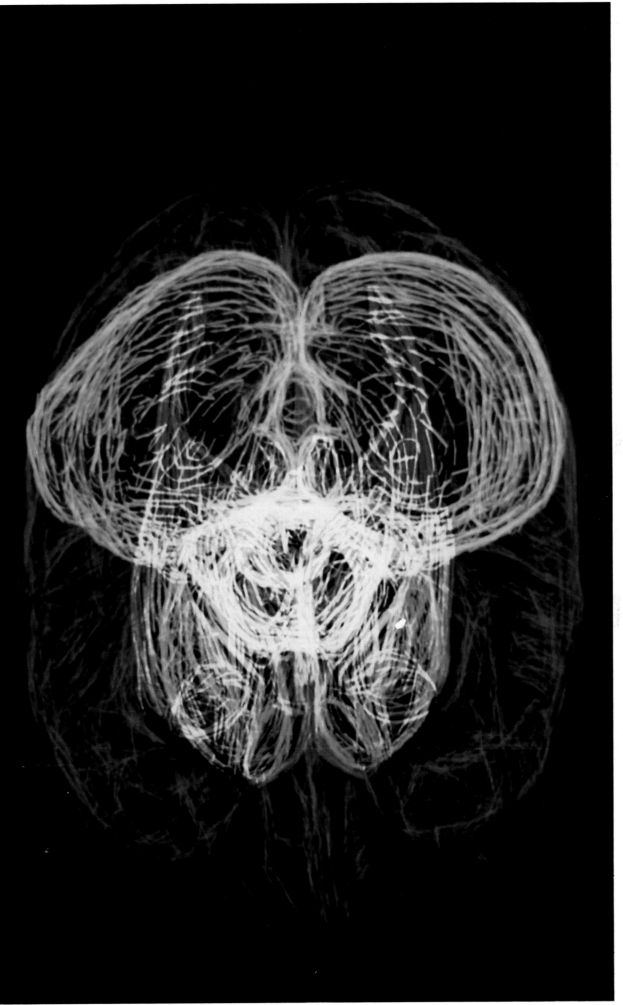

5.12

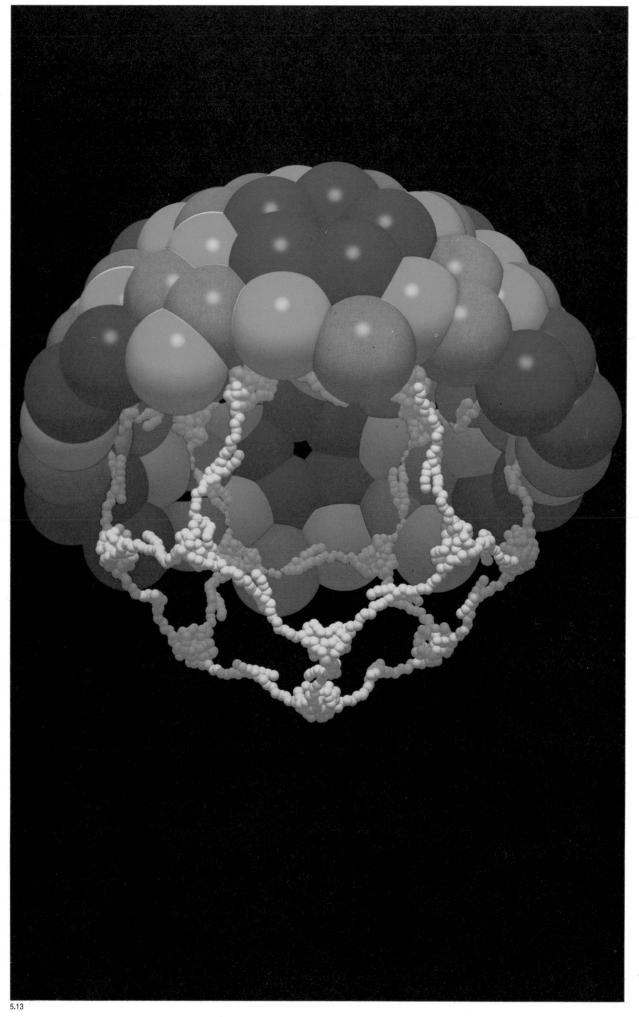

be effective.

When our scientist has reached a conclusion about the nature of his subject he must express it in some way. If he were Newton studying the way a body falls under gravity he could write just one simple equation which would exactly predict the way all real objects fall and which would be the last word on the subject. If he were Keynes, however, and wished to tell us about the way the economy of the world works, a book may not be enough. Moreover, Newton could measure the rate of descent of his apple, show us a corresponding value obtained from his formula, and then go to lunch secure in the knowledge that we believe him – whereas Keynes might have to prepare himself for an eternal argument about the soundness of his thoughts. How can a scientist use his theory to predict the behaviour of a system, and therefore confirm his

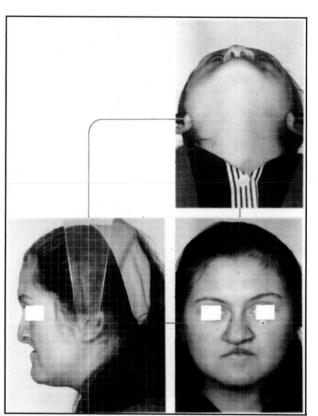

5.14.1

**5.13**: Tomato bushy stunt virus, Nelson Max and Arthur Olson. A raster display shows parts of this virus, which attacks tomato plants, as a hemisphere of amino acid subunits with chains of single amino acids (in yellow). The whole virus could be visualized as a complete sphere, and the yellow chains would be inside. They link to the red spheres, which are differentiated from the light blue and dark blue spheres because these have different symmetry environments. Chains for the blue spheres are not shown. The representation of the parts of the virus as shiny spheres is largely due to established conventions in chemistry. The advantage of choosing such symbolic conventions for this purpose is that a three-dimensional image of each subunit makes the structure of the virus easy to understand. Alternative vector-based symbols are appropriate to different purposes, such as real time interactive experimentation with artificial vaccines.

5.13

theory, when the theory applies to something which is too big or too complex to write equations for – a weather, economic, or galactic system? The answer lies, yet again, in the use of the computer model, but with a new ingredient – simulation.

We can create computer models that describe the physical world, the economic world, the galaxy, write programs which manipulate those models according to the rules embodied in our weather theory, our economic theory or our cosmological theory and then compare the way the models behave with the real world to see how well we have done. One use of simulation in science consists of doing just this, and of improving the theories or the models until real life and simulation behave similarly. Then the simulation model can be critically examined to gain insight into the working of the real life system and

from this, perhaps, understanding of what a new, simpler and more concise model may be like – one equation to describe our economy perhaps.

Simulation coupled with computer graphics can also be used to aid in the investigative side of science. Large molecules, such as proteins, are not rigid structures but, on the contrary, are continuously twisting, turning, vibrating and distorting. Molecular dynamics is the study of the way in which this happens. It is important because the dynamic properties of a molecule are thought to influence the biological function of the material which they constitute; for example, the way an enzyme behaves may be influenced by the molecular dynamics of its proteins. At the IBM UK Scientific Centre in Winchester, computer scientists have designed a system which can simulate the dynamics of a molecule and generate an animation of it on the screen of a vector display at a

rate of 30 frames a second. The computer model used for the simulation is a map of the way energy is distributed in the bonds between the various constituent atoms of the molecule, the lengths of these bonds and their angles. During tha animation the user is free to rotate the molecule, zoom in on it and pan across it; he can freeze the action, see it in reverse or see it faster or slower. In this way processes which occur within time spans of a few millionths of a millionth of a second can be closely observed. A complementary system can take the results of a molecular dynamics simula-

Science and simulation 71

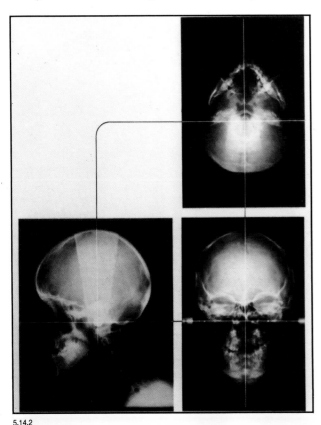

5.14.2

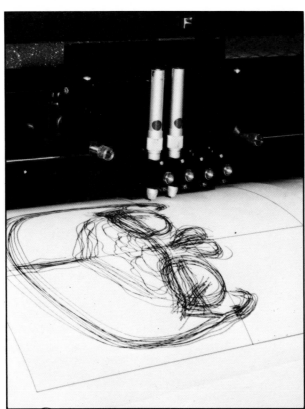

5.14.3

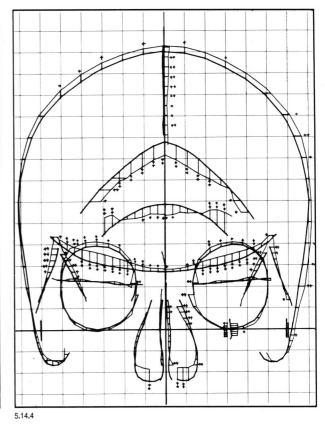

5.14.4

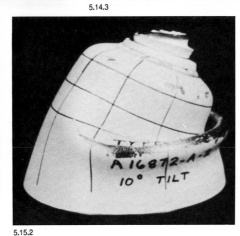

5.15.1

5.15.2

**5.15.1/2**: Conical form with and without stress deformation.
*B. Brown, Lawrence Livermore National Laboratory*

**5.14.1–4**: Morphanalysis is a medical imaging technique to analyze how the shapes of patients' heads and faces deviate from the norm in consequence of numerous medical conditions. It is an aid to physicians and surgeons which accurately denotes what plastic surgery or other treatment may be required. X-ray images and photograms are taken simultaneously to record the patient's condition. Subsequent image processing provides line drawings whose angles and dimensions are easily measured
*Morphanalysis Unit, Manchester University.*

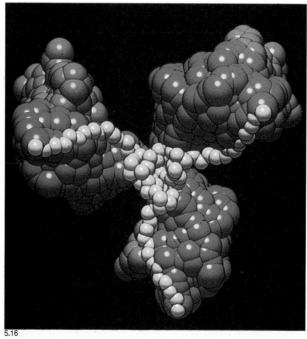

5.16

tion and graphically plot the way the position of an array of points on the molecule changes between subsequent frames of the simulation, so helping in the interpretation of the data.

At this point we leave our survey of the applications of computer graphics and simulation in science, although there are many other areas which we could look at, and turn to one of the most challenging technological applications of computer graphics: ship and flight simulation.

It would obviously be a bad idea to allow a novice naval officer to have his first experience of navigating while on the bridge of a real ship. Besides, over 70% of shipping accidents are still due to human errors, presumably by experienced people, so the need for periods of refresher training is apparent. A simulator can train new senior officers or train experienced officers to deal

**5.16/17**: Two types of DNA. These raster display spheres use standard chemical colours, except that carbon is not black but dark blue to distinguish it from the black blackground. Outlines are computed on a CDC-7600, and coloured on a Dicomed D-48 film recorder.
*Nelson Max, Lawrence Livermore National Laboratories.*

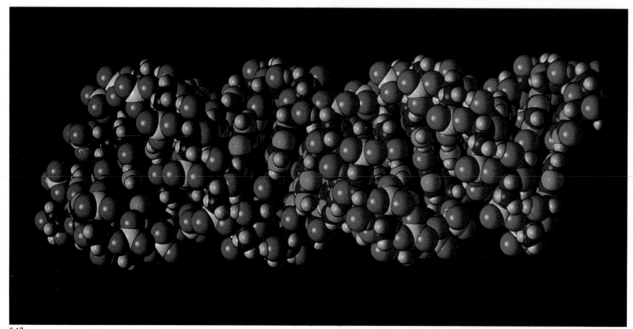

5.17

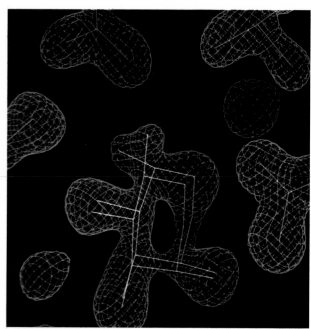

5.18

**5.18/19**: Vector-based visualization of a crystallography experiment at Rice University. The picture shows the complexes between two forms of the L-arabinose substrate and binding protein. Evans & Sutherland PS 300, with a CSM Colour Display giving 1800 programmable colours.
*Courtesy Evans & Sutherland Computer Corporation.*

**5.20**: Vector-scanned DNA. The double helix surface and skeleton are viewed down the axis. Evans & Sutherland PS 2 with a CSM colour display. University of California at San Francisco.
*Courtesy Evans & Sutherland Computer Corporation.*

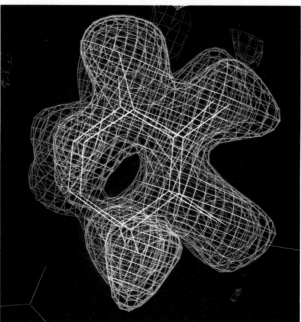

5.19

5.20

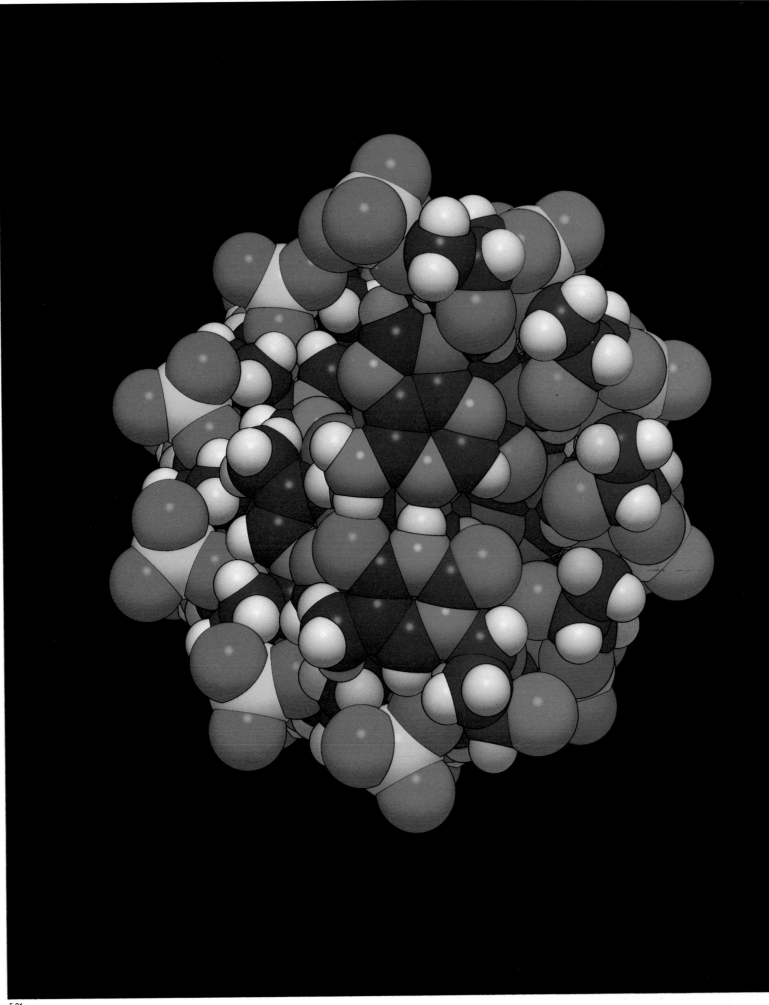

**5.21**: B DNA, top view, with shadows. This picture is a computer-drawn simulation of the coloured plastic space-filling molecular models used by chemists, with spheres at the Van der Waals radii of the respective atoms. The colours are the ones used with the standard models: hydrogen is white, nitrogen is blue, oxygen is red, and phosphorus is yellow. An exception is carbon which is not coloured black, but dark blue, to distinguish it from the black background. The outlines of the visible part of each atom are computed on a CDC-7600 at Lawrence Livermore National Laboratory. They are coloured in with shading and highlights on a Dicomed D48 colour film recorder, controlled by a Sperry Univac V75 minicomputer. *Nelson Max, Lawrence Livermore National Laboratories.*

with new routes and new ports. There are many other applications – research into the design of the ship's bridge and how information is presented there, research into the design of ports and navigation aids, and the analysis of past accidents are some notable ones.

A typical ship simulator comprises a mock-up of the bridge, complete with all the normal instruments and equipment, facing on to a panoramic viewscreen. Depending on the detail required in the display and the resolving power of the image system, the field of view can span from 40 to 280 degrees. Seven image projectors may be required for the widest view. The Marconi Tepigen ship simulator can display two million colours and eight thousand edges (two thousand four-sided figures, or one thousand eight-edged figures, etc.). These figures can be assembled to represent fixed features (land, navigation lights),

moving vessels or four different types of sea texture – an important visual cue in determining the motion of the ship.

It is in flight simulation, however, that we see the culmination of many of the techniques that have been developed in computer graphics; modelling, simulation, interaction and realism. The formidable requirement that the scenes which are to be displayed should be realistic but at the same time should be dynamic (particularly in military applications) means that such systems inevitably are highly complex and very expensive.

A typical flight simulator consists of a number of component parts. First there is the mock-up of a cabin of an aircraft mounted on a table that can be tilted by hydraulic pistons to convey to the trainee pilot the physical sensations associated with the manoeuvre he is performing. Then there is the imaging system which must

convince the pilot that he is looking out the window of an aircraft, rather than at a display screen. There is a substantial amount of computer hardware and other electronics. Finally there is the computer software, which models the aircraft characteristics, the weather and atmospheric conditions, the terrain and other aircraft, and also advances the simulation and controls the entire system.

The Evans & Sutherland CT5-A system is at the top end of the range of commercially available simulators and represents the current 'state of the art' in this technology. An outlay of between $2 000 000 and $5 000 000 will buy you a system which can display pictures composed of up to 2000 polygons per channel (a simulator typically comprises several channels) shown at a refresh rate of 50 frames per second, perform smooth shading and anti-aliasing (see chapter 3),

5.22

**5.22**: Simulation of Saturn with rings and Voyager probe.
*Dr James F. Blinn & Jet Propulsion Laboratory, for NASA.*

**5.23**: **Yaks at Sea**. Simulation of a Soviet Kiev Class U/STOL aircraft carrier with deck markings and five YAK-36 VTOL aircraft. This visualization includes sun glint on aircraft canopies, shadows of aircraft, white cap waves on the ocean and horizon glow. It was produced on a VAX 11/780 with an Adage/Ikonas RDS 3000 (1024 × 1024 × 24 bit frame buffer), and filmed on a Dunn Instruments 632 camera with CMS (Contour Modelling System) software.
© *Intelligent Light 1984.*

5.23

**5.24/25**: Scenes from a helicopter cabin as viewed in the TRIAD system, which combines a simulation computer with a real helicopter. Thus the pilot uses the same machine for ground-based simulation and for actual flight. The scene is edge-defined with two-dimensional texture to enhance realism, with an SP3T viewing system by Evans & Sutherland. TRIAD is a Rediflight product, jointly marketed by Rediffusion Simulation and Off-Shore Logistics. *Courtesy Evans & Sutherland Computer Corporation.*

**5.26**: Two A10 ground support aircraft over a landscape with local cultural features in Western Europe. This CT5A simulation tests the pilot's ability to follow relevant moving surfaces a lead or target aircraft. *Courtesy Evans & Sutherland Computer Corporation.*

5.24

5.25

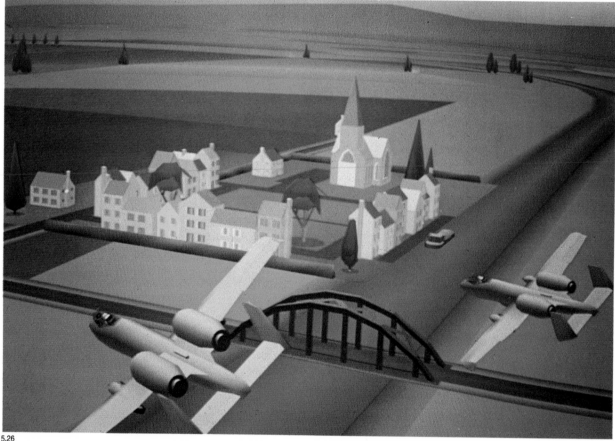

5.26

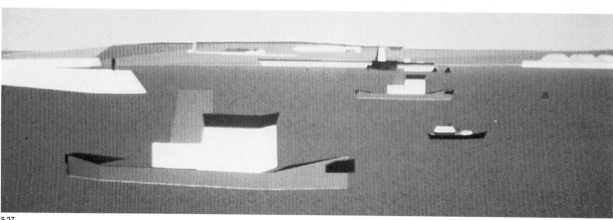

5.27

5.28

which supports Sun-like illumination of objects and allows transparent features to be shown (like the glass cockpit of an aeroplane). A number of different coordinate systems can be in use simultaneously; one coordinate system will apply to the simulator, the rest will apply to the simulated aircraft which can be viewed from it and which can be 'flown' in their own right in their own coordinate spaces.

All the objects displayed are modelled using a polygonal mesh representation (see chapter 2). A subsystem called 'level of detail management' ensures that when the object is far away imperceptible detail is suppressed by discarding some of the polygons, allowing a more complex overall picture (since the total number of polygons which can be displayed at one time is limited). The imaging system consists of raster graphics screens whose images are split up and then recombined in such a way that the pilot must focus his eyes at infinity in order to see the images properly in focus. This considerably increases the illusion of reality but does not make it complete because unfortunate parallax effects can be experienced by the pilot if he moves his head around. A recent development in imaging is to have a number of projectors mounted above the cabin mock-up whose outputs are directed at a parabolic mirror which curves around in front of the aircraft simulator's windscreen and on which the pictures are viewed. This method does away with parallax problems and gives the illusion of complete reality.

The main applications for the CT5-A are in engineering (Mercedes Benz possess one) and in military flight simulation. The high degree of realism this system offers is absolutely necessary for the training of combat pilots, whose lives might depend on the correct recognition of an enemy aircraft or good reading of landmarks during low flying. It has been found that something apparently as insignificant as another aircraft's skid marks on a runway can be an important visual cue during a landing approach. Other aircraft must be faithfully rendered so that the trainee pilot can gain experience of close formation flying and in-flight refuelling.

A flight simulator for a civil aircraft has a different set of requirements to those for a military aircraft. There is no need for smooth shading or high realism; most important is the capacity to provide visual cues for the movement of the aircraft. The Novoview SP3-T is a flight simulator costing between $600 000 and $1 500 000 which is produced by Evans and Sutherland specifically for the simulation of commercial flying.

The SP3-T can display fewer polygons than the CT5-A but can display texture (see chapter 3). The textured surfaces of grass, sky and sea convey an impression of height and motion as well as of realism. Another important difference between the two simulators is the way the SP3-T renders light sources. Obviously, lights are crucial when landing at an airport at night. The strobing approach lights to a runway are extremely bright and are often the first indication of the presence of an airport the pilot sees. Some of the lights are highly directional and disappear as the aircraft strays off the correct approach course. A raster scan display, such as is employed by the CT5-A, cannot produce the intensity which is needed to suggest these point sources realistically. The SP3-T uses vector display techniques for light sources and superimposes the image thus produced upon the rest of the scene, which is produced with rasters.

It is very important to be able to render fog, in its various guises, in a convincing manner so that the pilot can experience dangerous situations and learn how to cope with them before they happen to him 'for real'. Patchy ground fog can suddenly obscure the vision of a pilot during the final crucial seconds of an approach to a runway. The ragged edges of a cloud, called scud, can induce a pilot to dive below a cloud in an unwise attempt to gain clearer vision. The beacons on an aircraft generate glare in fog which can spoil what little visibility there might be. These occurrences, and others, can all be simulated on the SP3-T.

It is appropriate to finish the part of the book

**5.29**: The view from an AV-8B Harrier II multi-role combat aircraft of another aircraft of the same type, as seen on a CT5A computer imagery system for tactical visual simulation.
*Courtesy Evans & Sutherland Computer Corporation and Rediffusion Simulation.*

**5.30**: Two F 16 fighters in wing formation as seen from a third fighter. The CT5 system used was the precursor of the CT5A.
*Courtesy Evans & Sutherland Computer Corporation and Rediffusion Simulation.*

5.29

5.30

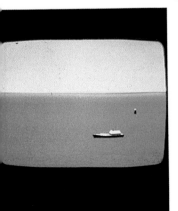

**5.27/28**: A panoramic view for the ship's bridge is obtained by positioning video projection screens side by side in a concave arc. Despite the simplicity of the method, it gives the impression of a real three-dimensional environment, with the operator's ship moving forward through the water. The display depicts the view from the bridge of a gas carrier approaching the new port of Bin Tuly, Sarawak.
*Marconi Tepigen Dusk-Night-Day Visual System. University of Wales Institute of Science and Technology/ South Glamorgan Institute of Higher Education.*

Science and Simulation ■ 77

5.31

**5.31**: Aircraft with reflections and texture on sea. SOGITEC, France.

**5.34**: Saturn rising, seen from Titan (one of Saturn's moons). Simulation by Dr James F. Blinn and Jet Propulsion Laboratory.

which deals with the technology and techniques of computer graphics with an example of one of its most spectacular achievements. The fortunes of flight simulation and those of computer graphics are intimately bound together; each new advance in computer graphics will be incorporated into the next generation of flight simulators, and the requirement for flight simulators with more and better features will spur the development of new techniques.

There are many aspects of computer imagery. The next chapter looks at the way artists are making use of them.

5.32

5.33

**5.32**: The exterior of a flight simulator designed by SOGITEC, France, with back-up technicians at work stations.

**5.33**: Airliner taking off, with runway detail and aircraft shadow. *Courtesy Evans & Sutherland Computer Corporation.*

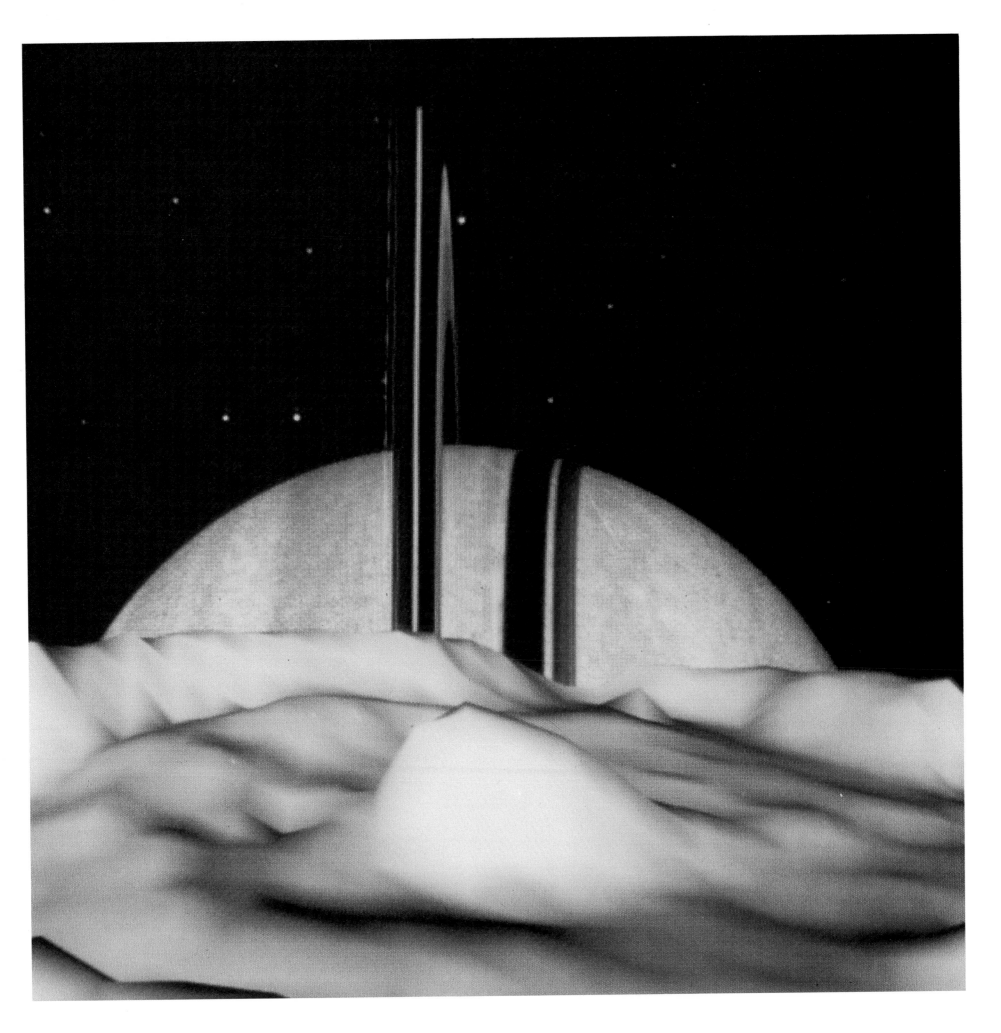

# 6 Art

The images in this chapter have been accepted for exhibition as works of art. The classification of images according to application (art, science, industry, etc.) is a useful way to approach computer graphics, but there are of course images that may be art as well as science, or art as well as a demonstration of an industrial technique. This chapter focusses on those images firmly labelled as art by their producers. We believe that computer graphics in art presents a strong challenge to conventional methods of making pictures, just as it does in science or industrial design.

If computer graphics can be art then the question arises as to where precisely the art is located. Is it in the program or the output? Analogies with more established art forms cannot be exact. Computer art is sometimes like photography – there is one original program, which can

**6.2**: **Triangle Draw**, James Hockenhull 1980, in Apple Integer BASIC Hockenhull discovered computers in 1979. He sees the program in non-interactive computer graphics as an art form. The various runs are the implications of the idea. The basic shape in *Triangle Draw* is the triangle, and the way it is repeated in different pictures gives various expressions of the theme. The modules for such procedures are difficult in the BASIC programming language. Hockenhull now uses 'microspeed', derived from the Fortran langauge.

**6.1**: **The Gallery**, Roy Hall, Cornell University. Cibaprint 16 × 20 inches VAX 11/780 and Grinnell frame buffer. Software by Roy Hall 1983. This print was photographed on a Dunn Instruments 632 camera from a 512 × 512, 48-bit display. The software uses ray tracing, focussed light sources and a reflection model for metals. Technical support by Chas Verbeck.

**6.3**: Art gallery scene with geometric primitives on plinths – homage to the 'building blocks' technique of solids modelling by John Whitney Jr and Gary Demos. *Information International Inc. 1981.*

6.1

produce pictures on any number of runs, as there is a photographic negative and many prints. But when a program incorporates randomness, the output of one run is so different from another that the minor variations of photographic prints are insignificant by comparison. Perhaps, then, computer art is better compared with painting, for in the case of a painting there is one image whose copies are reproductions of little intrinsic value. Yet it would be hard to identify in computer art an equivalent of the unique artefact produced by the painter's brush. The image on the screen of the computer is not unique – it appears any time the program is run. Again, the program is repeatable – it can be copied and run on any compatible computer.

Music might make a more logical companion to computer art; it is equally diverse. A piece of music can be played many times, as a program can be run many times, and each performance may be more or less different depending on the musician (or the user of an interactive computer program) and the instrument (or the computer system).

James Hockenhull, a theorist as well as practitioner of computer art, likens the compositions arising from one program to the products of a particular phase of an artist's work as, for example, in Picasso's blue period. Hockenhull's *Triangle Draw* or *Painter* series are variations, or rather different interpretations, based on the same underlying concept. One of his programs draws symmetrical shapes, asymmetrical shapes, jagged lines and straight lines; the fact that a program may generate dozens of images in a few minutes while Picasso, prolific as he was, needed several years to work out a theme, is only a quantitative difference. Art, Hockenhull argues,

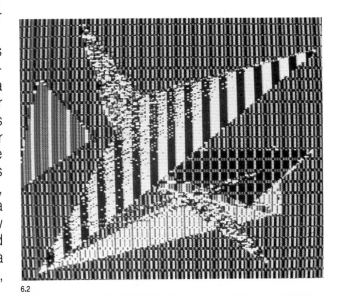

6.2

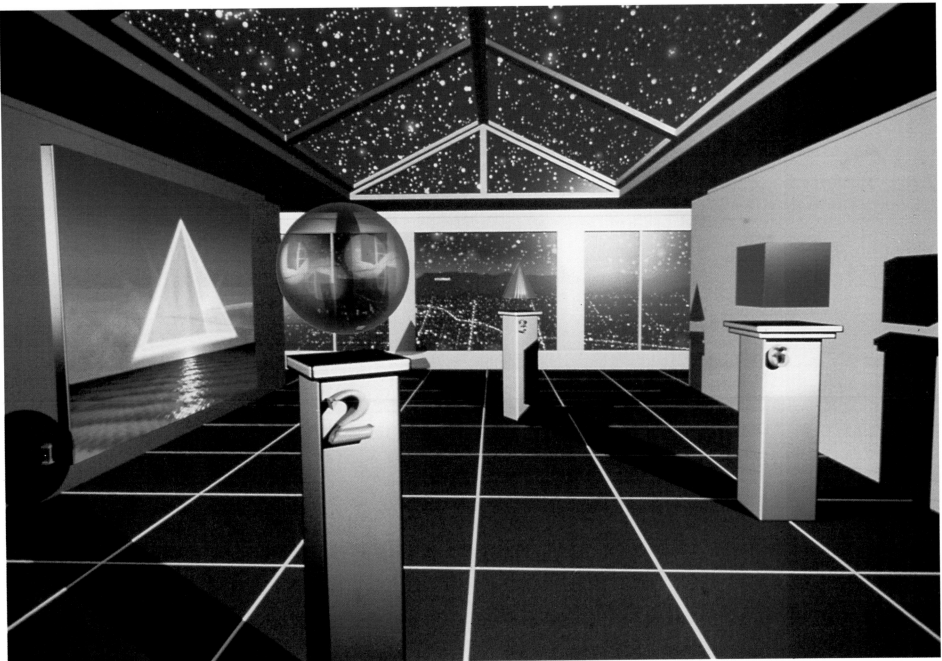

6.3

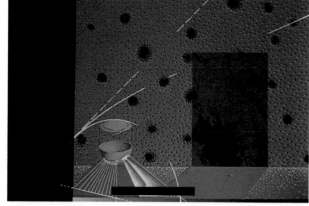

6.4

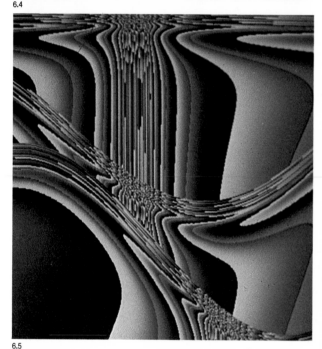

6.5

6.5: **Softy 3**, Frank Dietrich, West Coast University. Cibaprint 20 × 24 inches, VAX 750 and AED (Advanced Electronic Design) 767 display, Fortran software by Dietrich and David Coons.

is in the program and the individual realizations of it.

If this is so, is it possible to possess computer art in the same way that original paintings are possessed, and is there an artefact which is the unique expression of an artist's ideas? In computer art the expression includes all the hardware, the programming and the product of each run of the program; it may even include interaction with the viewer, whose movements near the screen may trigger new images. The output of a program can easily be duplicated, so possession of some forms of computer art is easy but exclusive possession of any computer art is almost impossible. It is certainly difficult to give an object any artificial rarity value in the way that photographers, engravers and etchers can make their prints more valuable by producing limited editions and then destroying the plates or nega-

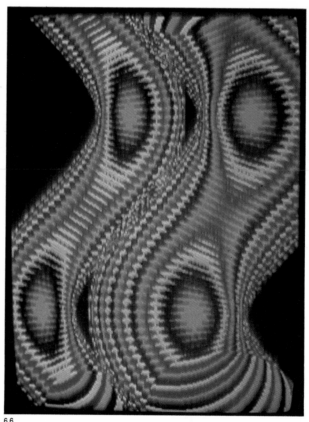

6.6

6.6: **Snake 82**, Frank Dietrich and Zsuzsa Molnar. The image is programmed with the ZGRASS language, which is easy for non-technical people to learn and can create complex effects. It was run on a Datavax UV-1, 1982.

tives. Indeed many computer artists believe that if you destroy a computer program that is capable of producing many new variations then creativity itself is being lost rather than just a creative work. All that does have rarity value is the production hardware.

The clearest way computer art can be possessed is in the way that music can be possessed – through the means of playing it. A music manuscript or an original computer program could have value as a high-class souvenir but it is the presence of instruments and musicians or a cassette or disc which enables us to appreciate the actual music. In computer art a videotape or videodisk is obtained and played on a domestic television set or, alternatively, the consumer goes to see the output of a high-resolution system as if going out to a concert.

Controversy rages over the importance of image resolution. The purists such as John Whitney Jr say that domestic television sets can never present computer art properly because they display images on their relatively few raster lines. Whitney estimates that a high-contrast colour photograph has a resolution equivalent to 18 000 lines and only very expensive machines can offer anything approaching this quality.

Many people would object to this, saying that in most cases there is absolutely nothing wrong with the image resolution on a domestic television set. As long as it is tuned correctly and remains a sensible size, not exceeding about three feet by four feet, the image quality is excellent. There is no reason not to rent a video for £1.50 a night and experience computer art as deeply as the person with the 4000 line display.

It is impossible to make a judgement on this point until both high and low-resolution systems are widely used. It is possible that the purists are confusing the very real problems of resolution in producing images with the far less burdensome problems of receiving images. Radio engineers know they need excellent microphones and studio equipment to produce broadcast quality speech because by the time the signal is reproduced on normal radio receiver the loss of signal quality on the way will be severe. In television this principle is even more important. An original image may be recorded on film, transferred to videotape, put through some special effects, broadcast, received, recorded onto a domestic videocassette and finally displayed on an out-of-tune television set in a bright room. With so many generations of image the quality deteriorates all the way and it is therefore important for computer graphics designers on television to work with high-quality monitors. Where does this leave the would-be possessor of computer art?

The implication is that as long as the original image is drawn to a high resolution then enough quality will be transmitted and there is no need to purchase a super computer or even a high-quality monitor (unless you want a giant-sized wall screen). High-resolution images can be piped to the home on cable, beamed from satellite or ground station or purchased on a videodisk and retain acceptable standards.

However the quality of equipment is impor-

6.7

tant when generating pictures. Although it is theoretically possible to produce equally great art with a tin whistle as with an 80-piece orchestra, the economic prospects for tin whistle composers are not encouraging. In computer art it is theoretically possible to produce rich artistic statements with the eight colours and aliased lines of a simple home computer, but it is a lot easier to make an impact when you have access to extensive computer memory, almost instantaneous computation and sophisticated input–output devices. Artists such as Mike Marshall,

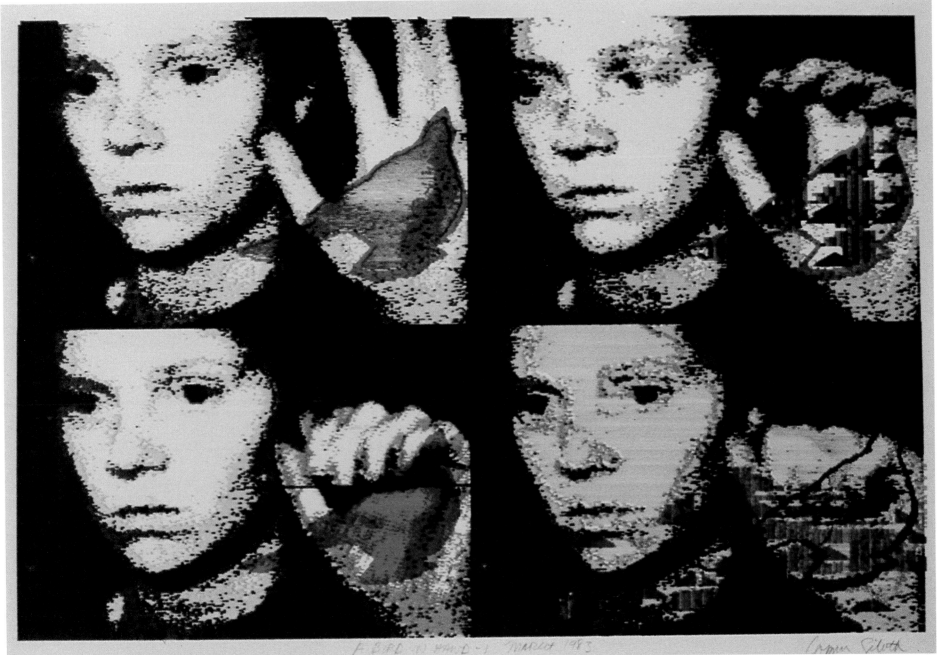

6.8

Fred Polito and now Frank Dietrich are fortunate in having access to custom-built facilities at universities that can afford the latest and most powerful equipment. Computer corporations have also employed artists, who have produced exciting work on successive new generations of mainframe computers.

One of the problems with these systems is that they are mutually incompatible. There has not been as much cross-fertilisation as might have been expected, and artists whose access to equipment is limited have gained little benefit in the form of exposure to techniques they can copy and extend. On less expensive and more widespread systems such as the 'Paintbox' systems described in chapter 8 artists can enter into a dialogue with each other because of the uniformity of the equipment. One key to 'portability', the ability of one person's programs to be used on another person's machine, lies in the use of standard graphics packages such as GKS or GINO-F. These standardize the sort of drawing operations which are available over a wide number of machines, so that methods can be developed to produce interesting effects which can be used on a number of different computers and displays. Standard programming languages also aid portability of programs but few of them were designed with artistic graphics in mind.

Among the programming languages which have attracted significant interest among artists are Kenneth Knowlton's BEFLIX for mosaics, John Whitney Jr's user program at UCLA and especially the GRASS and ZGRASS languages developed by Tom De Fanti in Chicago. De Fanti has been the most energetic promoter of the use of computer graphics by artists; he turned to an early video games system, the Bally Arcade, to make cheap computer images in the late 1970s. Artists working with him, such as Frank Dietrich, did the same and a community of artists developed in Chicago using the Bally system and a dialect of the BASIC language. Dietrich's and Zsuzsa Molnar's work at first resembled Knowlton's BEFLIX patterns but were extended to other low-resolution styles by S. Wenegersh and others.

From there De Fanti advanced to using a computer at Illinois University and his team developed the GRASS system. Images generated by the mainframe are displayed on the screen and filmed with a videocamera. The signal is transmitted to an analogue image processor and displayed again. De Fanti's collegue Don Sandin designed this processor to make real time interactive graphics flexible and accessible on low-cost equipment. The work possible on this system is extremely varied, lending itself to abstract images with woven texture and shimmering ripples of colour.

ZGRASS, developed purely for graphics, is based on a simple microprocessor system and an ordinary television display. It is very easy to learn but creates complex images as in *Snake 1982* produced by Dietrich and Molnar, who have been collaborating in video, computer and performance art for several years. In 1983 Dietrich abandoned ZGRASS and exhibited *Softy 3*, a new departure for him in the smoothness of its surfaces and the sense of depth. This was produced on a VAX 11/750 mainframe with software written in the Fortran language by the artist and David Coons.

At the present state of technology it would be unlikely that *Snake 1982* and *Softy 3* would be produced on the same system. Each combination of hardware and software provides opportunities and constraints, which inevitably means that there are similarities between the creation of different artists on the same system, but in the same way one artist working on different systems will tend to produce different styles using the same artistic vision. Thus Dietrich's work is made less restricting in terms of personal style but more powerfully expansive by the varying media he chooses.

However, versatility does not always depend on using different kinds of hardware. Joanne Culver's *Frozen Sun Cones* is produced using ZGRASS as is Dietrich's *Snake 1982* but the two have no obvious visual similarity. Other artists using the same system, such as Copper Giloth, one of the leading exponents of computer art, show a range of creative expression that is entirely her own. One example of the use of ZGRASS is the extremely witty film *Nuke the Duke*, which uses only simple video game graphics. It was made by Charles Kesler and Jaap Postma of East Carolina University and uses the visual imagery of the amusement arcade. Its subject is the effect of nuclear radiation which may have caused John Wayne ('the Duke') to die of cancer but despite the serious subject, the film has style, zest and engaging humour.

If sharing a common computer language is unusual among artists there is nevertheless a common interest in types of presentation such as multiple images, animation, and interactive art, in which the viewer affects some aspects of the work displayed. Interactive art enables the viewer to explore the range of an artist's vision through the ways the pictures can be changed, and also to recognise the formal structure of a piece by noticing what cannot change. With the advent of interactive videodisks, this kind of art need no longer be restricted to galleries, although the resolution on domestic television sets remains a problem for fast-moving detail.

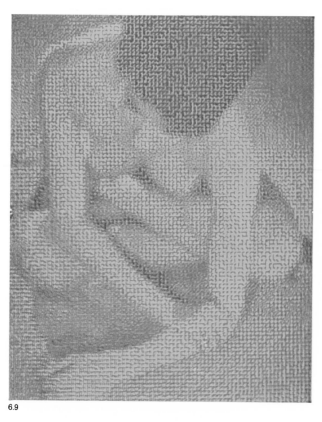

6.9: **Nude**, Lillian Schwartz and Kenneth Knowlton.

6.9

Lillian Schwartz, an established artist who became interested in animated graphics, occupies a special place in the history of computer art. Unlike other artists who have experimented with computer art, such as Stan Van Der Beek, James Whitney and Ed Emschwiller, her interest in computers has been continuous and her work has ridden on ever higher technology. She has worked with facilities made available though IBM and Bell Telephones, rather than striking out independently in Tom De Fanti's manner. Although she still works in other media, she admits to the seductive power of computing in leading her from producing still pictures to animation:

'I initially became interested in computers as a way of producing still graphics. Then I discovered that a simple change in the instructions given to a computer would produce a variation in the design. These variations ultimately become animation. While my sculptures had involved elements of movement, sound, colour and time, and I had always been interested in film, I never saw this work as leading to animation. I became interested in that area after about a year, but the computer pushed me into it.'

What the computer pushed her into was successively more flexible and powerful types of artist-machine interaction. Her first film with Knowlton, *Pixillation*, had to be typed into a keyboard number by number and pixel by pixel in slow batch-mode programming. A still image from the same period, *Hippie 1970*, had random patterns in each pixel chosen by the computer while everything else was typed in by hand.

The use of a flying-spot scanner enabled her to input source pictures more quickly and to maintain them, with results reminiscent of Picasso's cubism. Her portraits of her collaborators, Knowlton, Harmon and Vallaro, on a pseudo-Egyptian background (1969) were a step towards less abstract work which she continued in her influential film *Pictures from a Gallery* (1976). Her pointillist and cubist (or divisionist) views of her family portraits give them an austere authority that contrasts poignantly with the homely subject matter. This quantizing technique is now commonplace in many areas of visualization. It was a short step from using still picture sources to using film sequences. Athletes for *Olympiad* (1971) and 128 frames of a bird's flight for *l'Oiseau* (1976) were transformed, distorted and coloured in a number of ways. Parts of the image were manipulated while the rest remained static, and pseudo-colour was generated.

Her most recent film work takes up the theme of dance with live dancers and computer feedback. The film is a record of their interactive effects on a visual computer system and is called *3 K*. Rebecca Allen's sequence *The Catherine Wheel* also involves dance and is a demonstration of how closely human movement can be simulated (see chapter 3). The sequence is part of a *pas de deux* between a human dancer, Sara Rudner, and the computer-generated dancer. The latter is completely human in shape but the contours of the body are composed of dashed straight or curved lines which follow the limbs of the body. When the computer dancer moves, the live dancer tries to echo the movements – with such success that it prompts the very thought that it will soon be impossible to tell the difference. The whole theatre piece was directed by Twyla Tharp and lasts 90 minutes. The perfection of the computer dancer's performance symbolizes the perfection of St Catherine as contrasted with an ordinary

**6.10: Reflecting spheres**, by Hsuen-Chung Ho. These coloured spheres reflect light from the light source to the viewer's eye. The precise angle at which all the rays would actually bounce off is a matter of argument. Ho's ray tracing and subdivision alogrithms create a realistic effect. Cranston–Csuri, Productions Inc., Columbus, Ohio.

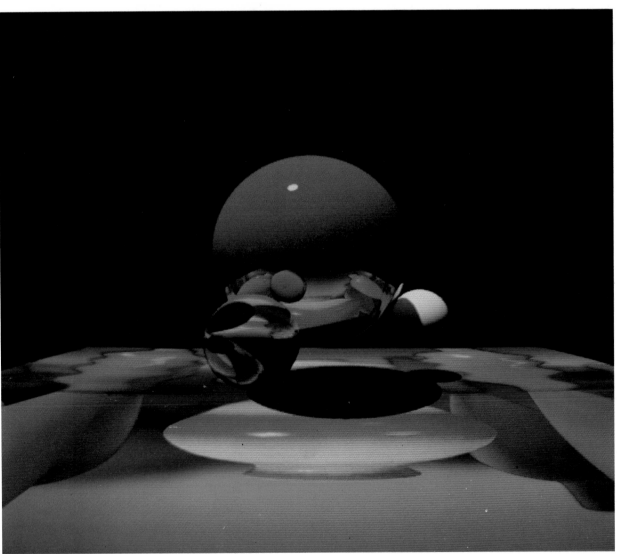

6.10

mortal, although to some eyes at least the human dancer is still ahead on points.

As computer visualization approaches the realism of photography, it is natural that artists should explore the contrasts between 'live' and 'digitized' actors. Still images in a book, unfortunately, cannot demonstrate this kind of interaction – another sign of the essential dynamism of computer graphics. As Tom Duff, programmer for the films *Star Trek II: The Wrath of Khan* and *Star Wars VI: The Return of the Jedi* put it at the end of a paper to the London Computer Graphics Conference, 'the way things move is much more important than how they look. Our most effective models . . . are just clusters of dots and lines that don't look very exciting in still images. It is their motion that brings them to life.'

This opinion of course comes from a film maker, not a stills artist, and the selection of

6.11

images displayed in this chapter lend support to the contrary view. What is noticeable about many images is not that they ought to be moving but that they ought to be paintings. The computer seems to be re-inventing the techniques and styles of twentieth-century movements in art as well as classic forms such as portraiture and landscapes. This must in part be due to the art establishment's resistance to the computer. A notorious example of this occurred in 1969 when Lillian Schwartz submitted a computer generated print to a competition in New Jersey. It was rejected. In 1970 she submitted the same print, this time masquerading as a hand-made silkscreen print. It was accepted and bought for the Trenton Museum's permanent collection.

Establishment resistance of this kind is breaking down fast. Artists do not emulate constructivist use of typography, silkscreen

**6.11**: Digital Effects New York.

**6.12**: **See the Beautiful Sea** (book 1), Margot Lovejoy. Xerox print. Amdahl computer, line printer output. Multiple image etchings based on geodetic data, 1982. *See the Beautiful Sea* is one of a series in which the theme is worked out in successive images. The computer gives great opportunities for this kind of exploration.

6.12

**6.13**: Alyce Kaprow. 1983.

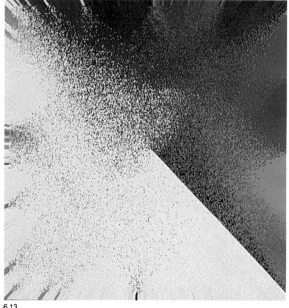

6.13

**6.14**: **Moz Ocean**, L Gartel. 5 × 5 foot, 324 × 70 Polaroids. Cromenco Z-80 computer, video synthesiser, special effects generator, 1983. Unusually, Gartel is a fine artist who employs one of the 'Paint' systems described in chapter 8. The 324 separate Polaroid prints of the *Moz Ocean* are best appreciated in the original large scale of the piece. Multiple images like this are a major theme of contemporary art from Andy Warhol onwards and the computer readily lends itself to such concepts.

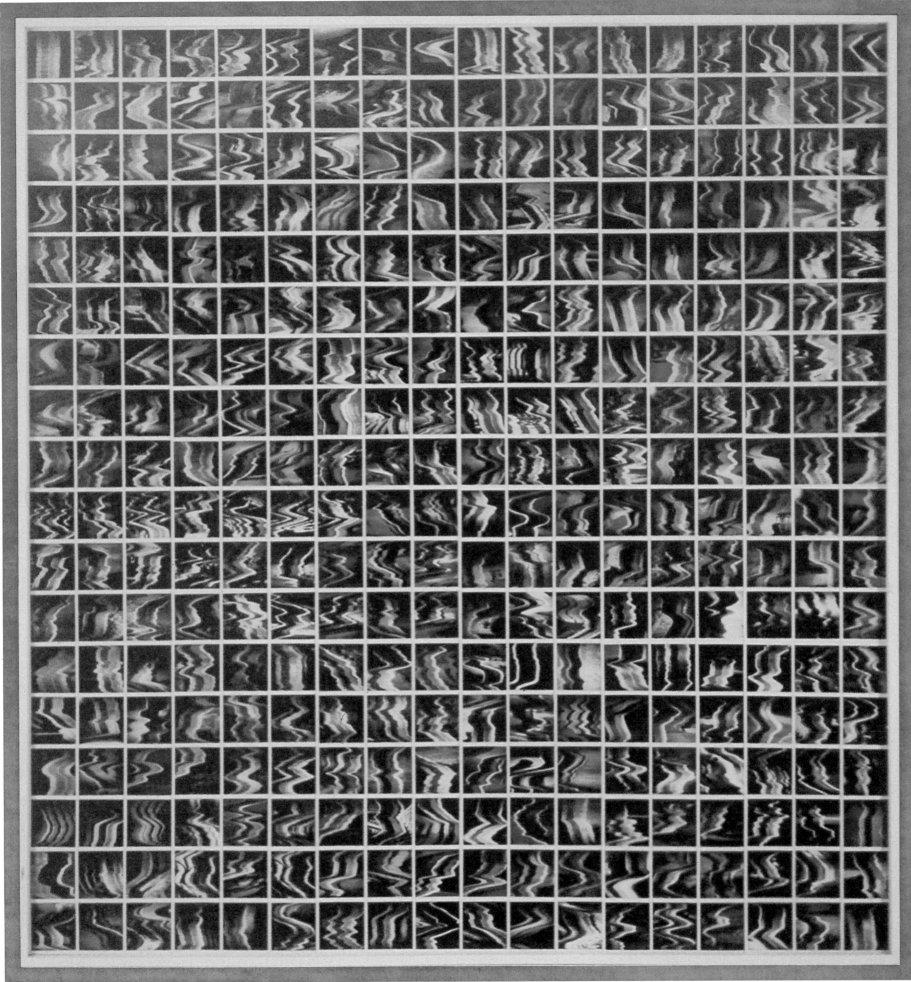

6.14

printing, surreal still life or abstract expressionism not because they are timorous or unoriginal, but because they are part of long artistic traditions. The demands of a new medium have to be understood in terms of previous forms of artistic expression before the medium can be utilized freely by the artist and appreciated properly by the viewer. This is not to say that every viewer, or every artist, must be aware of computer graphics techniques. It does mean that we have to be aware of the range of visualization possible for computers in terms of art which is relatively

familiar before we can presume to comment on the aesthetics of each new piece of work. Photography had to rival painting before it could take up a distinct space in the spectrum of the visual arts, and computer pictures have to relate to photography, performance and painting before they can establish their own unique ground.

Only when such an aesthetic has been developed will there be room to comment on whether a picture is really a graphic illustration, a piece of fine art, or an avant-garde experiment. At the moment, an image such as *Planetrise according to Mandelbrot* may be considered to be art and entered for the SIGGRAPH Art Show. Alternatively it may be shown by Mandelbrot himself with its cousin *Planetrise over Labelgraph Hill* as examples of the varied images made available by his fractal geometry. It may also appear in hardware catalogues to show the resolving power

of a Ramtek display system. So is it art, an illustrative geometric diagram, or a demonstration of machine technology? While the pictures for this chapter claim to be art and those in the rest of the book have other functions, there is no hard and fast distinction to be drawn between them for any reason other than cataloguing, so the answer must depend on the way a particular viewer sees the world and on the viewer's interest in any particular picture.

Some steps towards the appreciation of computer art are being made by teachers and artists introducing fine art or fine art-oriented students to the generation of images by computers. John Whitney Sr works with a dozen graduate students each quarter and sets each of them the assignment of making a one-minute composition on the Chromatics CGC 7900, a task in composing which, in Whitney's words, 'has

6.16

6.17

**6.16: Cosmic Code**, Marget Lovejoy 1982.

**6.17/18: St Catherine**. Computer-generated dancer accompanying a live dance choreographed by Twyla Tharp entitled *The Catherine Wheel*. By Rebecca Allen at NYIT.

6.15: **Hallo Plugs**, Joe Pasquale, Digital Effects Inc. Cibaprint 20 × 24 inches. IBM 3441, PDP 11/34. Software: Digital Effects' Vision System, 1983.

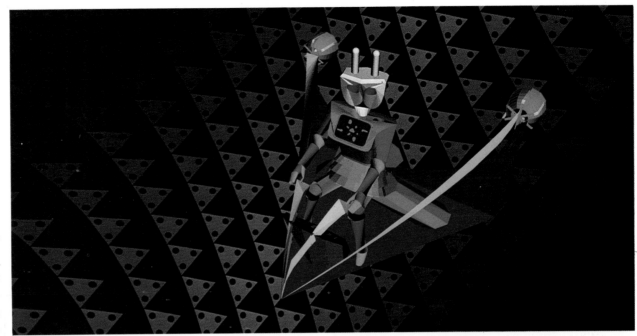

6.15

integrity as a stand-alone which is the same as composing a piece of music, a melody'. Whitney sees his own work since the 1940s as having great continuity, something he finds astonishing. 'The one thing that's more astonishing than that', he maintains, 'is how much better and more advanced it is now with these modern computers, such as the Chromatics. I'm expecting a lot of other ones before long.' Both in his own work and that of his students Whitney seeks what he calls 'digital harmony' – a sense that the artist and machine are working together in a fashion akin to musical composition and performance. His continuing creativity in the field is fuelled by the instant interactive response of a new generation of computers, and his book *Digital Harmony* attempts to lay down guidelines for fruitful development in the future.

The Thalmanns, like the Whitneys, are a family creatively involved in computer graphics, though Daniel and Nadia are husband and wife rather than parent and son. They collaborated with their student, Philippe Bergeron, at Montreal University to produce a 13-minute masterpiece of vector animation, *Dream Flight/Vol de Rêve*, which won the 1982 London Computer Graphics major award and shows a witty, ingenious and touching apocalypse (New York sinks into the ocean because its inhabitants reject an alien visitor). The Thalmann's main work is in computer-aided design rather than fine art and their MIRA graphical system is meant for design. *Dream Flight* took 14 months to produce. The process of developing MIRA and introducing it to students has lead the Thalmanns to deeper insights into the artistic use of computer graphics. The complexities of animation, they feel, are such that it is a good idea that the programming is invisible to the user. Rather than program each movement, animators can use a 'key frame' system which gives a synchronized, smooth movement of specified objects at specified locations at specified times. Unfortunately, such 'in-betweening' of intermediate pictures in a time sequence nearly always looks too automatic. For a more creative involvement in the computer image, artists have to become involved in its programming. A purpose-built system, however quick, user-friendly and reliable, may only produce predictable images. As the Thalmanns put it, 'programming is time-consuming, but user-friendly systems are limitative'.

6.18

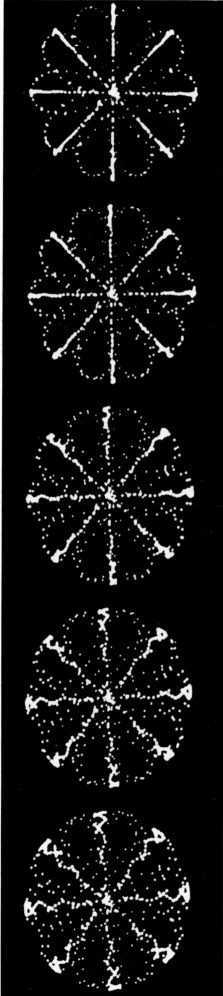

6.19

Further support for this view has been expressed by Brian Smith of the Royal College of Art in London. He feels that illuminating results do not depend on a linear, numerate approach to programming but are more like artist's or natural scientist's experimentation. If every interaction with the computer is a voyage of discovery, the chances are that 'pugs' (picture bugs) will occur and, like the slime mould which lead to the discovery of penicillin, these mistakes may lead to rich areas of aesthetic innovation. It is notable that the artists like Lynn Smith and Schwartz also pay tribute to the value of mistakes.

A wide-ranging view is taken by Gene Youngblood, author of *Expanded Cinema* (1970), the seminal work on electronic art. He has experimented with the techniques he describes and firmly believes in an imminent explosion of user-friendly systems for generating high-resolution images. Gary Demos of Digital Productions suggested to Youngblood that machines like the Cray will soon be online to thousands of home computers, producing interactive home movies in high-resolution, fully shaded and coloured environments. The user could create characters and be involved in the movie, tapping into a variety of 'custom visual simulation' outputs from powerful super computers. There is already the Aspen Movie Map from MIT's Architecture Machine Group, which allows the viewer to choose a route around or into the buildings of Aspen, Colorado. In ten years the viewer will also be able to interact with the town's computer simulated inhabitants.

If this seems more like entertainment than art, Youngblood is keen to point out that computer graphics can also be interactive in a much more profound sense. Historically, art has been monopolized by those who possess the time, wealth, skills and technology to produce and appreciate it. The experience of current practitioners seems to confirm this – pictures can only be made effectively and creatively with the programming skills, time for serendipity, and expensive machines. However, the costs of hardware are falling. The very large scale integrated circuit chip and the transputer will allow the average home user to own $1000 \times 1000$ 32-bit pixel displays and with this technology local groups will be able to produce environments, objects and actors limited only by their own imaginations. The real problem, according to Youngblood, is that unless communication is genuinely two-way conversation on an equal basis, we shall remain the consumers of a few networks' offerings rather than participate in our own space and time.

This warning is salutary. The enthusiasm of the prophets of user-friendliness and universal creativity for computer graphics is reminiscent of the extravagant claims made for hand animation since the first developments of the cinema. Hand animation seemed to many people to offer a three-dimensional world of movement which would become the 'eighth art', the summation of

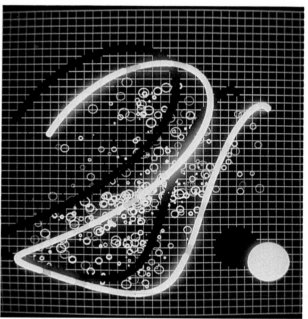

6.20

**6.20**:, Mike Marshall. Cibaprint 20 × 24 inches. Calma Design System, Data General Eclipse, Lexidata frame buffer, 1982.

**6.19**: A mandala by John Whitney Sr.

visual, oral, musical and physical expression. In the 1980s animation is still largely restricted to childrens' cartoons of a very limited quality. It would be very unfortunate if computer graphics is as untrue to its potential as animation has been.

The spread of home computers is one way to guard against the misuse of the potential of computer art, just as the supercomputer's ever-more accessible realism is another way. A third is the way computer graphics enhances art media other than computer pictures as such. There is a

**6.21**: **Sword in the Forest**, Richard Chuang, Pacific Data Images 1983.

6.21

**6.22**: **Artist's Table**, Glenn Entis, Pacific Data Images.

6.22

6.23

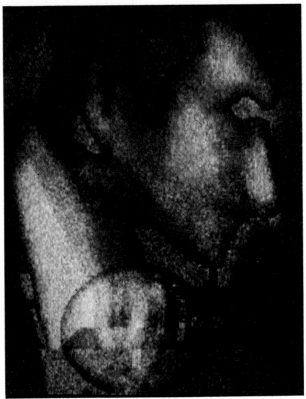

6.24

**6.23**: **Dream Flight**, Philippe Bergeron, Nadia Magnenat-Thalmann, University of Montreal. This 13-minute film uses vector graphics for extraordinarily effective narrative and design. In this image the Statue of Liberty faces the World Trade Centre prior to the arrival of a flying visitor whose poor reception by the natives leads to disaster. Made with the MIRA graphics and animation system, designed by N. Magnenat-Thalmann & D. Thalmann, University of Montreal.

**6.24**: **Ça Roule**, Herve Huitric and Monique Nahas. Ektachrome print 16.5 × 23 inches. LSI 11 frame buffer, 1981. Huitric and Nahas are computer science researchers at Université Paris VIII, currently involved with texture mapping, ray tracing and local modulation of forms.

6.25

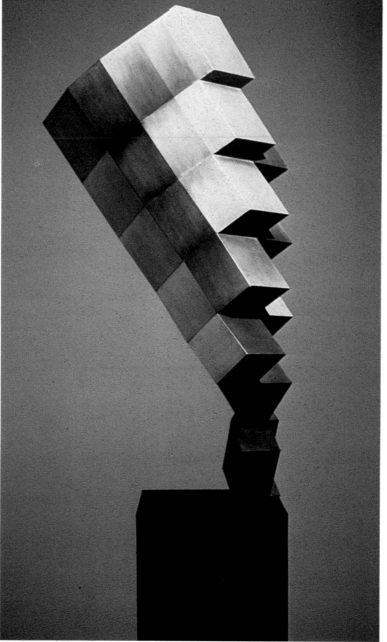

6.26

**6.25**: **Cloud Book**. Margot Lovejoy. 1983.

**6.26**: Sculpture, David Morris. Trans-package software on a Datamax UV-1, 1983. David Morris has produced a number of computer-aided sculptures whose top-heavy appearance – they balance on a slender support – has been modelled many times in the computer to combine a feeling of weight with grace and structural stability.

6.27.1

**6.27.1**: Schematic graph of curves in Rob Fisher's sculpture *Northern Lights*, programmed by Fred Stocker on his Adage 30 minicomputer.

**6.27.2**: Model of curve forms in *Northern Lights*.

**6.27.3**: The finished sculpture: 5000 pieces of glass, brass and cable, 60 feet deep. The sculpture is sited in the Playboy Club, Atlantic City.

very wide and blurred crossover between computer and video but apart from this there are also great contributions from computer graphics in the field of crafts in general and to sculpture in particular. Computer-aided sculpture is similar in techniques to CADCAM, with the difference that the design decisions are in the last resort aesthetic, although engineering considerations are important along the way.

As long as popular knowledge of computer graphics remains patchy and the applications of computer graphics extend so quickly into diverse areas, the place allotted to art will remain highly controversial. If Youngblood's prophecies are fulfilled and every home can receive and store high-resolution images, processing them and generating self-created images as well, then perhaps we shall be closer to the society of which William Morris dreamed, in which every home contained not just art but artists too.

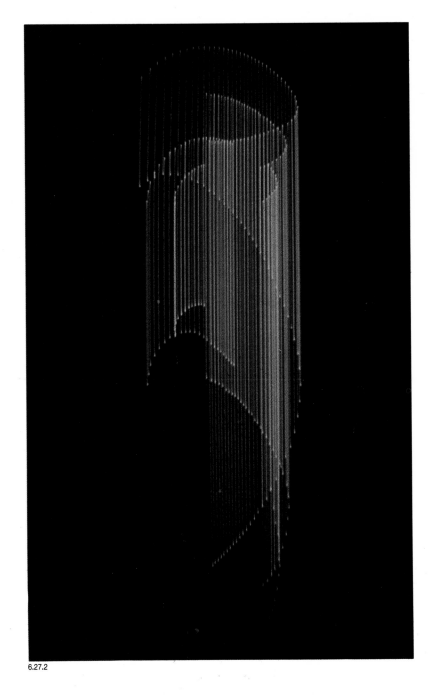

6.27.2

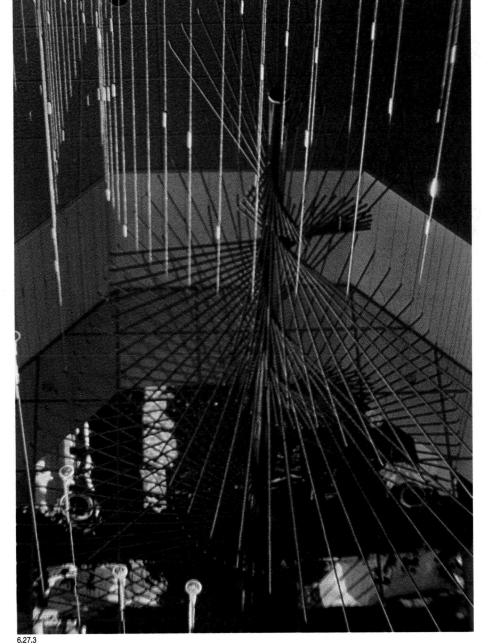

6.27.3

6.28

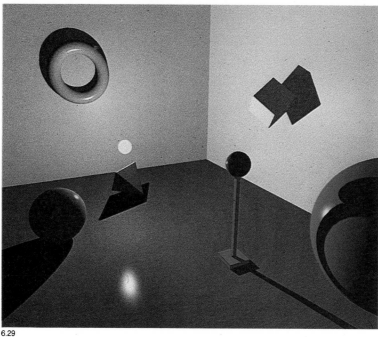

6.29

6.30

**6.28**: **Ed's Dendrite**, Mike Newman, DICOMED Corporation. Cibachrome 11 × 14 inches. Dicomed Imaginator, Design Station Dicomed; D148 SR film recorder, 1983.

**6.29**: Geometric primitives on floor with moulded patterns. John Whitney Jr, Gary Demos, Richard Taylor, Information International Inc. Cray 1 1981.

**6.30**: Barsky, De Rose, Dippé, University of California at Berkeley.

**6.31**: **Santy Fold**, Harry Holland, Carnegie–Mellon University. Cibachrome print 15½ × 17 ⅛ inches. PDP 11/03, AED 512 display. Software by Warren K. Wake.

**6.34**: Barbara Sykes, 1982. Barbara Sykes is a regular contributor to computer art shows; *Video Haiku* is one of her other pieces.

6.31

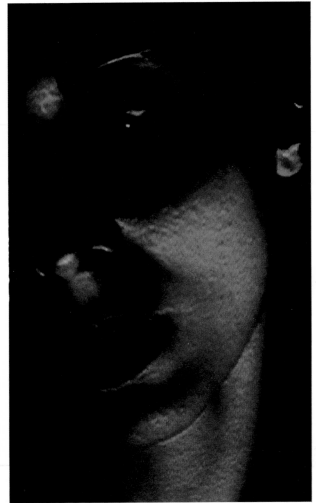

6.34

6.32

6.33

**6.32**: **Changing Pictures, TRW**. Robert Abel & Associates.

**6.33**: **Prismiance**, Edward Zajec. Hard copy from Calcomp plotter. CDC Cyber 170/720, DEC System 10 with LIGHT frame buffer. Software: Pascal (initial development with M. Hmeljak), 1983.

6.35

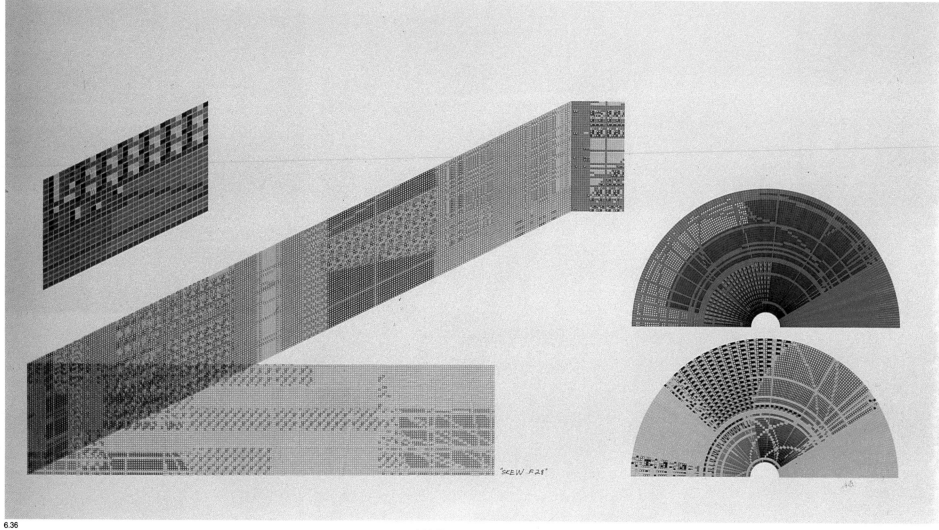

6.36

**6.36**: **Skew F28**, Mark Wilson.

6.37

**6.35**: **Untitled Landscape**, Ned Greene, NYIT Computer Graphics Laboratory, 1983. This is one frame from an animation sequence depicting flight over terrain. The landscape was modelled with a program that makes a data-base for a polygon mesh from a depth image and in this case the depth image was painted. The texture mapped on to the mesh was made by interactively editing the colour map of the depth image to get the desired overall colouration and then processing the resulting image in various ways. Z-buffers were used to perform depth cueing so that objects in the distance would appear hazy. Polygon renderer by Paul Heckbert, mesh modelling program by Lance Williams, depth cueing programme by Ned Greene, modelling, animation and rendering by Ned Greene.

**6.37**: **Soft Computer**, Brian Reffin Smith, Royal College of Art, London, 1983. Television image of Research 380Z computer processed and plotted on Calcomp 81 plotter. The angle of each line represents the brightness of each pixel.

**6.38**: **Columns and Arches**. This image is by Rick Balabuck of the Computer Graphics Research Group, Ohio State University. The data was constructed using a combination of hand techniques and a data-generation program written by W. Carleson which allowed two-dimensional drawings on a tablet to be converted interactively into three-dimensional shapes by projection, rotation, lofting and tubular processes. The image was displayed on a custom frame buffer built by Marc Howard using software developed by Frank Crow. The image was calculated on a VAX 11/780 minicomputer. Frank Crow's scene assembler program allowed the use of multiple coloured light sources, transparent objects and texture mapping.

6.38

**6.39**: **Untitled**, Manfred Mohr. A wooden construction, plotted by computer, of all 24 diagonal paths of the diagonal 000–111, generated from a four-dimensional hypercube.

**6.41**: **Cubic Limit V: Restriction**, Manfred Mohr. The artist describes his work as follows: *Very different results, visually and semantically, can be obtained through different procedures, all related to the structure of the cube, an omnipresent metastructure of my present work. While always maintaining the rigid structure of the cube, I destroy the three-dimensional illusion as well as the symmetries of the cube, drawn in two dimensions thus creating generators of two-dimensional 'êtres graphiques'. In V: Restriction a cube is cut through its centre point into two half cubes, which can be rotated separately around this common point. Both parts create independent signs and their visual aspects change when seen under different angular projections*

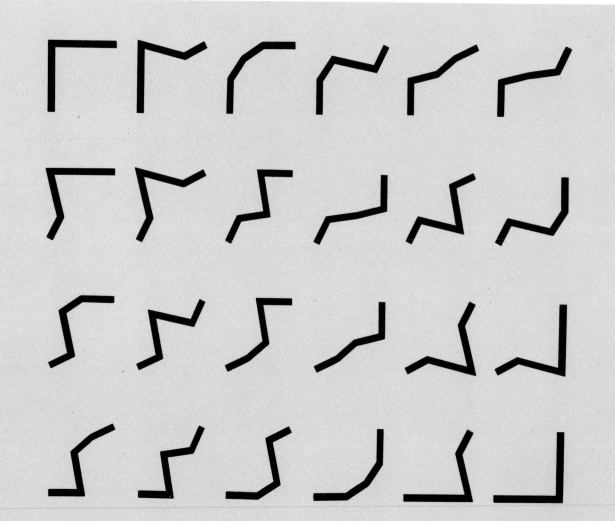

6.39

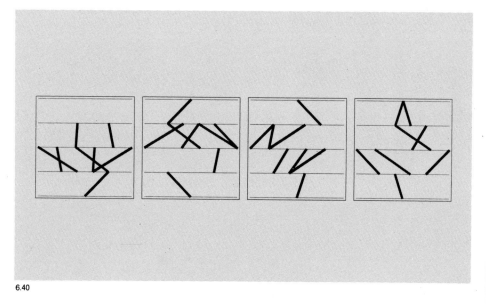

6.40

**6.40**: **Zeichnung**, Manfred Mohr.

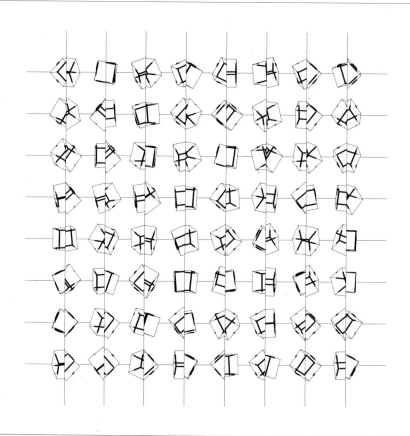

6.41

**6.42**: **Cubic Kennedy**, a study of John F. Kennedy in wireframe boxes. One of a series based on a portrait by the Computer Technique Group, Japan.

**6.43**: Photographs of the kudzu plant, the source for Scott Daly's ECAZ series.

Scott Daly describes his work as follows: *These images were made on the LP-2 Laser Printer at PEC Laboratories. This is a computer imaging system using an RGB laser scanner to create hard copy transparencies with resolution high enough (6000 × 4000) that the film grains would be the limiting factor in resolution rather than a computer-based sampling pattern such as pixels or scan lines. In this series I used a real photograph as the input for computer manipulation. The original image input is shown on the left and is my backyard in North Carolina where the Japanese kudzu plant is taking over the forest. Two versions of computer processing in consecutively higher degrees follow from left to right. The program is a shift-variant transform, meaning that the impulse response of the transform is not constant throughout the image. Basically the transform is a one-dimensional (horizontal) image stretcher, compressor and folder. The stretching is most evident in the middle image, in the centre, where there is a region of horizontal lines connecting fairly regular leaf patterns. This stretching takes all the colour values along a vertical slice and repeats them horizontally until they rejoin with the other side of the leaves.*

*The compression and folding are more easily grasped in the third image of the series, where the folding leads to symmetries and the compression causes the flora to appear as thin totem poles.*

*Of interest is the fact that many viewers see faces in the image, due to the excessive symmetries. In fact, in all of my images where I've used this folding program, faces appear out of non-facial input elements due to the resulting symmetries. To me this implies a basic neurophysiological detection mechanism for faces based on symmetry, this being the primary feature common to all animal faces. The title makes reference to novelist Frank Herbert's ECAZ, the planet which is the sculptor's paradise, being totally covered with rapidly growing vegetation whose directions of growth can be altered by telepathic thoughts of the sculptor.*

**6.44**: ECAZ#1, Scott Daly.

**6.45**: ECAZ#2, Scott Daly.

**6.46**: **LIFO**, Gregorio Rivera. 'Last in, first out' is a parametric stacking system used in programming. Polaroid print 20 × 24 inches. Perkin-Elmer 3220 CPU, Grinnell frame buffer, Reticon CCD scanning camera. Software: VLW, MIT Visible Language Workshop, 1982.

**6.47**: **JSDD 2**, Joel Slayton, Visible Language Workshop, MIT. Polaroid print 10½ × 12⅝ inches. Perkin-Elmer 3220 CPU, 1981.

6.43

6.46

6.47

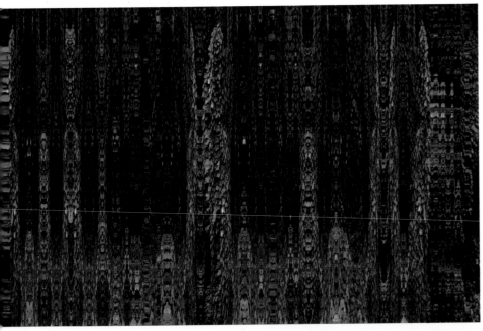
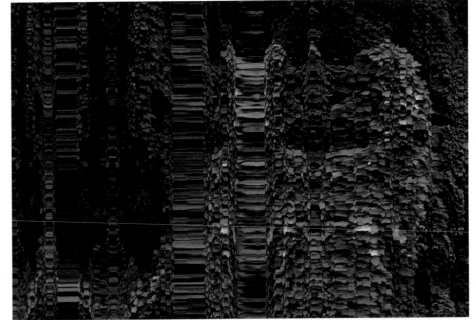

6.45

6.48

**6.48**: Texture study on a three-dimensional mask. Etienne Beeker, Jean-Charles Hourcade, Alain Nicolas. The face of Alain Jean of the styling department at Renault France was digitized for this study, which uses the UNISURF system. Institut National de l'Audiovisuel, France, 1983.

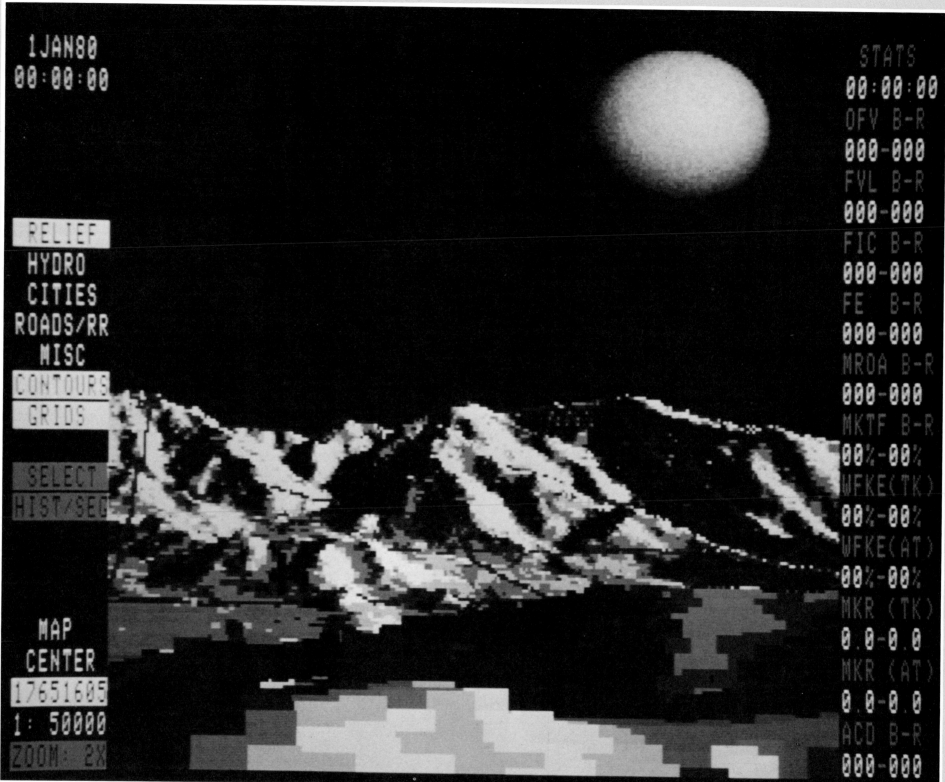

6.49

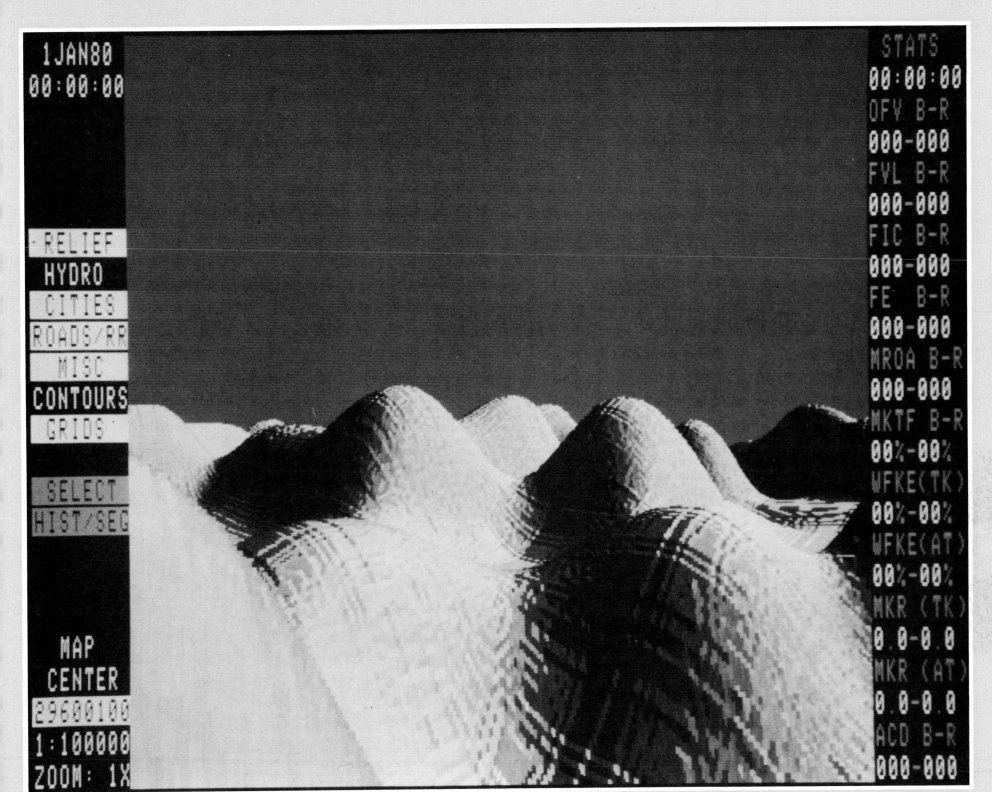

6.50

**6.49**: A sphere rises over a simulated terrain, Brad de Graf.

**6.50**: Simulated terrain, Brad de Graf. Both images were created with software by the artist on a VAX 11/780 with a Deanza 512 × 480 frame buffer.

**6.51**: **Fazes**, Alyce Kaprow, MIT.

6.53

6.52

**6.52**: Alyce Kaprow, MIT. Perkin-Elmer 3230, Grinnell frame buffer, MIT Visual Language Workshop SYS software.

**6.53**: **Flux III**, Margot Lovejoy, 1982.

6.54

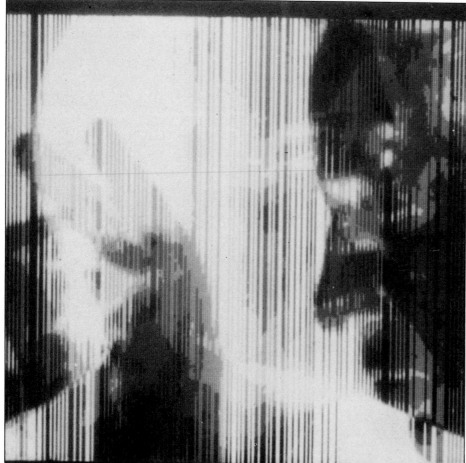

6.55

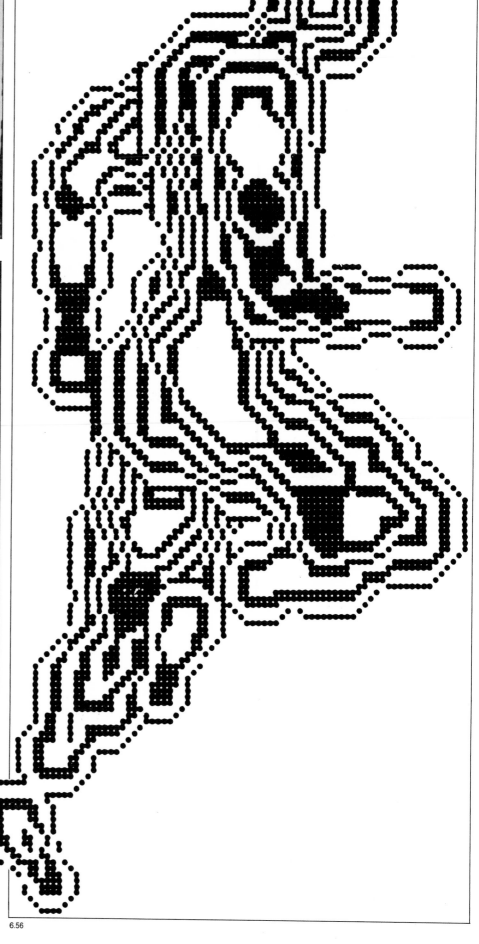

**6.56**: **Olympiad**, Lillian Schwartz, 1971.

**6.54**: **Courtyard**. Rick Balabuck. Produced at Computer Graphics Research, Ohio State University.

**6.55**: Alyce Kaprow

**6.57**: Male Torso. *Cranston–Csuri for The Body Machine.*

6.56

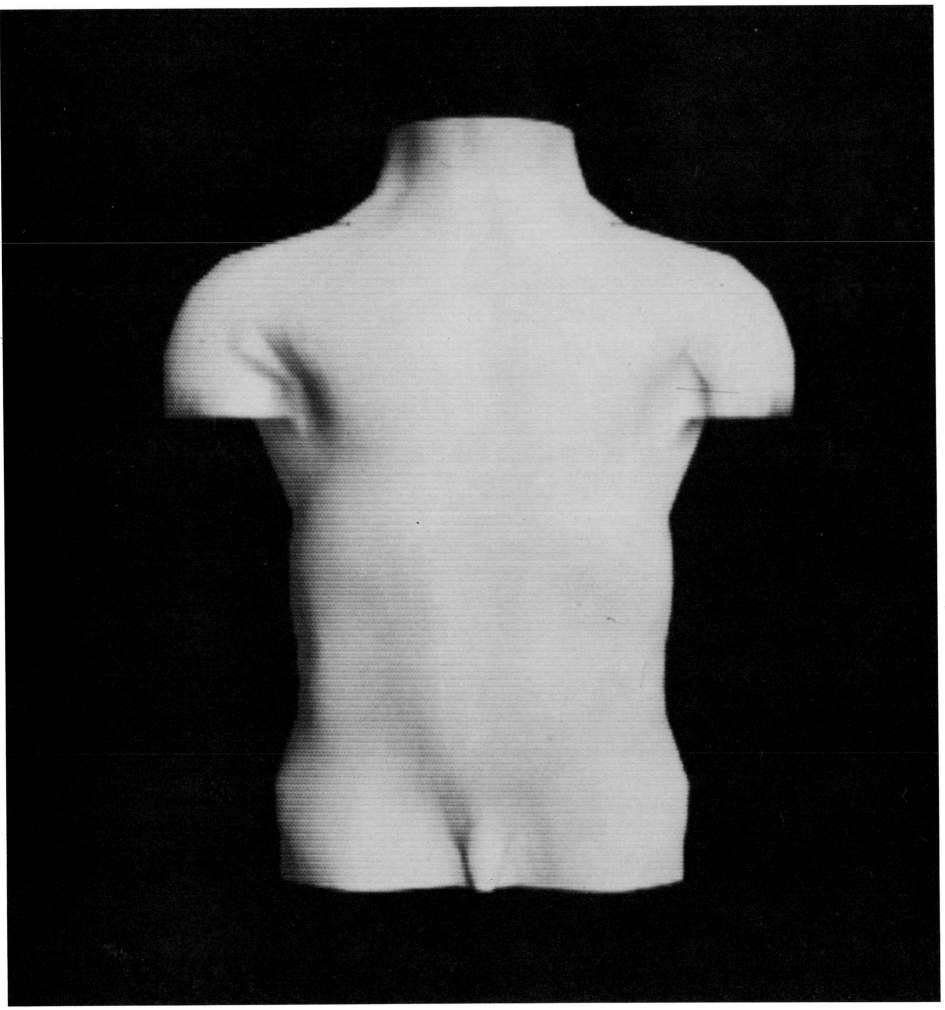

6.57

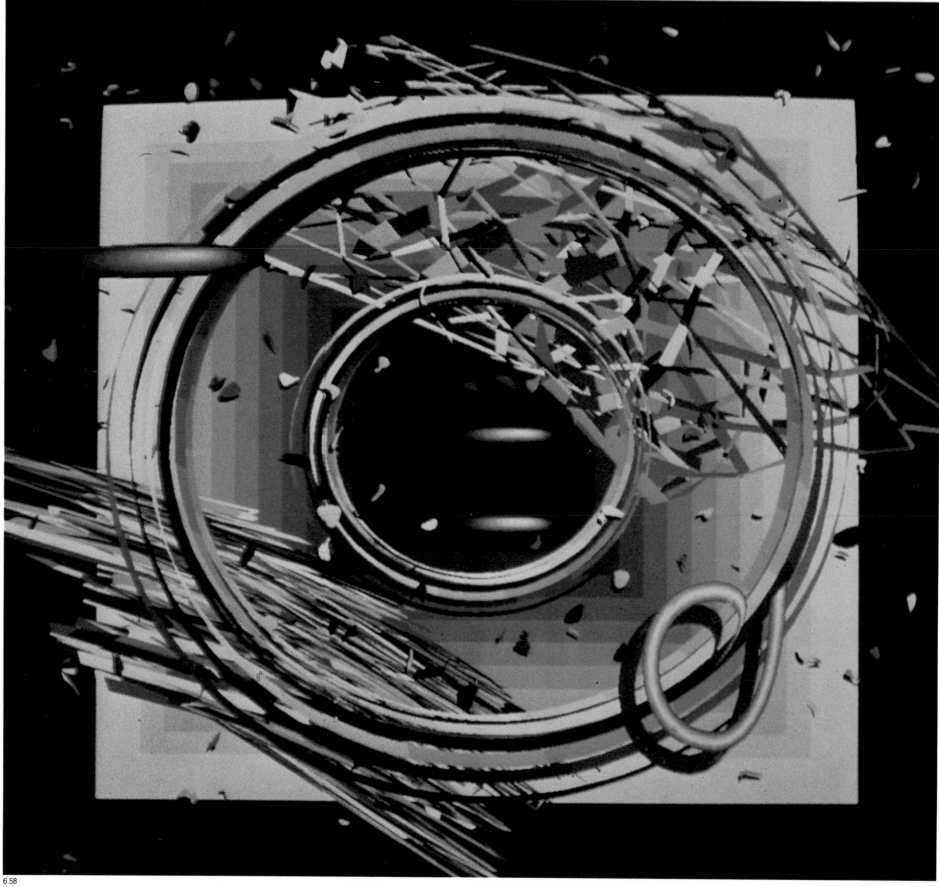

6.58

**6.58**: **Target**, Mike Marshall and Fred
Polito. Data General Eclipse, Lexidata display. Software: ART DEMO
by Mike Marshall.

6.59

**6.59**: Skyscraper with spire reflected
in neighbouring glass tower block at
sunset. Turner Whitted and David
Weimer, Bell Laboratories.

# 7 Feature Films

**7.1**: Original drawing of a 'light cycle' for Walt Disney's *TRON*, by Syd Mead. He designed the look of the vehicles in *TRON* as well as the feature films *Star Trek I* and *Blade Runner*. The electronic process of 'rezzing up' mirrors the design process at the drawing board as well as computer graphics methodology.

© 1982 Walt Disney Productions

Building up his last reserves of energy, our hero, Flash Gordon, leaps the ravine to escape the evil clutches of Ming the Merciless. He points his laser pistol at the pursuing soldiers and pulls the trigger. Despite no visible signs of being hit, several of his enemies drop dead. He rushes to his rocket ship and takes off, his rocket motor emitting puffs of white smoke as he goes. Judging by the way the ship wobbles and lurches, he will not escape Ming's clutches for very long – but we know he will live to fight another day and continue his crusade against tyranny in next week's thrilling instalment.

A child in the 1930s would wait in eager anticipation for the next instalment of his hero's adventure. Although these early science fiction films now have a charm all of their own, they no longer stir up the same excitement in today's young cinema-goer. He has been brought up on a diet of *Star Wars* and *TRON*, (not to mention real adventures in space and on the moon) and is liable to find the special effects in programmes like *Flash Gordon* amusing rather than convincing. This is not to say that *Flash Gordon* did not appear realistic to the cinema-goer in the 1930s, just that expectations have changed. To quench the seemingly never-ending thirst for realistic, action-packed adventures, it is increasingly becoming the task of the computer animator to produce spectacular and above all believable special effects.

Computer graphics have been helping to solve the entertainment film industry's problem of declining cinema audiences. While television and latterly video have expanded, the number of screens in conventional cinemas has continued to decline – in the UK from 30 000 in the 1940s to about 1500 today. Until video came along, X-rated pictures could keep the cinema going, but now that cable television, satellite television and videodisks are joining videocassettes in the competition for viewers, cinemas no longer monopolize the adult audience and must seek to recapture the teenagers who have always been the cinema's mainstay. Ideally for film makers, a film should be excellent on the big screen and profitable in small screen distribution too. The current trend is towards ever bigger and better special effects. It is for these that producers are looking to computer graphics. If the film has heroes and heroines who do not die and do not get married, all the better – a series may then be possible.

The results were such film series as *Star Wars*, *Star Trek* and *Superman*. Even Walt Disney Productions largely abandoned conventional cartoon animation to make *TRON*, the film which to date makes the most use of computer graphics. Computer graphics were introduced into feature films slowly and cautiously. In the 1970s, the era of the vector display, practically no feature film producer took advantage of this relatively cheap and adaptable technology which could give a stylish, high-tech look. In the 1980s, with so many more variations available, the wireframe display still suits the imagination of directors. Superman's body was analyzed by the computer in *Superman III* as a configuration of glowing green lines, as was the landscape of an alien planetoid in *Alien* five years earlier. There are even examples of

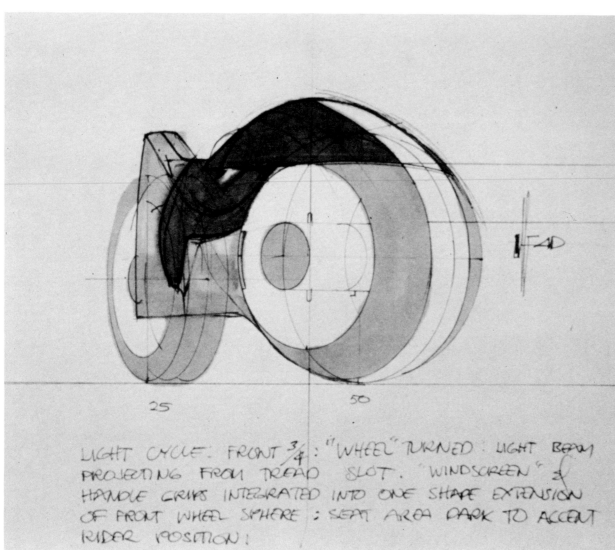

25      50

LIGHT CYCLE: FRONT ¾: "WHEEL" TURNED: LIGHT BEAM
PROJECTING FROM TREAD SLOT. "WINDSCREEN" &
HANDLE GRIPS INTEGRATED INTO ONE SHAPE EXTENSION
OF FRONT WHEEL SPHERE: SEAT AREA DARK TO ACCENT
RIDER POSITION!

7.1

directors asking for the hidden lines to be put back into a computer visualization so that the picture is more obviously a computer image. These include George Lucas, referring to the 'blueprint' views of the trench around the Death Star in the first *Star Wars* film to be produced (known as *Star Wars IV* because there were 'prequels'). The images were used on the consoles of the pilots' vehicles to show the target of the heroes' missiles.

The first application of computer graphics in feature films was in *Westworld*, produced in 1977 and featuring a robot gunman (played by Yul Brynner) whose eyesight took the form of a mosaic of 'quantized' patterns. The sequences were, at the time they were produced, an effective, dramatic and visually stimulating representation of the way a robot sees. This idea is now a familiar video effect, often seen on television and posters, although it is by no means as hackneyed as the wireframe grid of glowing green lines. The technique used for *Westworld* involved sampling the pixels of a photographic image, averaging the intensity of the light from 50 to 60 pixels at equal intervals and separating the red, blue and green signals. The resulting large squares of colour were enough to provide a recognizable image of a previously known object, especially when the object moved.

Gary Demos and John Whitney Jr, the son of the computer graphics pioneer, were responsible for this achievement. Along with Richard Taylor, they soon became key figures in the Entertainments Technology Group of Information International Inc. (Triple I). Their influence was particularly important at this stage since there was a great resistance among feature-film professionals to the idea that computer graphics could be 'realistic'. With the powerful Cray computers available through Triple I's computer print compositing system and microfilm plotter business, Demos and Whitney demonstrated that computer-generated images could approach the realism of photographs.

On the whole though, computer graphics in feature films has been contained within the confines of an 'alien viewscreen' or an 'X-wing fighter pilot's console' or some other device which separates graphic images from human actors with a clear border around the graphic image. The Death Star of *Star Wars IV* has already been mentioned. There were increasingly sophisticated views of the Death Star in *Star Wars V: The Empire Strikes Back* and *Star Wars VI: Return of the Jedi*.

*Return of the Jedi* brought the alien viewscreen into three dimensions with a 'computer-controlled hologram projector', which is used by the rebel space fighters to plan their attack on the Death Star. The actors appear to surround a large green globe, representing the Forest Moon of Endor, with a partially constructed red Death Star orbiting it and protected by an energy field emanating from the moon. The Moon of Endor, the Death Star and the force field in this sequence were given some solidity by a number of fast, swirling dots mapped on to their surfaces. These gave a 'swimming' but credible actuality to the translucent shapes.

A simple Hewlett Packard 9845-B computer was used for instrument panel readings in *Buck Rogers in the Twenty-Fifth Century*, the story of a comic strip hero who travels into the future. The instrument panel showed vector images originally created for motion control systems (computerized control of camera movements). High-contrast pictures were photographed from a VDU as still images and coloured using manual operations.

*Alien*, the space horror film in which an alien being is found on a barren asteroid, featured a brief screen display of a landscape. It was designed by Lodge-Cheeseman Ltd and generated by Systems Simulation Ltd, one of the very few computer graphics facilities outside the US providing computer graphics for motion pictures in this period (1976). The first intention for *Alien* was to digitize a polystyrene model landscape for a database which would provide a grid-like display on the screen. However the landscape was complex: rugged mountains and hills sloping down to a central valley. The database would have been enormous. Instead of this approach, Alan Sutcliffe of Systems Simulation attempted a program which would generate mountains at random, but was constrained to diminish their height towards the centre. The valley was parametrized separately and the whole display was given a convex curve as if on a small celestial body. Another routine roughened up the curves of the hills to give a more natural, weather-beaten look. The scene was realized as a network of large grid squares with hidden lines removed.

Among many other minor appearances of computer graphics on alien viewscreens and the like, one that made ingenious use of the Scanimate analogue system developed by Computer Image Corporation was *Hanger 18* (1980). There, an alien television set appears to scan a cube of space while it warms up for making a fully three-dimensional image. Image West produced this effect, designed by Peter Sorenson.

When feature film makers were satisfied with the images computers could produce on futuristic screens and instrument panels the next step was to use the computer image for special effects: to help characters materialize and dematerialize, fire lasers glow or explode. Triple I again led the way with the materialization of Samurai warriors in *Futureworld*. A still photograph of the warriors was digitized as geometric patterns on the VDU. Each point in the pattern could be used to generate a geometric shape; a few dozen points were chosen and became foci for triangles which diminished in size, became more numerous and returned to the simple live action image. A form of computer visual enhancement was then used so that the warriors could be placed in a real background. Instead of relying on optical techniques in which the foreground character is filmed in (normally blue) limbo, Triple I averaged the information in two scenes, one with Samurai and one without, and the computer recorded the differences – the Samurai in various stages of their materialization. The Samurai could then be inserted back into the landscape when holes of the right size and shape were electronically cut into the background image.

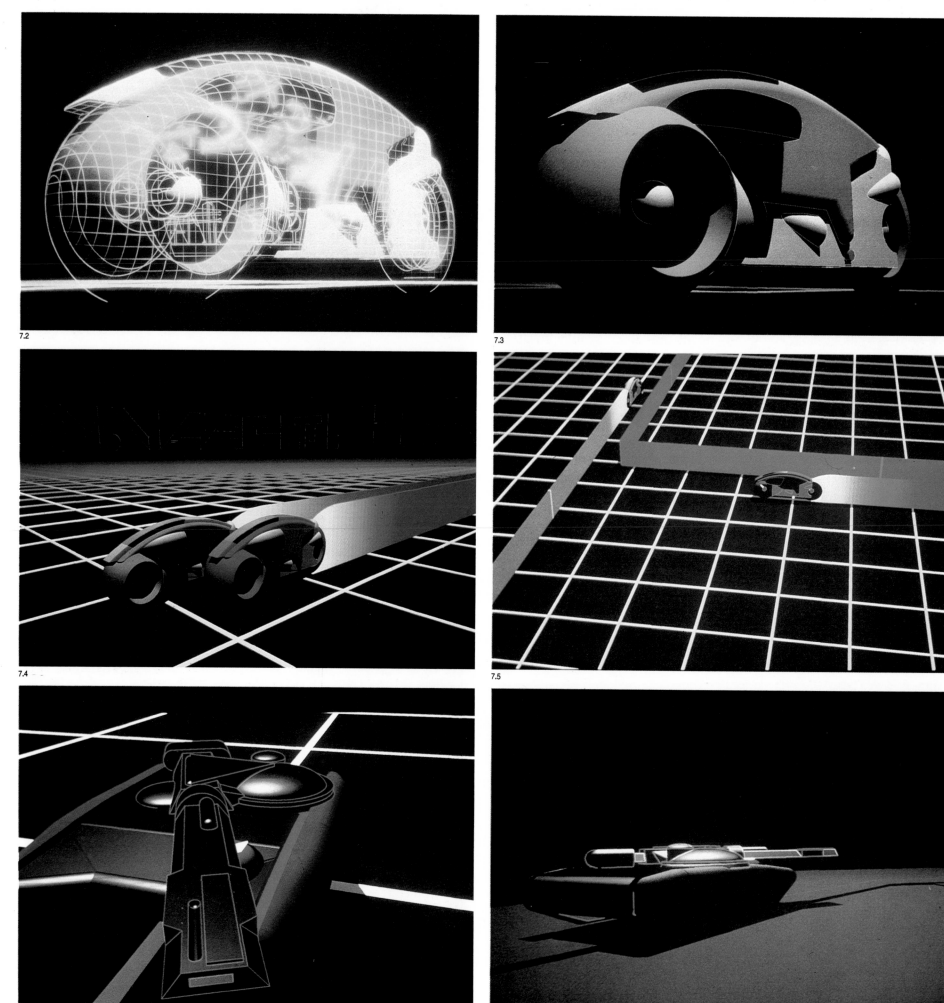

7.2

7.3

7.4

7.5

7.6

7.7

7.8

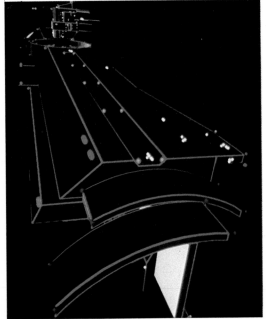

7.9

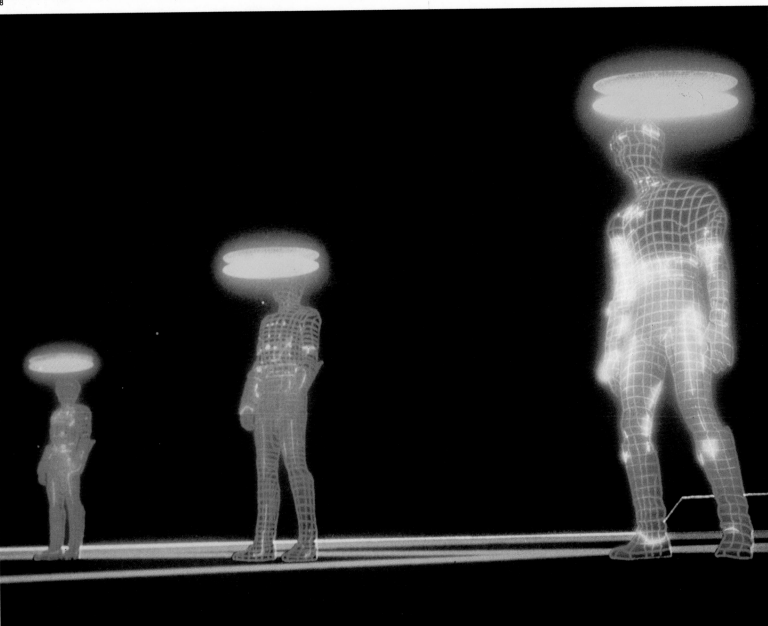

7.10

**7.2/3/4/5**: The light cycle 'rezzes up' in preparation for the life-or-death race around the games grid. Computer-graphics by MAGI Synthavision, New York.
© 1982 Walt Disney Productions

**7.6/7**: Another MAGI contribution to TRON is the group of battle tanks which chase the hero, played by Bruce Boxleitner, down corridors and along precipices. The constructive solid geometry (basic shapes) production method allows the tanks and 'recognizers' to distintegrate excitingly into pieces when required.
© 1982 Walt Disney Productions

**7.8**: A recognizer hovers menacingly over the video game grid. MAGI Synthavision

**7.9**: Towards the climax of TRON the evil Sark, played by David Warner, flies this stately battle craft over the computer landscape. The vehicle was created by Information International Inc.
© 1982 Walt Disney Productions

**7.10**: Three video game warriors – in fact human actors with glowing red lines added optically. It appears that they change into wireframe light cycles – the rider becomes the machine.
© 1982 Walt Disney Productions

The *slit-scan* effect, which can simulate a high-speed journey or a radiance of coloured lines around a central object, was first created manually for the film *2001: A Space Odyssey* (1968). Since then several companies producing television commercials have made great use of it. One of the most interesting examples was for a feature film, *Demon Seed*, using Scanimate at Image West. Using this technique, it was possible to appear to zoom through space and to give the triangular image used for the film's emotional computer a pulsating halo of streaks, varied to express moods from anger to orgasmic ecstasy. The same system was used to create force fields, laser blasts and glowing vehicles for *Logan's Run*.

Computer graphics began to affect feature films more radically when applied to the creation of vehicles rather than glowing lines around them. Up until this point, science fiction and adventure films had relied on the model maker's art for their more spectacular journeys, crashes and chases. For *2001* a 55-foot model had to be manipulated by a skilled team to simulate the slow flypast of a huge, detailed spacecraft. It is now possible to do away with the physical model completely. A computer may hold a representation (a model) of the object internally and produce views of this model on its screen, or directly on to film, as required. This three-dimensional computer model

may be produced by one of two basic methods: (i) a real, or imagined, object may be digitized and its surface modelled; or (ii) the object may be produced by combining basic shapes (cubes, spheres, cones, etc.) to produce the shape required – this is referred to as constructive solid geometry. At Triple I the first method was used to realize a flight of five X-wing fighters for *The Empire Strikes Back*. Because of financial disagreements, the film eventually went back to using hand-made models, but the demonstration had convinced George Lucas that computer graphics was capable of photographic realism. He set up a group to provide a computer facility within his own organization. He also controls a more conventional special effects company, tantalizingly called Industrial Light and Magic Inc., and claims that, rather than competing with this company, the computer company has independent long-range goals.

Lucas' Computer Development Division is designing hardware-based animation systems called PIXARS. These will be much cheaper than the Cray supercomputer which Gary Demos' and John Whitney Jr's new company, Digital Productions, are using to produce very high-quality sequences. However, being designed as special purpose animation computers, rather than just very fast general purpose computers (like the Cray), PIXARS should be just as capable of highly realistic detail. At the time of writing, the PIXAR's potential for computer graphics is as secret as Digital Productions' own feature film, *Starfighters*, which aims to out-Lucas Lucas.

Until this or similar films appear, the best showcase of computer graphics for general consumption is found in *TRON*, a Walt Disney production directed by Stephen Lisberger in 1981. In a largely computer-generated environment, a number of computer-generated vehicles demonstrate a variety of computer graphics techniques. Several different computer graphics companies were involved in the making of *TRON*. They include MAGI Synthavision, Robert Abel and Associates, Digital Effects Inc. and Triple I.

The computer-generated vehicles in the film were produced by MAGI (Mathematical Applications Group Inc.) and Triple I. MAGI used constructive solid geometry to create models for the 'tanks', 'recognizers' and 'light cycles', whereas Triple I digitized imaginary vehicles to produce the 'solar sailor' and 'Sark's battle craft'. Since making *TRON*, MAGI have developed a system called Synthamation, which is said to be able to produce in two months what took ten months for *TRON*. MAGI's first contribution in the chronological order of the film's story is the materialization, or 'rezzing up' in *TRON* jargon, of

the 'light cycle' – a motor cycle with fixed spheres for wheels and a cockpit completely enclosing the rider. The process of rezzing up illustrates the stages in designing an object as well as the increasingly complex ways in which the model may be rendered: wireframe grid, then solids modelled and hidden surfaces removed, then light sources and texture. MAGI's basic shapes system is simple compared with Triple I's digitized coordinates, but the scene in which the light cycles race in zig-zags across an apparently vast arena (winning by blocking the opponent's exit) was the result of one of the most complex programs ever written for computer graphics – although the light cycle had no discrete moving parts during operation.

In the eight minutes of *TRON* designed by MAGI, two other types of vehicle, apart from the 'light cycle', appear – low-slung tanks with enormously long barrels, and machines, called 'recognizers', which look like flying gantries with two menacing legs. When these were wrecked the basic shapes system came into its own – the primitive shapes used to model them flew apart in spectacular fashion.

MAGI's base during this production was in New York, while Disney was at Los Angeles. To check the computer animation from MAGI, *TRON*'s special effects directors viewed tests, piped down a telephone line from New York, on a high-resolution graphics terminal. Planning and execution were so disciplined that only four or five scenes needed to be changed more than once. Computer personnel and Disney animators working on *TRON* often used two very different kinds of language to refer to the same thing. MAGI were able to improve communication by developing 'Director's Language', a code based on the English language which moves objects and specifies speed, distance and rotations, and may both be understood by humans and interpreted by a computer. They tested the animation on low-resolution 200 × 200 displays, up to 200–300 frames at a time, but the very high resolution filming with a Celco film recorder was done under clinical conditions, physically and electrically isolated from the rest of the world in order to minimize mistakes.

In *TRON*, the combination of live and computer-drawn characters was achieved by filming actors on sets with reference points whose positions could be used by the computer to check the orientation of a scene before generating a background for it. MAGI's subsequent work with Disney has involved combination of hand-animated characters with computer environments, building on the animation strengths of both man and machine.

The advantages of the MAGI system for the film makers was that it could operate quickly and flexibly. Triple I contributed the detailed, fully-realized vehicles which appear at the end of the film and move in a more stately and restricted fashion. One of the most memorable of these is a kind of aerial aircraft carrier which takes the villainous Sark towards his evil leader, the Master Control Program (MCP). A point line scanner exposed each frame, in which the carrier appeared, three times – in red, blue and green. To build up solid shapes and subtle colours the scanner required up to 30 minutes for a single frame of film – at normal projection rates, one second of film requires 25 such frames. Therefore Richard Taylor, who directed the computer graphics, decreed that five minutes per frame had to be the average. Even so, Triple I's six minutes of film took 49 days of continuous filming to produce.

Perhaps the most elaborate vehicles in computer graphics come from NYIT's Computer Graphics Laboratory, founded and funded by Alexander Schure and directed by his son Louis. Their unfinished feature film *The Works* contains no less than 25 robots including a mechanical ant whose head houses two robot pilots, named Clyde and Ipso Facto. Every detail of the robots and driving controls is meticulously represented, from the shiny metal texture to working dials and levers. Whatever their value as entertainment, the sequences completed and shown so far include the most believable and striking moving objects yet made by computer graphics. NYIT uses electronic tablets and 'wands' to input general outlines of the robots and then basic shapes, as at MAGI, fill in the spaces. Thus, NYIT has a kind of hybrid of the Triple I and MAGI systems. The primitive shapes can be stretched and squeezed at will by the designers to fit the desired form. Textured surfaces of any kind are possible, although the style of *The Works* demands polished metal.

In the capable hands of MAGI, Triple I, NYIT and others, computer graphics has helped to realize an impressive fleet of imaginative vehicles. Naturally, these vehicles need environments in which to operate and computer graphics has again been enlisted to create the right surroundings for the light cycle, the mechanical ant and even the human actor. Computer-generated environments, including landscapes, space scenes, interiors and fantasy environments offer great scope for computer graphics techniques. Walt Disney's *The Black Hole* featured a vortex of apparently cosmic forces, produced by Robert Abel and Associates, in which the varying dimensions of the funnel and the changing viewpoint

created a dramatic impression of the black hole's mystery and power. Shortly after *The Black Hole*, *Star Trek: The Movie* (or *Star Trek I*) also included a computer vortex effect, more elaborately realized than the green line grid used for *The Black Hole*. The sequence shows the view from the spaceship Enterprise in 'hyperspace' amid spiralling stars, which are then 'sucked down a tube' as if the spaceship is being sucked back into normal space.

*Star Trek II: The Wrath of Khan* provided an impressively complex sequence of photographic realism in the 60-second 'Genesis bomb' sequence. A deep-space probe carries the notional camera as it flies towards a barren planet, spirals down on its near approach and ejects a 'pod', which falls to the surface of the planet. On impact an explosion generates a disk of flames which expands around the planet. From the ever-spiralling probe, the edge of the disk is seen as a wall of fire. When the whole planet has been covered, gases are given off to give a planetary atmosphere; mountains grow and seas flood the valleys. As the planet recedes from the probe's view, vegetation fills the land and another world is ready for human colonization. The idea of 'terra-forming' planets for human life is popular in science fiction, but this is the first time it has been convincingly realized in visual form.

The production of this sequence required a coordinated input from eight designers and up to ten exposures of the film were needed to create the various parts of the image. The choreography of probe and planet were first decided upon, including, at a late stage, a scene where the flames disappear below the horizon and then spring into view again in dramatic close-up. The appearance of the barren planet was then painted with the aid of a program for making craters, executed by Tom Duff. The effect of the wall of fire was the result of an innovative idea by Bill Reeves using particle systems, as described in chapter 3. Reeves realized that to produce convincing-looking flames it was possible to make use of the random generation of particles and particle systems. These particles may be thought of as points of light ejected in a random direction by the initial explosion, following suitable paths through space, fading in brightness and eventually dying – very much like sparks thrown up by a bonfire. As particles died more were generated by randomly-created particle systems representing secondary explosions. The initial explosion of the 'Genesis bomb' created 25 000 particles; later in the sequence when fire had engulfed the whole planet, there were 750 000 such particles. The position of each individual particle was computed for each frame so that it could be drawn in the

correct position. In fact, each particle was drawn as a short straight line representing the path of its motion during that frame (instead of one instantaneous position). This is called 'motion blurring' and ensures that the particles appear to move smoothly, rather than jumping between frames. Since every particle was drawn, many particles could be drawn on top of each other; the number of particles at each position was used to determine the colour of the image on the screen. If only a few particles passed through a pixel in a given frame then that pixel was coloured red; the more particles that passed through the pixel, the more yellow it appeared, representing the heat at the centre of a fire.

The 'Genesis' sequence in *Star Trek II* was brief, though spectacular. The challenge of making computer graphics environments for *TRON* was of another order of magnitude. In *TRON* there are 15 minutes of purely computer-generated images and 200 other scenes with computer-generated environments. *TRON* was a more ambitious computer graphics project than any other yet completed and required great accuracy in registering the foreground characters against the backgrounds. In the latter stages of the film, this registration was achieved by filming the actors in a dark, blank set, whose proportions were mirrored in a computer database. Four 'witness points' (light sources) at key positions in the set enabled the computer to match the live set with its memory and to reproduce the visualization with the same viewpoint, focal length of lens and viewpoint movements. While the shape and size of the set were fixed, not least by the need for correct perspective around the actors, the colours of the set could be varied at will; indeed, the colours of the 'walls' vary in most of the settings for *TRON*.

**7.11**: **Wild Things**, a test sequence by MAGI Inc., Elmsford, New York, builds on their experience with witness points and human actors in *TRON* in order to provide a unique service. A client's cartoon character can be incorporated in a three-dimensional computer-generated environment.

**7.12.1–8**: Images from the 'Genesis' sequence at the opening of *Star Trek II: The Wrath of Khan*, which continued the adventures of Captain Kirk, Spock and the rest of the crew of the starship Enterprise. The story has Captain Kirk watching a videotape of a science fiction process in which a dead planet becomes suitable for human life when a space probe fires a 'pod' at it. The pod explodes on impact, engulfs the planet in a wall of fire. And the result is an Earth-like globe of green continents, blue seas and swirling clouds. *Star Trek ® II: The Wrath of Khan.* © 1982 by Paramount Pictures Corp.

**7.12.1**: The pod burns in to the cratered, inhospitable planet.

**7.12.2**: The planet catches fire.

**7.12.3**: Fire sweeps across the landscape.

**7.12.4**: The camera is almost caught in the flames.

**7.12.5**: The planet cools and the surface of hills begins to appear.

**7.12.6**: Mountains are formed and stand out against the night sky, whose

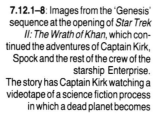

7.11

7.12.1

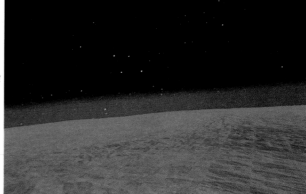

7.12.5

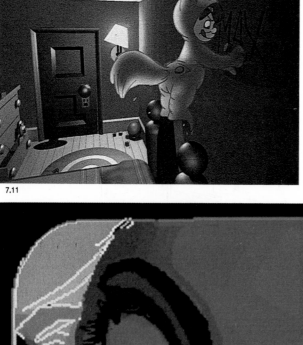

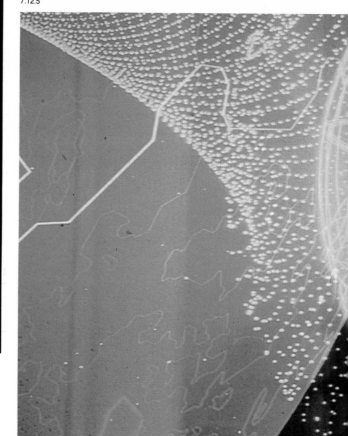

**7.13**: An image developed for the film *Videodrome* Digital Effects, New York.

**7.14**: **Death Star** scenes from *Star Wars VI: Return of the Jedi*. Each frame is composed of up to eight separate elements. The large green sphere is the 'Forest Moon of Endor', and its background and foreground continents and lakes make up four elements. The Death Star (in red) and the yellow 'force field' which links it to Endor are a further two elements, and mattes for Endor and Death Star complete the 'holographic display' (a science fiction term not yet current in computer graphics). The mattes are partly transparent to allow the live scene to be visible through the computer-generated image.
*Evans & Sutherland monochrome by William T. Reeves and Tom Duff.* © *Lucasfilm Ltd. All Rights Reserved.*

7.14

stars were computed to resemble an actual configuration, not as seen from Earth, but from Epsilon Indi.

**7.12.7**: On the daylight side of the planet the peaks are snow-clad above the blue sea.

**7.12.8**: As the probe pulls away into space, the continents and cloud formations show that the planet is now ready for human colonization. *Star Trek ® II: The Wrath of Khan.* © *1982 by Paramount Pictures Corp.*

**7.15**: **Night Castles**, Ned Greene, NYIT Computer Graphics Laboratory. Another famous image, also featured at SIGGRAPH. The shape of the castle is reminiscent of graphics by M. C. Escher and the moonlight effects on the waves help to create a magical effect.

7.12.2

7.12.3

7.12.4

7.12.6

7.12.7

7.12.8

7.15

Perhaps the most spectacular environment in *TRON* is the single vector graphics sequence known as 'Flynn's Ride', after the character who is drawn from his workstation into the heart of the computer. Vector graphics were also used for one of the characters, Bit, whose binary characteristics are to change shape for 'yes' and 'no', while floating near the hero's head. Unfortunately, Bit's extensive role in the film was curtailed to two minutes for scheduling reasons, but it remains one of the most memorable characters in the film – not bad for a pint-sized polyhedron. Bit was

generated by Digital Effects Inc., but Flynn's Ride, together with the titles and trailers for *TRON*, were made by Robert Abel and Associates, who showed how far they have come since *The Black Hole*. The Flynn's Ride sequence was realized as a series of ever-diminishing horizontal planes. At first they resembled Los Angeles at night – huge vistas of street lighting and jewelled clusters of neon tubes. As the camera travelled down through these scenes, they resembled more and more a fantasy-enriched stack of circuit diagrams, while the traffic became the passage of electrons along metal pathways. These images helped to point up the theme of the film, which is the parallelism between human civilization and the way programs work in computers. Views from the villain Dillinger's office and the final emergence of Flynn from inside the computer to the streets of a metropolis were used to reinforce the theme at

the beginning and end of the film. Despite somewhat low-key critical reviews, *TRON* succeeded financially and technically. It was a great achievement for director Stephen Lisberger and a courageous move by the Walt Disney organization.

Perhaps the most challenging application of computer graphics to the entertainment world has been in the creation of believable human characters. This should be distinguished from the various ways in which cartoon animation has used computer graphics. In the case of a cartoon, the character is realized as a humorous two-dimensional drawing and the computer's contribution lies in animating the image, colouring it or matching it with backgrounds. The character itself, being flat, cannot be entered into the computer as a three-dimensional model and so cannot be manipulated by computer means. A pilot sequence for the feature film *Raggetty Ann* animated the character using the computer at Triple I; another feature, *Rock and Rule*, also depended on computer techniques. Neither, though, used original character designs apart from conventional hand drawings.

Computer generation of human figures, on the other hand, is among the most exciting goals of computer graphics. A first demonstration was made by Demos and Whitney for *Futureworld*, the sequel to *Westworld*. Peter Fonda was asked to pose in white make-up while a grid was projected on to his face. He was photographed simultaneously from two directions and the resulting images were placed on a digitizing tablet. The important grid intersections were digitized and the computer then had a rough three-dimensional model of the actor's face. In the film, the paper-thin surface of the face and the sides of the head was revolved for the camera and seen from front and back. The latter stages of constructing the face in solid flat polygons as opposed to a wireframe were also seen. These polygons were at first large and sharply angled, giving the face a faceted shape and a dull white texture. The polygons were then smoothed out around the edges, light sources were added and the face was seen as a shiny, artificial but very recognizable portrait.

The Triple I team under the direction of Richard Taylor, developed this technique further with the 'Cindy Head' for actress Susan Dey in *Looker*. Like Peter Fonda, she was photographed in white make-up with a grid projected onto her face. This time the pictures were taken from several angles. The resulting database of grid intersections was more complex than for the Fonda face and allowed the whole head to be modelled, including the ears. *Looker* was directed

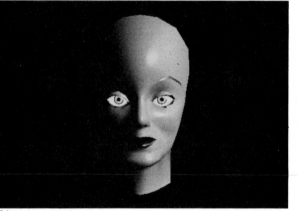

7.16.1

7.16.2

7.17

by Michael Crichton, as were *Westworld* and *Futureworld*. His intention was again to show the viewer successively more realistic views of the head. The grid coordinates were encoded by Art Durinski and Larry Malone to produce a cranium like a geodesic dome and a much tighter network around the facial features. Onto these were mapped the solid polygons for the skin, including lips and nostrils. The eyeballs were given their own spherical shading model and the faceted head became much more realistic as the angles where polygons met were smoothed away. Colour was added for skin tone, lips, pupils and geometric eyebrows. The expression of the face however was bland and could not be changed.

The next step up the ladder was reached when a complete human figure was digitized by Triple I to form 'Adam Powers', a top-hatted juggler whose body could be articulated at joints such as knees and elbows. In the first films of Adam Powers in action, the face did not change. However, the same database was adapted for the character of the Master Control Program in *TRON*. Adam Powers' face was stretched horizontally around a pillar and endowed with sinister converging eyes, a wide flared nose and full, sneering lips. The facial movements during speech were convincing, but a high degree of realism would have been inappropriate to a character who resembled a column of multi-coloured light rather than a human being. Total realism was therefore not sought.

While Adam Powers and the MCP were very successful, they were still based on an actual human face which had been digitized. Expression could not be varied a great amount. The generation of a human head inside the computer from first principles was not attempted. At NYIT however, Frederick I. Parke has been doing just that. He works on both the surface shape of the face and on the underlying muscles. Neither system is effective on its own as yet, but the judicious combination of the two parametrized graphical models can form realistic facial expressions. The result is similar in appearance to the masks in *Adventures in Success*, a promotional video for the song of the same name by Will Powers (no relation of Adam!).

Parke's system allows for 50 independent facial actions, which may occur separately or in any combination. It is worth quoting at length from Parke's August 1982 paper on the subject to show the painstaking detail that realistic rendering of human faces must involve:

'The expression parameters found useful for the eyes include: eye pupil dilation, eyelid opening, the position and shape of the eyebrows and where the eyes are looking. Useful expression parameters for the mouth include: jaw rotation (which controls mouth opening), width of mouth, mouth expression (smiling, frowning, etc), position of the upper lip and positions of the corners of the mouth. Other useful expression parameters include: the size of the nostrils and the orientation of the face (head) with respect to the neck and the rest of the body. The ability to orient and tilt the face was not included in early models and was obvious by its absence. With 15 or so parameters it is possible to develop a model which allows interesting expression animation and the ability to animate to a spoken sound track.

To allow changes in the conformation of faces (those aspects which vary from individual to individual and make each individual unique) requires a different set of parameters, which have not, as yet, been fully determined. Some conformation parameters apply globally to the face. These are the aspect ratio of the face (height to width ratio), skin colour and a transformation which attempts to model facial growth. The colour (and texture in more elaborate models) of the

**7.16.1–8/7.17**: Facial parameters developed by Dr Frederick I. Parkes, director of NYIT's Computer Graphics Laboratory. Parkes' system was applied by Rebecca Allen in her music video for singer Will Powers and Island Records.

7.16.3

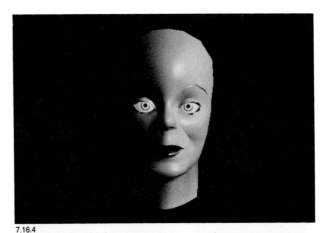

7.16.4

7.16.5

7.16.6

7.16.7

7.16.8

various facial features such as eyebrows, eyelashes, lips and iris of the eye are controlled by conformation parameters. Other conformation parameters consist of relative size, shape and positioning information. These include parameters which control: length and shape of the neck; shape of the cheek and cheekbone regions; shape of the chin; position and separation of the eyes; size of the eyball; size of the iris, shape of the forehead; width of the jaw; length of the nose; width of the end of the nose; width of the bridge of the nose; scale of the chin; size of the eyelids; scale of the forehead and scale of the mouth to eyes portion of the face relative to the rest of the face.'

Though the faces presented here are less than perfect as regards the shape of the eye and the eyelids (among other factors), the potential for this system is immense and *The Works* will be a first showcase. This is the beginning of the most revolutionary step that computer graphics can take in the feature film world, supplanting not only special effects men, set designers and animators, but also the actors themselves. However, it is very easy to under-estimate the amount of work required (both human effort and computer time) to produce even relatively simple computer-generated scenes. Since many tens of thousands of frames must be produced for even a short feature film, this problem is obviously increased; Alvy Ray Smith has a cautionary last word: 'It would take 400 years to make a fully computer-generated feature film on present equipment'.

7.18

7.19

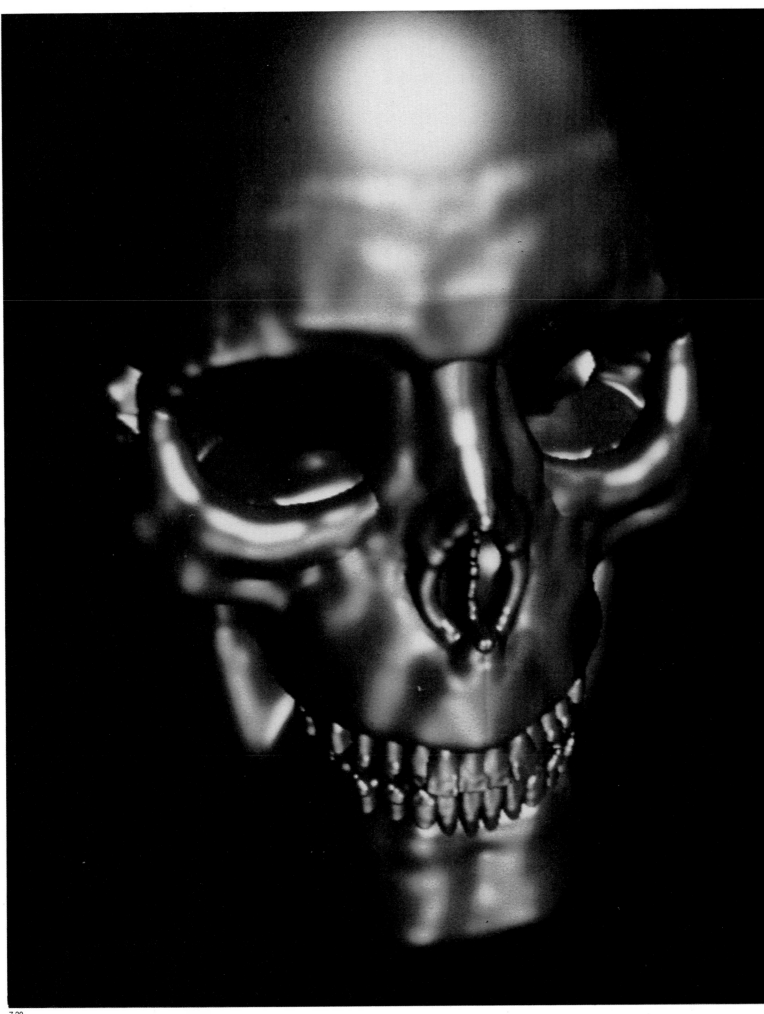

**7.18**: Mechanical ant construction worker from NYIT's unfinished feature film (or showcase of computer animation) entitled *The Works*. The writer and director is Lance Williams, production design is by Bill Maher, and Dick Lundin made the ants.

**7.19**: **Clyde in the cockpit**, Dick Lundin, NYIT Computer Graphics Laboratory. The mechanical ant is driven by a robot called Clyde. A previous robot driver, Ipso Facto, has been made redundant. The cockpit is ergonomically designed to accommodate Clyde's unusual physique – the chair fits only his body and the joystick controls are adjusted by his hands. He can monitor all the details of ant walk performance on the cockpit instruments. Desert texture mapping is by Paul Xander Jr.

**7.20**: The skull from *GOLGO 13*, a Japanese animated feature film. Like Kawaguchi's film *Growth: Mysterious Galaxy* (see chapter 2), the skull was made on a Links 1 multi-micro system of 64 computers. The skull has 600 control points and was rendered by ray tracing.
*Hitoshi Nishimura and Yoshi Fukushima at Osaka University.*

7.20

# 8 Television

Thanks to television, we all know about computer graphics. Commercials, children's programmes, science documentaries, news programmes and Britain's Open University broadcasts and titles – all have drawn on the resources and flexibility of computer graphics.

The most frequent application is to titles, which present a perpetual design problem. Visual appeal is a must when television stations need to identify themselves, future offerings have to be listed and the stars' portraits need captions. With computer graphics it is easy to make names and logos come alive with dazzling movement and dramatic lighting.

Television would seem ideally suited to computer graphics on a technological level – you just plug your home television set into the computer and there you are. Unfortunately, it is not as simple as that. High-resolution, cinema-quality computer graphics for television is still some way in the future. The gap in image quality between the top-flight system's VDU, or film, and the home-viewer's television set is still very wide. The advantage of computer graphics for television lies in the array of visual techniques it can muster, not the technical superiority of the image. Also the image-originating system need not be expensive compared with other equipment at the television station. A Cubicomp CS-5 system with solid modelling (smooth shading) was advertized in 1983 at under $10 000. The BBC/CM Video Flair is also microprocessor-based and similarly priced.

At the top end of the market however, computer imaging for television is still beyond the means of most design groups. The Ampex *AVA* system, first retailed for $200 000 in 1981, includes PDP 11–34 computer, a display controller and a DM-9160 disk drive. The system was designed in its basics by Alvy Ray Smith, whose work at NYIT led him to realize that a system was needed which would provide flexible visualizing methods for designers with no computer literacy. The AVA system is interfaced to the artists by two monitors and an electronic stylus on a drawing tablet. One monitor is used for menus and text, the other monitor for the finished article. Like other 'paintbox' systems, AVA offers a wide range of brush and pen-strokes, resembling watercolour, pencil, acrylics or ink sketching. Drawn objects can be painted instantly and re-arranged in varying orientations and combinations. They may then be transmitted directly or mixed with other video signals to form a composite television image. Circles, rectangles and other geometrical shapes can be generated from minimal reference points and over 200 colours can be used.

In fact, this number of colours is quite small when compared with other systems. Flair gives a basic 256 colour blocks, which can be combined. There is only one monitor to work from so the menus for palette and brush-stroke are positioned on the side of the drawing table and the artist

8.1

**8.1**: **Hairpiece**. An example of artwork produced on a Flair system. Graham McCallum, BBC TV.

touches them with a stylus to specify, say, a chrome yellow italic style of handwriting. Flair also has an airbrush facility which scatters spots at random around the tip of the stylus, building up a solid area of colour if the stylus remains in the same position for any length of time. The picture resolution on Flair is 768 × 576 lines (the other 49 lines in the European 625 line system are not visible on the screen). This is somewhat better than the 512 × 512 raster used in many computer graphics systems, but there is still frequent staircasing on Flair images.

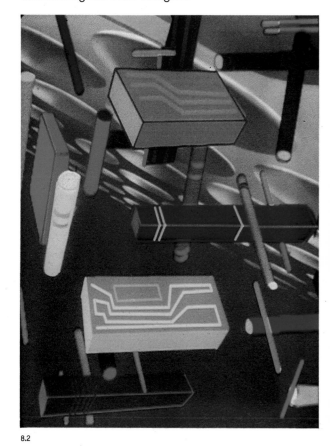

8.2

**8.2**: Building blocks in space. The raw material for . . .

**8.3**: . . . vector images on MPC system (fibre optics).
*Moving Picture Company Ltd.*

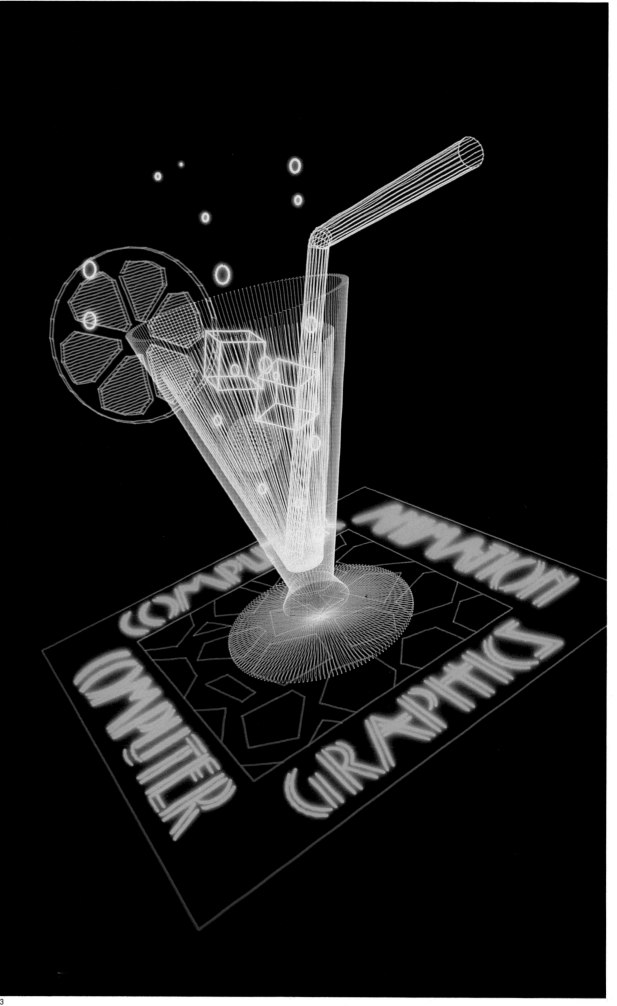

8.3

**8.4**: Artwork produced by Antics. *Grove Park Animations Ltd.*

**8.5**: **Hi-Fi** – television commercial by Robert Abel & Associates.

8.4

8.5

**8.6**: A video effect or computer graphics? The point is arguable, but this kind of image, in which original input is altered by an analog computer, is more conveniently pigeonholed as a video effect (although its earliest models, CIC's Animac and Scanimates, were the first commercial computer graphics systems for television). Now that digital techniques are universal, these blurs and wobbles seem not to fall into the same area of visualization. *Synopsis Video.*

8.6

The Quantel Paintbox is about the same price as AVA and gives better definition than Flair. Colours are practically unlimited in their combinations, but subtleties have to be avoided if the output is to be broadcast. Nevertheless, it is important that the artist has a high-resolution monitor to work from. The down-grading process as the image passes from original output to domestic reception is limited by the excellence of the original.

A paint and animation system that has received little attention in the West, mainly because its designers are based in Japan, is the Antics system devised by Alan Kitching and Jim Harker. Antics has a long history and was originally meant purely for animation. Alan Kitching's 'primordial' Antics was first seen in 1973. The 'paleolithic' model was sold to Swedish television in 1978 and used to animate the smiling or frowning faces of politicians in the general election there. The 'stone age' Antics of 1983 was a rival to other Paintbox systems of the time in the inclusion of soft-shading (or airbrushing), a standard range of 700 colours (which can be transparent or opaque) and a range of graphic and animation functions. The configuration of equipment in the stone age Antics includes a text (or menu) screen, a wireframe display for line-testing and a colour screen for art work, together with a hardcopy unit to produce output on paper.

Although Antics has been out of the mainstream of computer graphics, it is, at least, designed by artists for artists' use. The hardcopy output is described as an essential production tool. It is much easier for artists to visualize changes in a picture by scribbling on a piece of paper than by talking in the abstract or changing line-test or colour-screen images, which might result in loss of the best ideas down the gremlin-filled circuitry of the data store. It is true, as Ampex AVA advertising claims, that messy bits of dog-eared cardboard are no longer needed – but they may be desirable. It is very frustrating for designers to be denied access to paper copies of their work, for doodling, restructuring or merely as a record. The computer is an excellent way to create images but not always the safest way to preserve them or the easiest way to visualize alterations to them.

However much computer graphics may seem to be the right technological answer, when dealing with people you have to consider psychological and sociological factors. This could be one reason for the relatively low impact of computer graphics on television commercials and for the very limited range of computer graphic styles that have found acceptance among advertisers. Computer Image Corporation (CIC) has been pumping out computer graphics for commercials since 1969 but it is hardly a household name. In fact, CIC's 1974 system, CAESAR (Computer Animated Episodes using Single Axis Rotation), is still less known than the Scanimates which preceded it but are still employed for cheap 'computer animation' when required.

Computer graphics effects first made a significant impact on television in the 1970s. Viewers were assaulted by a deluge of wobbly, tumbling titles produced on analogue computers. Due to over-saturation these effects are currently out of favour amongst television producers. Dolphin is one of the best known computer graphics production houses in New York and mastered such techniques at an early stage. The titles they produced for the Public Broadcasting System programme, *The Scarlet Letter*, deliberately resemble hand-animation. Alan Stanley, Dolphin's president, claims that 'you'd never dream it was computerized'. This may be a matter of opinion but it was probably largely true when said in 1980. Even today, a major resistance factor against computer graphics on television is its association with the primitive graphics of previous generations of hardware. As in feature films, the glowing green line wireframe grid is still associated with a high-tech image. This is somewhat ironic, since, in computer graphics circles at least, the vector display used to produce these images (together with the images themselves) is considered very much out of date.

The prevalence of the glowing green line has had an inhibiting effect on television commercials. While one client of a leading production house in 1983 was still insisting that the 'jaggies' (staircases) be put back into the lines of his product, thus wasting a lot of expensive anti-aliasing (smoothing), many other would-be clients assume that the jagged jittery image is all that is available and investigate no further. Perhaps it is not surprising that advertising agencies are wary of computer graphics when every company using it takes great delight in making their system sound fantastically complicated and unique. The jargon is super-complex, when in fact the only computer that is essential to a particular production is the one that prints out the schedules and invoices.

No producer of computer graphics for commercials is immune to the joy of mystifying the customer with high technology, but Bob Abel, one of the most successful commercials producers of the computer graphics world in the early 80s, is more immune than most. His string of commercials for Levi's included the advertisement with best audience penetration ever. His company, Robert Abel and Associates, uses a whole range

of techniques, including vector or raster graphics, on an Evans & Sutherland Picture System 300 to provide model-making and live action. Like a number of others in the field, Abel met John Whitney Sr in his formative years and turned from an engineering background to industrial design and then film. Abel's company became successful partly because the Evans & Sutherland display is a reassuring tool for visualizing commercials in line form before the client is committed to high costs. It can also be used for the final commercial, as in the Chevrolet Corvette film which incorporates many different kinds of image-making and uses a VAX/11–750 as a basic processor. Abel makes good use of purely raster techniques as well, as in his promotional film for the *Anti-friction Drive*, which replaces cogwheels in a gear chain with components based on toroidal rings. The computer graphics clearly demonstrates a new

8.7

8.8

8.8: Quatro. Commercial for four-fruit soft drink.
*Jankel and Morton at Cucumber Studios. Computer graphics by SOGITEC.*

8.9: **Braun**, electric razor commercial by Robert Abel & Associates. The movements of a live action camera and the product were matched by the motion of a wireframe computer image.

8.9

and complex process to the most unmechanical of minds.

Abel's main strength is the combination of different media. He originally used a computer only to check the smoothness and speed for complex live-action camera movements before setting up an expensive shot with a Mitchell studio camera. With the Braun commercial, the line drawing from an Evans and Sutherland vector tube was mixed with live action to simulate the progression from an idea on the drawing board to the finished product. An even more remarkable Abel creation, *Panasonic Glider*, is a wireframe journey through Chicago, showing off the outlines of the many highrise monuments to twentieth century architectural experiment. Thus, in commercials at least, vector (line) drawings still have a high-tech image and for as long as the public continues to associate the wireframe grid with technological advance and reliability, we shall continue to see mock engineering drawings as we are told, say, that 'Braun's feed-in comb aligns even long and woolly hairs'.

A commercial which managed to enhance

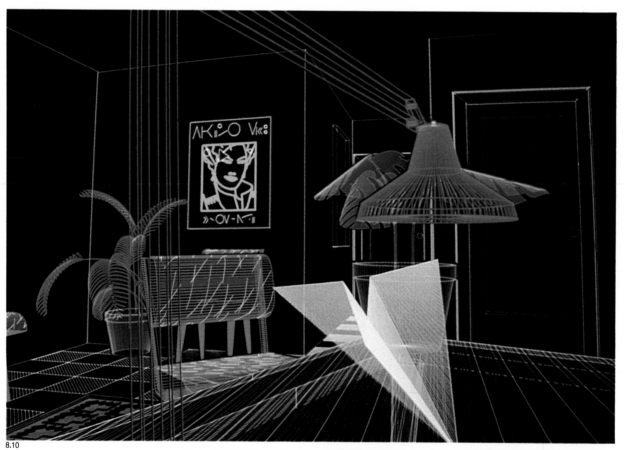

8.10

8.10: **Panasonic glider**. A remarkable journey out of the office and through a simulated Chicago, in a commercial for National Panasonic by Robert Abel & Associates.

8.11: An electronic calculator and other pieces of equipment fly towards the camera in this dramatic commercial for sharp office systems, entirely computer-generated by SOGITEC, France.

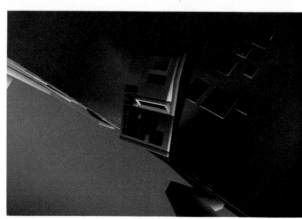

8.11

8.12/13

8.14

the wireframe look was Cucumber Studios' *Pifco: Food Processor*. An EMI system, since taken over by Electronic Arts, did the outline vector animation of a food processor in action, into which was introduced a super-real hand-animated vegetable. The computer animation was supplied as black lines on celluloid with no hidden line removal. The 'hidden lines' were then removed by hand and negative photo-mechanical prints made. This high-contrast film was photographed frame by frame with the hand rendered animation matted into the sequence.

The *Quatro* commercial, by Cucumber Studios, combined solid-surface raster computer graphics with hand-animated and rendered fruits. This soft drink commercial is a combination of live action/animation/computer graphics and special effects. After shooting the live action, the computer graphics were used to go from a live-action vending machine through a 'transparent' side of the machine and into the computer graphic world. SOGITEC, who created the computer graphic interior of the machine, supplied outlines of the fruit which were then animated, rendered and matted into the computer graphic machine interior.

Another British company, Lodge–Cheeseman, has made a speciality of slit-scan techniques. They are also involved in image origination, having modelled realistic space fighters for a commercial for KP Spacers snacks. They also worked with Digital Pictures Ltd to produce a solid surface commercial for Michelin Tyres with a fully-solid Michelin man, and with Electronic Arts to produce one of the first almost totally computer-generated commercials to be seen on British television – the pop-up book effect for Norwich Union Insurance.

8.15

8.16

**8.14**: **Glaxo**, a poster for the drug corporation Glaxo by Digital Effects Inc. The surreal landscape is reminiscent of Walt Disney's *TRON*, to which Digital Effects Inc. contributed.

**8.15**: **Michelin Man**. The first computer model of the familiar character from Michelin tyre advertisements was designed by Lodge–Cheeseman Ltd and computer animated by Digital Pictures Ltd.

**8.16**: One of a number of key frames produced for viability study of computer graphics versus conventional methods in the production of animated commercials. © *Intelligent Light 1984*.

**8.17.1–7**: **Pirelli** tyres commercial, produced by Cucumber Studios, London with computer graphics executed by Digital Effects Inc. New York. This sequence shows how the tyre was built up and then revolved as a fully-realized solid image. Few viewers would have realized that this tyre never existed outside a computer.

**8.18.1–5**: **NBC Nightly News Identification**. The lettering arrows down into the globe in a suitably urgent style for a networked US news programme. The globe was covered with photographs of people and places in the news by a technique involving laser scans for transparencies. These were then mapped onto the sphere. *Digital Effects Inc.*

8.18.1–3

8.18.4

8.18.5

8.19

8.20

8.21

**8.21**: **NHK Identification**. The Japanese equivalent of the BBC, Nippon Hosai Kyoko, used this station identification designed on their Antics system by Sig Sakai.

**8.19**: **RFP Antenne 2**. Another SOGITEC production, this is a trailer for a French television programme on the Antenne 2 network. The three-dimensional composition of the apple with the raised lettering is crisply executed.

**8.20**: **Sharp** office systems commercial with computer graphics by SOGITEC, Boulogne. A very detailed visualization of office machinery (more than 10 000 polygons or surfaces in each frame), it took 20 minutes per frame to compute. The result is a smooth juggling in space of VDUs, keyboards and other equipment, which all assembles into a normal configuration as the commercial ends. The modelling was based on blueprints of the machines sent by their manufacturers in Japan.

8.22.1

8.22.2

8.22.3

8.22.4

8.22.5

**8.22.1–6**: *Think Electric*, designed by Ken Brown, was made with back-lit artwork generated on Electronic Arts' computer in London in 1976. It was an early trail-blazer among digital computer-generated commercials, and stimulated awareness of the role of electricity in everyday life. Electricity Council, UK.

The American computer commercials scene stretches from New York to Los Angeles via Indiana and Denver. The main commercials producers are still in New York and Los Angeles, but CIC has been in Denver since 1969 and Computer Creations, a digital image company, in Indiana since 1975. The facilities which dominate the scene in design and technological terms are the companies which worked on *TRON* – Digital Effects, MAGI, Robert Abel and Triple I (whose leading computer graphics personnel are now at Digital Productions) – along with relative newcomers such as Cranston–Csuri and Pacific Data Images, and the original dominant influence, the New York Institute of Technology.

Digital Effects Inc., based in New York and now Los Angeles, has grown fast. Their Dicomed 48 film recorder leads to feature-film quality 35 mm images. Unusually, they have also made an impact in print advertising. The pointillist image of Brooklyn Bridge for Harris Computers was an early example; the mysterious landscape image for Glaxo Inc. is more recent. In 1981 Cucumber

**8.24.1–4**: LWT's news discussion programme, *Weekend World*, uses computer-generated pictures of real places in the title sequence designed by Robinson Lambie Nairn and generated by Digital Pictures.

8.24.1

8.24.2

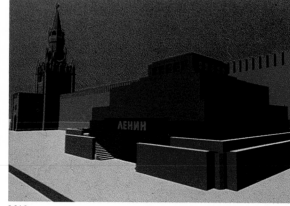

8.24.3

8.26.1

8.26.2

**8.26.1–5**: Title sequence for BBC TV *Sportsnight* designed for the BBC by Electronic Arts.

**8.27: NBA Basketball Promotion** trailer for the televised opening of the National Basketball Association season on CBS TV.
*Designed by Bill Feigenbaum, Feigenbaum Productions, and produced at NYIT, computer graphics by Kenneth Wesley.*

8.27

8.28.1

130

Television

8.22.6

8.23.1

8.23.2

8.23.3

Studios commissioned from Digital Effects a solid-surface computer graphic 30-second sequence for Pirelli tyres. This film was the first completely computer-generated solid-surface television commercial on British television. In this film the viewer hangs over what looks like a perfectly real car tyre as it is rapidly created from nothing, being built up through the various stages of manufacture into a perfect photographic representation of a brand new tyre. It is only because the representation is perhaps too perfect that you might suspect it is aided by the work of an airbrush artist. It was in fact never a painting or a photograph, but created entirely within the computer.

To save on data storage, the representation of the tyre was organized in repeatable sections; each zig-zag was a copy of its neighbour. Furthermore, there was never a whole tyre, but only the section which would be viewed. A wireframe model of a three-dimensional tyre was designed first, then the relevant two-dimensional perspective views were calculated. A visible surface algorithm removed the hidden side.

**8.23.1–3**: **LWT**. The striped pattern of the lettering is laid across the screen as if randomly placed, until the lines are truncated to form the intials of London Weekend Television. *Electronic Arts Ltd.*

**8.25**: **Scientific American** commercial by Digital Pictures. A series of television spots of images related to articles in the magazine.

8.24.4

8.25

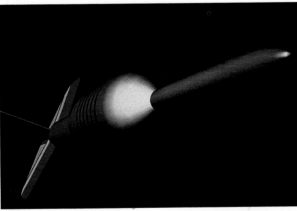

8.26.3

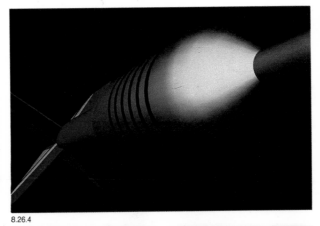

8.26.4

8.26.5

8.28.2

8.28.3

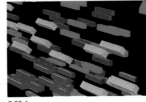

8.28.4

8.28.5

8.28.6

**8.28.1–6**: **Channel 4**. This second version of the logo for a new British television channel was designed, like the first version, by Robinson Lambie-Nairn. This time the computer animation was by Digital Effects Inc.

Imaginary light sources were created for the diffuse and specular light, and colour was added to give a good solid black, a range of grey tones and an embossed 'Pirelli' on the tyre.

France's most successful computer graphics company is SOGITEC of Boulogne. An elegant visual style is apparent in their commercial for Sharp Office Systems, which won the Computer Graphics 1983 award for computer-generated television advertising. It featured a number of pieces of office equipment floating in space,

which were then brought into a functional relationship by blue laser lines.

There is clearly a vast amount of expertise ready to work for television commercials, but it is not always exploited to the full. The massive success stories such as Abel and Dolphin attract many others to the field, but the patronizing attitude of 'give them what they think they want' adopted by producers can lead to a stultifying reliance on glowing lines or gleaming logos.

The computer-generated television title is a creative area which is specialized but spectacular.

Such titles have a distinctive quality which makes them effective as buffers between television programmes, and they can make relatively unexciting captions interesting and enjoyable to watch. The graphic excellence of some of them depends on motion, which alas cannot be demonstrated in a book, but others are just as good in still form.

Digital Effects have produced a dramatic sequence for NBC Nightly News, in which the lettering enters from beyond the viewers' left shoulder and shoots into the centre of a brown globe, there to explode in brilliant white light. Pacific Data Images used a similar dramatic meeting of sphere and rectangle in their title for Brazil's Globo Television Network. Across the Pacific, Sig Sakai has used an Antics system to make a great transparent 'NHK', hovering above a blue grid and under a night sky for Japanese television. Feigenbaum Productions' 1981 sequence for ABC News, with two red and orange wireframe globes touching a tiny blue and white Earth, is a powerful symbol of the opposing forces threatening the planet. Finally, Britain's Channel 4, having the great advantage of a single figure 4 to show both name and channel number, is identified, in two different versions, by the way the component bricks of the figure 4 fly apart and come together in a risky (as testified by a number of unsuccessful line-tests!) but ultimately successful venture. The second version was commissioned from Digital Effects by Robinson Lambie Nairn, while the first was worked on by several companies including Systems Stimulation though finally produced by Triple I.

Longer sequences give more scope for creativity. British television producers are just beginning to explore the possibilities for computer-generated title sequences for programmes. Two notable front-runners are the BBC's *Sportsnight* and LWT's *Weekend World*. The *Weekend World* title sequence was designed by Robinson Lambie Nairn, who commissioned the computer graphics from Digital Pictures in London. It shows a computer-generated flypast of the world's major cities, generated by Digital Pictures. It involved building a highly-detailed model of famous landmarks such as Westminster Clock Tower (Big Ben), the Post Office Tower, the Kremlin and the Empire State Building. The view from an imaginary aeroplane is then used to produce a breathtaking, but all too brief high-resolution sequence. *Sportsnight* uses a dramatic sequence, covering such sports as motor-racing, football, darts and snooker, providing a bright, fresh start to the programme, complementing the jaunty theme tune.

Another memorable sports sequence was made by Bill Feigenbaum for CBS's coverage of

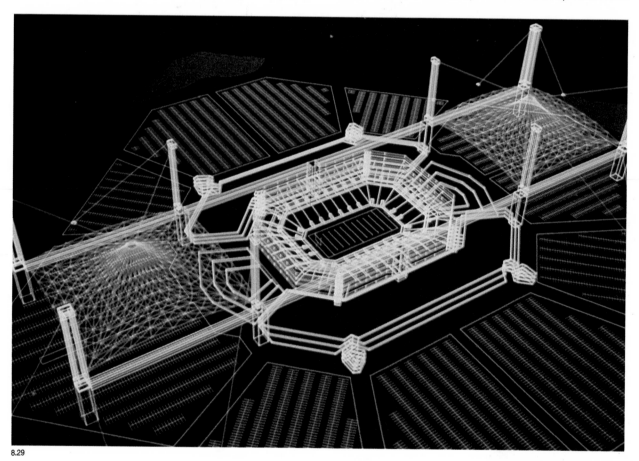

8.29

**8.29: Dade County Stadium.**
Another pioneering achievement by Robert Abel & Associates set the style for computer-generated sports promotions.
*Directed and designed by Bill Kovac and Nick Weingarten.*

the NBA basketball season. It shows the stadium from dramatic angles, brings in the electronic score-board and links it all to the CBS camera filming the action. Robert Abel's *Dade County Stadium* produces a similar graphic effect – designed, as is all Abel's computer work, by Bill Kovacs. Weather reports too offer good stimulus to the graphic imagination, although the presence of the weather man has tended to reduce the scope in the latter case to endless re-designing of clouds, raindrops and suns. One final gem needs mentioning, another Computer Graphics 1983 award winner. It was made by Bob English and Gijs Bannenberg at Electronic Arts as a trailer for Channel 4's general future programming and is entitled *Look Forward*. The camera moves down a series of corridors, turning left and right in new directions. On the walls are gentle illustrations of different types of programming in the style of Mexican murals, contrasting with the speed of the journey and winking in and out as the camera passes them. An excellent sequence for Britain's newest and most experimental television company.

The best computer graphics for television is probably never broadcast, but is often used to impress television people and advertising agencies. Like all commercial film producers, computer graphics houses produce showreels or demonstration tapes, which are used to attract business. If (as is often the case with computer graphics) the techniques are so new that no one has used them as yet, it is up to the people who have designed the system to show what is possible. The joint leaders in the showreel field for several years were NYIT's Computer Graphics Laboratory and Triple I. Since Triple I has sold off its computer graphics interests, this competition has ceased. The Computer Graphics Laboratory at NYIT continue to astonish audiences with new sequences from *The Works*, while also including commercials and other items, such as *St. Catherine*, designed and directed by Rebecca Allen (see chapters 2 and 6).

Another Rebecca Allen contribution takes the form of two promotional music video films for Will Powers and Island Records (*Adventures in Success* and *Smile*). As in the case of *St. Catherine*, these make a contrast between the perfect computer construct (here a mask or robot rather than a dancer), and the all too human performer. Music videos are an increasingly important showcase for computer graphics, and reach an enormous audience through television. One of the early examples was a brief vector scene at the end of *Accidents Will Happen*, directed by Annabel Jankel and Rocky Morton, a Cucumber Studios video for Elvis Costello: the

singer's face became an outline drawing which faded away with the music.

The depiction of people in computer graphics has come a long way since then; the arrival of computer graphics comedy is an indication of this. The climax of the NYIT showreel is possibly the only truly hilarious use of computer graphics to date. Dot Matrix (a busty blonde) and User Friendly (a warm, strong fellow) are the first computer-generated television presenters. They gush with suitably saccharine charm about the delights of their television programme, *3-DV*, and

**8.30**: **Lookforward to Channel 4**. A general promotional sequence in which the viewer moves along a corridor whose walls display upcoming attractions.
*Designed by Bob English (Channel 4) and Gijs Bannenberg, Electronic Arts.*

**8.31**: **Yellow Ball with Mirror**. *Cranston–Csuri Productions Inc.*

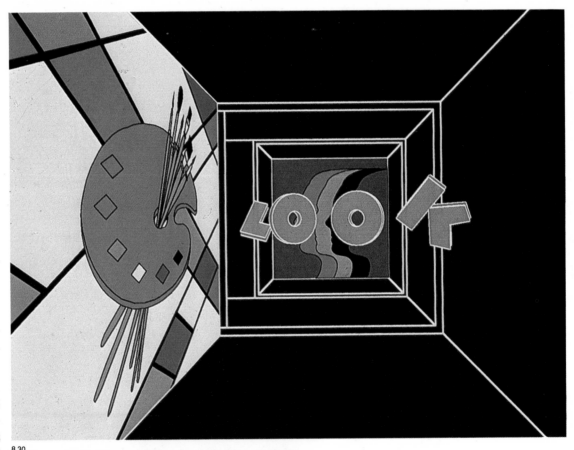

8.30

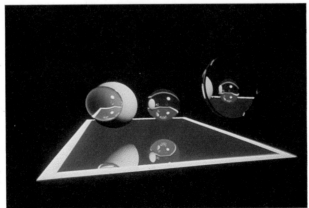

8.31

8.32

8.33

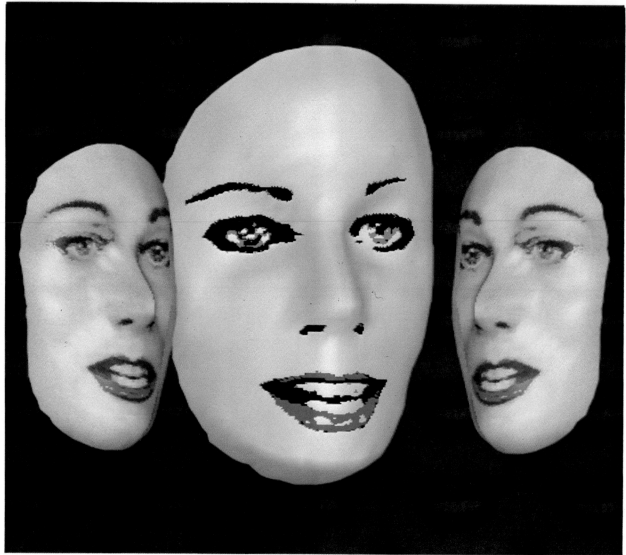

8.34

prepare us for the brash new age when the people on television will be just like real people – but much more fun to be with.

Though Triple I has now moved out of the computer graphics business, there are many other production companies ready to take its place in the showreel stakes. Triple I produced Adam Powers, their top-hatted juggler, or a Fabergé Easter Egg (in the style of David Em's contemporary art); a company such as Cranston–Csuri now uses bouncing balls on a mirror tray (entitled, in at least some incarnations, as *Yellow Ball With Mirror*) as their own particular continuity device while ranging from the animation of bones to skulls with smoking cigarettes, to an elegant Edwardian hotel with sunshades at each window, to the porch of a vast building with people entering it, to a forest of pencils (*Pencil City*) and back to the tray, astonishing the viewer once more by bouncing the ball not on the surface of the tray but a little below it – as if the tray is covered with a pool of mercury. The showreel is a superb demonstration of digital sophistication.

A relative newcomer to the field, Pacific Data Images, also produce an immaculate showreel. Their images range from television commercials for Plessey to a refrigerator with potato chips, dominoes, a grid globe, robots on a chessboard, folding geometric shapes, jagged and curled pipes, and robot teddy bears.

It is unfortunate for the general public that so much of the talent expended on producing showreel material remains unseen. Computer graphics has yet to establish a constituency in its own right. It is considered as a tool for commercials, titles or cartoons, but the entertainment value inherent in the extraordinary visual range of computer graphics is almost never taken up by programme controllers. It remains for an enterprising producer to produce a series subtitled something like *Computer Graphics Showcase*. There are useful precedents. Art animation films are given regular airings on various television channels, and music video films, which attract an enormous following on MTV cable network and other outlets, are similar to computer graphics productions in their brevity, lack of narrative structure and independence from verbal communication. As computer graphics technology and creativity progress, there is hope that this rich medium will soon be allocated a regular slot in television programming.

The rapacious speed with which television consumes images is, says Robert Abel, like the public's appetite for fast food. But there is one important difference: 'with the computer it may be possible to make fast food that's nutritious'.

**8.32**: Images from Cranston–Csuri Inc.'s 1983 demonstration tape.

**8.34**: Rotating masks from *Adventures in Success*, a music video with live and computer-generated human characters for singer Will Powers. Rebecca Allen and Paul Heckbert created the masks. As the masks rotate, an optical illusion occurs in which the rotation seems to reverse direction when the inside of the mask appears. *NYIT Computer Graphics Laboratory.*

**8.33**: Glass Balls on Tray.

**8.34**: Skull with Eyeball and Smoking Cigarette *Cranston–Csuri Productions Inc.*

# 9 Video Games and Home Computing

Two decades ago the thought of people standing in front of a television frantically pushing buttons while little shapes rushed around the screen would have seemed absurd. The possibility of a person owning a machine capable of complex business and scientific calculations, and with the ability to display the results of such calculations in colour on a television screen would have seemed equally far-fetched. But the fact is that home computers and their video game predecessors are now one of the most popular forms of entertainment in the Western world,

especially among the younger people, who readily accept the joy and challenge of this new application of technology.

The video game is the result of matching the rapid reduction in the cost of computing electronics with well-established television technology to produce a cheap machine which gave to the player control over the output of the television screen. When Nolan Bushnell invented *Pong*, a poor electronic imitation of table-tennis, it was an instant success. The only criticism from the users of the machine was that it stopped working when the coin box became full on the first day it was introduced. However it was Taito's *Space Invaders* which brought the video game into most peoples lives, to such an extent that the name is now often synonymous with video games as a whole. *Space Invaders* started the video game boom of the late 1970s, in which Atari led the way with a string of popular games such as *Asteroids*, *Battlezone*, *Centipede*, *Lunar Lander*, *Missile Command*, *The Tempest*, and others.

The technology of video game machines advanced rapidly as the players demanded faster and more exciting games. The simple monochrome display of *Space Invaders*, sometimes enhanced by putting coloured gels over parts of the screen, gave way to true colour displays. Raster technology, with its ability to display many colours and complex images, began to predominate over vector machines, which gave precise but slightly dull effects – although there were notable exceptions, such as the impressive three-dimensional graphics in *Battlezone* and the very popular *Asteroids*.

Most of the early machines had distinctly violent overtones, although the destruction was generally aimed at some unknown and overtly hostile alien force. The successful player needed fast reactions to cope with the increasing number of mobile but generally rather stupid opponents. Such games earned the title of 'twitch' games and they were generally lacking mental challenge. The trend soon changed however, spearheaded by the very popular game of *Pacman*, which involved outwitting four chasing opponents. Only occasionally did players actually have to destroy the enemy, although the violent element was not completely removed. One feature which has remained constant in all the different types of video game is the large number of games which

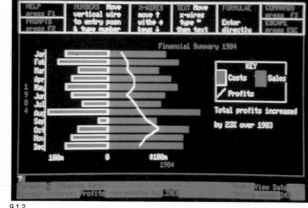

9.1.1

9.1.2

**9.1.1-2**: Financial planning layouts for a Spectrum home computer.

**9.3**: **Flight Simulator**. This is a complex game that depends on fast reactions but it is more of an executive toy than a street kid's pastime. Designed for the upper end of the home computer market and the businessman's quiet moment in the office, the flight simulator runs only on a disk-driven IBM Personal Computer. It gives a faithful simulation of the performance of a Cessna 182 single-engine aircraft, and will appeal to the prospective week-end pilot as well as the fantasist (to whom the only overt concession is a 'World War One' option involving dogfights and bombing runs). The graphics are superior to those of the arcade, and not too unlike the professional flight simulator. The major flaw is that it is keyboard-operated; you cannot wrestle with the steering column wheel or kick at pedals as you plummet towards the ground.
*Microsoft Corporation, 1982.*

**9.4**: **Laser Grand Prix**. A sophisticated laser-disk game in which realistic views of the race track, player's car and competitors' are displayed according to the cues from the controls operated by the player.
*Laser Vision*

must be played on any one machine to obtain a reasonable score and the considerable financial outlay that this represents.

Current advances in computer and video technology have been rapidly incorporated into the latest video games. New controls replaced the simple buttons of *Space Invaders* in the trackerball for *Missile Command* and the dual joysticks of *Battlezone*, speech and stereo hi-fidelity sound became common. The most recent games incorporate videodisks so that computer-generated action takes place in front of real-life film sequences, as in *MACH II*, and the player's actions affects the sequence of events in a film, as in *Dragon's Lair*. Among the possible advances in video game technology being studied at present are more direct controls using input taken directly from the players muscles and the use of biofeedback by measuring respiration, pulse and brain activity which are then used to adjust the game to suit each individual player. Most of these advances in technology are in response to the increasing discrimination on the part of the game player and the falling popularity of video games.

The boom in video games was short lived. By the end of 1983 Atari had lost well over $500 m in three quarter's trading, and some public opinion had turned against the violent nature of the games and the sleazy atmosphere of the arcades. In the US the Surgeon General warned that long stints of zapping space invaders might predispose children to violence, although Atari then hired a team of social psychologists who engaged in research which purported to show that the violence endemic in blowing up a space invader did not spill over in everyday life, and put forward the positive uses of video games in helping severely handicapped people and as a reward system for treating maladjusted or deviant children. Most of this effort was in vain, however. In an extreme case the citizens of Marshfield, Massachusetts succeeded in closing their electronic arcades on the grounds that they attracted crowds of teenage boys who were alleged to engage in gambling and drug trafficking, and that children were missing school and spending all their money playing video games. The overwhelming majority of video game players are young males and so the industry has tried to attract a wider audience to improve their image with the introduction of games such as *Ms.Pacman*.

The main cause of the decline in video game popularity, however, has been the advent of home computers, which have similar computing power to the arcade machines, usually involving the same microprocessor, but are designed for more general use. The owner of a home computer can obtain a version of most of the popular arcade games: this can then be used any time and on the better machines, is a very good approximation to the real thing. Besides, the flexibility of the home computer has led people to study computing in more detail and to learn to program for them-

9.2: **Roller Aces**. Graphics including mountains with clouds below them which make for a sense of wide open spaces. An arcade video game.
*Street*

9.2

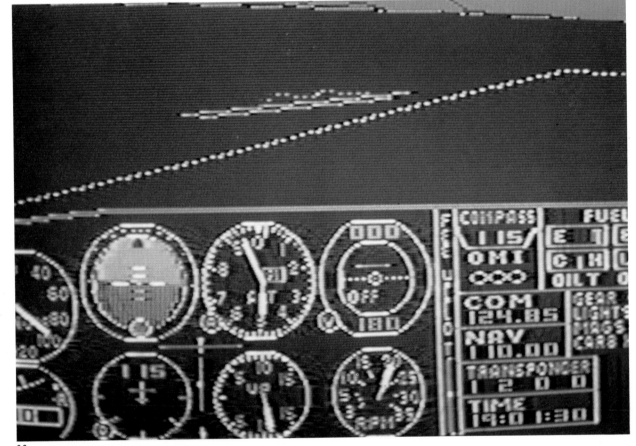

9.3

9.4

**9.5-6**: Viewdata systems, such as *Prestel* in the UK, send images down the telephone line to slightly adapted domestic television sets. Teletext systems do the same thing over the airwaves, utilizing the 49 or so under-used scan lines at the top and bottom of the screen. The image resolution of both systems is very low, but these images by Ralph Steadman show that there is still a lot of graphic potential.

selves; for many this has become a better game than any that an arcade machine could offer.

Atari, which made such a killing from the boom in arcade games, was slow to respond to the challenge of the home computer games. At first it seemed enough to convert the best arcade software into home games using plug-in cartridges to store the programs. These cartridges have several advantages, such as instantly availability compared to the slow cassette tape used by most machines, but they are expensive to produce and, once made, can be used only for the

game they have built in to them. Cassette tapes or the more expensive disks can be used to store any program, and if the game fails to sell, a new program can be stored on them, whereas any unsold cartridges are useless. Indeed, when Atari and their rival Texas Instruments moved into the home computer market the hit-making touch deserted them both; Texas Instruments pulled out of the home computer market altogether and Atari were left with thousands of unsold cartridges. Many of these were reduced to a quarter of their original price in a desperate sales drive, but eventually in despair Atari dug a big hole in the Nevada desert and in it dumped 14 truckloads of unsaleable cartridges.

In this respect Atari had failed to capitalize on the unique feature of the computer game; computer code does not need to be converted into a physical product to be distributed effectively. Combining this feature with the realization that computers do not have to be isolated but can talk to each other gives rise to the concept of computer networks. When connected to a network, a small computer can have access to a huge number of programs stored on a much larger computer at the other end of a telephone line; these programs can be bought directly without any physical transfer at all (apart from a few electrons going down the telephone wires). At the beginning of 1984 Atari saw this as the way to go and linked with Activision to send programs over the telephone network. British Telecom realized early on that its Prestel system could be used for personal computers and contracted with Micronet 800 to supply home computer software.

The possibility of connecting home computers to large machines has been too much of a temptation for some computer owners and has led to a considerable amount of electronic breaking into the computer systems used by large businesses or government bodies. This has been highlighted in the film *War Games*, in which a young enthusiast connects to a Pentagon computer and initiates a nuclear strike on Seattle. The Defense Department denied that such an event could ever happen but the subsequent exposure of breaches in computer security from home computers has not helped their credibility or eased the public's fears.

The popularity of home computers can be gauged by looking at the total number in use. In Great Britain, which has the densest population of home computers in the world, that figure was about 1.2 million by the middle of 1983 and with the constant stream of new computers coming on the market is growing very rapidly. Over half of these computers have been made by Sinclair Research, a proportion unlikely to fall in the near

9.5

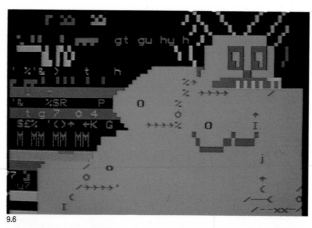

9.6

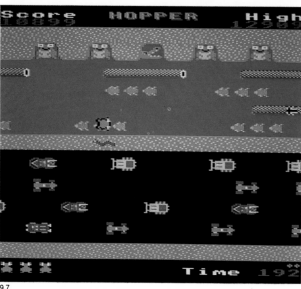

9.7

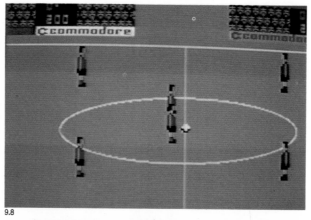

9.8

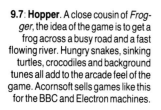

9.9

**9.7**: **Hopper**. A close cousin of *Frogger*, the idea of the game is to get a frog across a busy road and a fast flowing river. Hungry snakes, sinking turtles, crocodiles and background tunes all add to the arcade feel of the game. Acornsoft sells games like this for the BBC and Electron machines.

**9.8**: **Soccer**. A game which cleverly avoids animating 22 independent players by concentrating on the player with the ball and his closest opponent. The sound effects of cheers from the crowd as a goal is scored help to boost this game's attractions. *Commodore.*

**9.9**: **Barmy burgers**. A Donkey-Kong style maze game on ladders. *Blavy.*

future, given the release of the QL machine, aimed at both the home market and small business users.

In America and Japan the average spending on home computers is much higher, the top-selling machines being the IBM PC and NEC Personal Computer respectively, and the type of machine demanded by the different markets varies considerably. The Japanese regard colour graphics as the most important selling point and demand a high-resolution monitor; however, they are quite content to use slow cassette storage and to write in limited dialects of BASIC. This decision is partly driven by the need to display the Kanji, the complex characters used in Japanese writing, and the heavy computing demand made by such graphics means that the typical Japanese home computer would be considered in the West to be the basis of a business system.

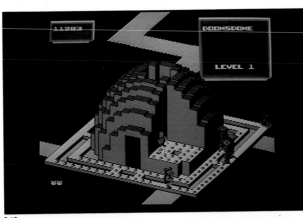

9.10

9.11

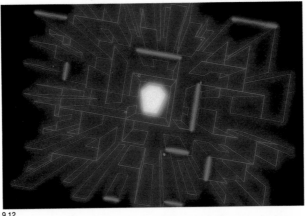

9.12

9.13

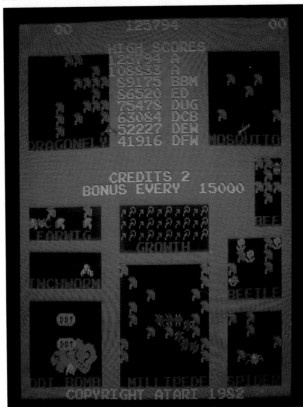

9.14

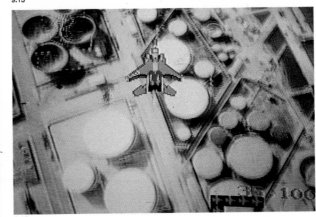

9.15

**9.10: Crystal Castles.** The cuddly bear, quest for gems and wicked witch in this game are designed to make it appeal to the *Pacman* market of girls and younger children. It is still a 'twitch' game though, and the appeal of testing reaction time and reflexes to the limit is apparently waning among the 8 to 14-year olds who are the most interested players. The next generation of players will design their own castle shapes rather than wait for the next trick from a middle-aged, 15-year old professional game designer. *Atari Inc.*

**9.13: Camels.** An game set in ancient Egypt. *Llama Soft.*

**9.11: Valhalla.** An adventure game in which the player must enter instructions to the 'hero' in order for him to take his place among the Norse Gods. *Legend.*

**9.14: Millipede.** This incredibly complex game of rapid thumb movements features mushroom-spawning millipedes, jumping spiders, bombing double-lived bees, zig-zagging dragonflies, diagonal mosquitos, poisonous earwigs, flower-planting beetles, accelerating inchworms, and the player as a princely archer. In reaction to the increasing proficiency of the arcade players and their increasingly low boredom threshold, games designers have had to pile it on thick to retain custom. *Atari Inc.*

**9.12: Major Havoc** is a descendent of a long line of games, from the original *Space Invaders* through *Galaxians*, *Lunar Lander*, *Space Wars*, *Black Hole* and many others. As in the newer games, of which the *TRON* video game was an important marker, the environment changes as the player achieves the immediate goal. In *Major Havoc*, there are waves of attackers (as in *Space Invaders*), a maze (as in *Pacman*), and even a 'game within a game' which is one of the oldest offshoots of *Pong*, known as *Breakout*. In *Breakout* a bouncing ball knocks out the bricks in a wall as long as the player can knock it back with a paddle. *Major Havoc's* other attractions are multiple viewports or windows, as in an instrument panel, and secret code numbers to activate extra weapons. *Atari Inc.*

**9.15: Mach 3.** The computer-graphics jet flies over a real photographic refinery in this hybrid laser-disk game. *Sega Laser.*

**9.16**: **Goblet** Sinclair's homage to Jim Blinn takes the form of a wire-frame goblet program in the introductory graphics package that comes free with the Spectrum computer.

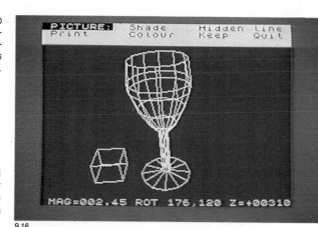

PICTURE: Shade Hidden Line
Print Colour Keep Quit

MAG=002.45 ROT 176,120 Z=+00310
9.16

**9.17**: **The Cry**, the painting by Edvard Munch, still retains much of its power in the limited graphic resolution offered by the Prestel Viewdata system.

ESS 444 44412374

9.17

There are a number of features which are greatly sought after in home computers. The most obvious of these is the ability to move shapes rapidly around the screen with the minimum of effort. In many machines this must be done by removing and drawing the image for each movement, but more recent machines have special hardware for just this purpose and can move multi-coloured objects, or 'sprites', with relative ease. More importantly, these sprites can be driven by fairly simple BASIC programs. Pairs of sprites can be linked to give 'player–missile' graphics, which are ideal for writing *Space Invader* programs. However, with such features there is a danger of losing the generality of a home computer by ignoring other features, or pricing the machine so high that it cannot reasonably be afforded by the average family.

The number of sprites, their size and their capabilities vary between machines, but they all require considerable memory to store the individual shapes. There is always a trade-off between the quality of the graphics and the memory taken to store the image. Acorn's BBC microcomputer uses 20k of an available 32k-bit memory when using 16 colours and a resolution of 256 × 160, while the Sinclair Spectrum reduces its memory requirement by restricting the number of colours which can be shown in a given area, thus reducing the flexibility of the display.

One of the most important features of a home machine is the ease with which it can be programmed. This depends to a certain extent on the whole philosophy of the machine and the complexity of the 'operating system', the program which looks after all the hardware such as the keyboard and the screen. The ability to draw lines and points is essential and it is highly desirable to be able to fill arbitrary areas with colour, so that complex pictures can be built up. An important consideration is the quality of the programming languages available, which in the first case usually means Basic. The quality of the Basic in home computer varies drastically from the very simple version on the Commodore 64 to BBC Basic, which contains a number of advanced features and is also very fast, despite the similar hardware capabilities of the two machines. For graphics the availability of Logo or similar graphics languages is highly desirable and this can be obtained for most of the popular computers. The future prospects in computer hardware look good as the price of microprocessors drops and the complexity rises. The QL is already offering a huge 512k memory and the BBC machine is growing with the addition of a 16032 second processor, giving home owners the same power as many of today's minicomputers and the ability to create complex images previously available only on large computer systems. Further in the future are products such as wall-sized television screens, direct voice input (no more one-finger typing) and, still further, three-dimensional holographic displays driven by lasers.

The prospects in the software field are equally promising. The first wave of software for the new machines was based around the arcade favourites. Most were twitch games of some sort, but the general home computer could not match the specialized arcade machine for crisp picture quality and, most importantly, for the specialized controls which have become the rule rather than the exception. So software has developed in other directions. Arcade game writers were limited to short games because, after all, they wanted as

9.18

9.19

9.20

**9.18**: **Astro Chase**. A 3-dimensional environment combining domestic and outer space imagery.
*Parker Bros.*

**9.19**: **Merry go round**. A graphics package for the Sinclair Spectrum.

**9.20**: **Island**. Sinclair graphics can bring you your own custom-built desert island, with optional coconuts.

many people to play (and pay) as possible. Home computer games are played far more frequently than arcade games, so that the simple games quickly become boring unless a large number of extra features are added or the game is particularly original and well programmed.

It would be wrong to assume that all home computer programs had their origin in video games, for people have been playing games on computers for many years. These games were initially limited to printed output on slow terminals and so developed a very different style to arcade games, but even the classic *Star Trek* had simple graphics, with a map of the galaxy drawn by appropriate use of characters. Programming of games such as draughts and especially chess have provided valuable test beds for research into artificial intelligence; it is probable that the majority of all computer usage goes into developing, studying or playing games.

The most important contribution to home computers from the larger computer systems must be the game of *Adventure*, based on the popular role-playing game of *Dungeons and Dragons*. The computer describes your surroundings in an imaginary underground dungeon and you give the computer simple commands such as 'go north', 'take lamp' and 'wave rod'. Most commands cause some response from the computer, and by finding the appropriate commands you can explore the underground world, a process which can take months to finish. All the descriptions from the computer are textural, so the scope for computer graphics in such games is enormous.

The transfer of adventure games to home computers has been very successful, to the extent that the whole of the original *Adventure* has been converted to run on a home computer with only 32k memory, including all the original messages and a number of extra rooms. The new games of this type are beginning to contain graphics, for example *The Hobbit* and *Valhalla* for the Sinclair Spectrum, which contain simple draw-ings with limited animation. These games also introduce the concept of other people living in the imaginary world with whom the player can meet and interact, although at present the depth of their personalities is rather limited. The basis for such games can be existing books, as in *The Hobbit*, or new works of the programmer's imagination based on existing mythology or history, as in *Valhalla*. The next generation of such fantasy games will exploit the new technology of machines to incorporate realistic sound, speech and full-colour animated graphics, and will be much more complex than existing games, with real characters to interact with and complex goals to achieve. Systems are being designed to allow authors with no computing experience to use their imagination to create this new generation of game, and there will be new drawing tools developed (or transferred from larger machines) to allow artists to add detailed drawings.

*Maze Wars* is a computer game which is the forerunner of a new variation to fantasy games. 'It is played on large computer systems and allows players to wander around a maze, with the exciting possibility of meeting another player round the next corner. The game uses fairly simple graphics to represent the view into a maze, with an eye representing the presence of another player in the game. With the rapid increase in computer networks will come the multi-player game, in which a number of players will inhabit an imaginary world and either combat each other or join forces to solve a common problem or meet a common foe.

The diversity of programs available on home computers is staggering, from games to cookery and star-maps to library catalogues. The business users of the small computer have begun to realise the potential of graphics with pie charts and histograms for presenting company performance, and word processors using colour and graphics to speed document preparation. Systems such as Lisa from Apple Computers give the businessman an aerial view of his desk with small pictures, or icons representing the different tasks he may wish to perform. He may have a number of different jobs on the go at once; the graphics enable him to select whichever item he requires in the simplest possible way.

Computer graphics has been used in many walks of life and more applications are being found all the time. At present one of the most demanding tasks a small computer can be given is the pro-duction and animation of complex pictures. With the development of a new generation of powerful machines capable of such tasks, the future of computer graphics in the home and in business is very rosy indeed.

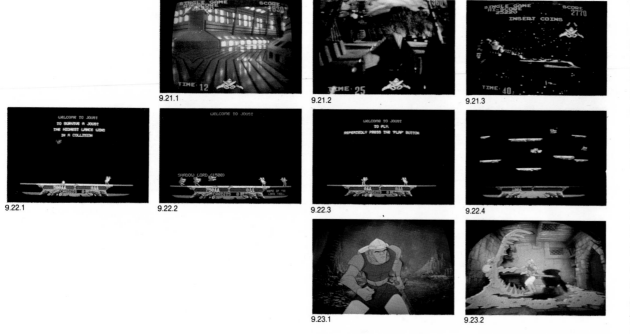

9.21.1–3: **Galaxy Ranger**.
*Sega Laser.*

9.22.1–4: **Joust**. A mediaeval tourna-ment with mythical creatures is the setting for this aerial combat game.
*Williams.*

9.24: This commercial won MAGI Synthavision the 1983 Clio award (the Oscars of television commercials) for best computer-generated commer-cial. *Worm War I* is the title of the commercial; *Worm Wars* is the video game it advertises.

9.23.1–2: **Dragon's Lair**. The first giant hit of the laser-disc generation of games, Dragon's Lair uses entirely hand-drawn cartoons, but stores them on a disc and allows the player to choose two or three alternative routes at various key points in his journey around a complicated castle full of perils. If he successfully fights off his attackers and rescues his pack and his sword, the hero arrives in the open air to find princess waiting to be freed from the dragon's spell. The hero fetches a special magic sword to dispatch the dragon, and a key to liberate the princess who swoons bustily into his arms.
*Atari Laser.*

9.24